THE BOOK OF
PROPHECIES

Fig. 10.

THE BOOK OF
PROPHECIES

DISCOVER THE SECRETS OF THE
PAST, PRESENT AND FUTURE

JONATHAN DEE

COLLINS & BROWN

To Rhiannon and Christopher,
Two travellers into a new age.

First published in Great Britain in 1999
by Collins & Brown Limited
London House
Great Eastern Wharf
Parkgate Road
London SW11 4NQ

1 3 5 7 9 8 6 4 2

British Library Cataloguing-in-Publication Data:
A catalogue record for this book is available from the British Library.

ISBN 1 85585 683 2

Editors: Susan Martineau and Amy Corzine
Design: The Bridgewater Book Company
Illustrator: Nicky Ackland-Snow
Picture research: Gabrielle Allen

Reproduction by Hong Kong Graphic and Printing Ltd
Printed and bound by Dai Nippon, Hong Kong

CONTENTS

PROPHETS OF DOOM OR PROPHETS OF BLISS?

The crystal ball of Dr John Dee (1527-1608), the most notorious magician and mystic of the Elizabethan era (see pages 80-83).

O ne may associate the idea of prophecy with the frail figure of the pariah mooting messages of doom, the religious extremist or someone ordinary who, once in a lifetime, prophesies an event due to sheer coincidence. However, our contemporary fix on the future is very much in evidence, and is so intricately interwoven with the minutiae of every-day living that it is almost indiscernable. From the weather forecast to horse-racing tips, election opinion polls to previewed fashion trends, we use practical prophecy every day to minimize risk and anticipate failure or success.

Modern-day prophets have a ready audience for words of wisdom. Tabloid newspapers are avid for their headline-winning predictions, reflecting the public's hunger for revelations about the future. Daily horoscopes in newspapers are thought to account for one-fifth of total sales. When gambling on the lottery becomes a quest for a glimpse of the future, acts of mundane prophecy fulfill an almost daily need for a sense of security about the coming weeks, and also the decades to be inherited by the next generation.

On a greater scale, prophets have influenced and advised those in positions of power, albeit on a discreet level, throughout history (see The Politics of Prophecy, pages 70-95). For some, however, consultations with mystic advisors become public knowledge. During the presidency of Ronald Reagan during the 1980s, he and First Lady Nancy Reagan changed the times of important meetings and travel arrangements to comply with the advice of their astrologer, Joanne Quigley. More recently, in early 1999, a report emerged that President Boris Yeltsin of Russia had frequently consulted an astrologer named Georgi Rogozin on matters of importance.

Saint Joan of Arc (1412-1431), under interrogation by King Charles VII. Joan believed that the voices responsible for her extraordinary bravery in battle against the English were of divine origin.

At this time in our history – the start of the new millennium – it is natural to speculate on our fate. There have been many prophecies throughout the ages which relate to this time, or are thought to relate to this 'Change of the Age'. The question remains: is this to be a time of calamity, of global destruction, of final judgement? Or is it to be one of reawakened harmony, the Second Coming of the Messiah, and the dawning of the new longed-for Age of Aquarius?

Oracles, augurs, psychics, seers, prognosticators, readers of omens, fortune tellers, shamans, witches, and visionaries: all are prophets of a kind. They have existed for thousands of years in all cultures, and in general were respected figures in the community, often combining their psychic roles with that of doctor, priest or even 'agony aunt'.

Paradoxically, however, these figures were also scapegoated for being the 'bearers of bad tidings' — and have been blamed for the very ills against which they have sought to warn. It may be that the

The virgin Mary was thought to have appeared to three children in Portugal, 1938, warning them of humanity's fate.

role of prophet requires one to stand somewhat apart from society, and in so doing incur suspicion. Understandably, not all prophets were saints, and this book includes those who were, and many who certainly were not (see *A Symposium of Seers From A to Z*, pages 170–181). You will find among them devout believers and charlatans, fools and tyrants, victims and persecutors. Prophet Edward Kelly, who predicted in 1583 the death of Mary, Queen of Scots, five years before her demise, was a notorious graverobber, spy and con-man; and Marie Lavaux, the Voodoo Queen of New Orleans, was said to have placed voodoo dolls in the bedrooms of wealthy households. Enterprisingly, the terrified victims would need to pay dearly to have the voodoo curses removed by none other than the Voodoo Queen herself

(pages 118-121). In short, in most areas of life, many prophets were as worldly and flawed as their neighbours, and the ability to foretell the future did not guarantee moral worthiness.

It may be that we all have the ability to see into the future, albeit on an unconscious level. There have always been people who seem to have an eerie sensitivity to disaster — it has been noted, following train and aeroplane disasters, that the number of passengers travelling on 'doomed' vehicles or vessels is less than on other days.

Before the RMS Titanic set sail on its fateful maiden voyage in April, 1912, there was an exceptionally large number of cancellations during the previous week. Most passengers had no explanation for their reluctance to travel, but one, an English businessman named J. Connor Middleton, had cancelled due to a nightmare in which he had seen the Titanic 'floating on the sea, keel upwards and her passengers and crew swimming around her.' The vision was so terrifying that he could not ignore this subconscious warning and set foot on board.

Middleton was not, and is not, alone in possessing this survival instinct. There have also been many who, often vainly, have tried to warn others of impending catastrophe. It seems likely that this prophetic urge is linked generally to dramatic situations, because in our day-to-day lives, it is simply unnecessary. This is why the dream can often be the most common vehicle for the predictive process. However, many of the extraordinary people who have developed their latent prophetic talent have used objects, concepts or even sounds to aid them. Yet it is to be remembered that crystal balls, tarot cards and tea leaves, for example, are merely paraphernalia which act as a focus while the unconscious mind gets to work.

Within this book you will find dream readers, oracles and those who sought the future in the entrails of beasts and in magic mirrors. Astrology and numerology are explained, as are the lesser-known techniques, all included in Parting The Veil: A Glossary of Divinatory Techniques (see pages 182-187).

Orthodox religions at least admit the possibility of foretelling the future, even if they disapprove of the practice, yet there is no known scientific basis for prophecy. Since in our age, science has generally replaced the great established faiths as the 'sole' repository of wisdom, can there be any factual basis for a belief in destiny and those who can perceive its shape? This would mean that in some sense the future already exists, and that we follow its course, only being aware of our immediate surroundings and the time which they occupy.

Nevertheless, the mystery remains. The uncanny, inexplicable accuracy of some prophets leads to the inevitable conclusion that it is not only possible, but likely, that the future can be foreseen. This book uncovers fascinating messages for today and our future, and it is your decision to believe, dismiss, question, and reinterpret the secrets revealed within.

A postcard of 'unsinkable' ship, the Titanic, 1912. The large number of cancellations received during the week before the Titanic sailed indicates that possibly everyone has precognitive abilities.

CHAPTER ONE

THE WISDOM OF
THE ANCIENTS

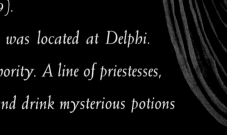

For ancient civilizations, the mysteries of nature – of the past and the future – were considered to be the realm of the gods. It is therefore understandable that great efforts were made to glean clues as to their will.

Foremost among the gods who were believed to speak to humanity via a medium was the deity Apollo, although his messages were often perplexing. He was known as 'Loxias', or 'The Riddler', on account of his obscure oracles.

Apollo was not the only power thought to reveal the secrets of the universe. The Egyptians worshipped a host of animal gods who were believed to do just that, and we should not forget

The Temple of Apollo at Delphi, Greece, where the Pythia, 'who spoke with the voice of Apollo', predicted the future.

the spirits of the dead – these souls, freed from the constraints of time and space, were also considered wise in the ways of the future. All these and more are treated in 'The Riddles of the Gods' (pages 12-19).

The most prominent oracle in the ancient world was located at Delphi. Here, the riddling Apollo spoke with the greatest authority. A line of priestesses, each known as the Pythia, would inhale vapours and drink mysterious potions

before going into a trance and revealing the future. The myster-

ies of Delphi are unveiled in 'The Voice of Apollo' (pages 20-25).

Delphi was much visited by the incomparable Alexander the

Great. Although firmly believing in his own divinity, he felt the

need to consult his Olympian relatives for constant resassurance. Stories of Alexander's visits to the

spiritual centres of his world are told in 'Alexander and the Oracles' (pages 26-31).

Arguably, the most famous prophecy recorded was uttered to Julius Caesar by an obscure

prophet named Vitricius Spurinna. Caesar chose not to heed his warning, and suffered the conse-

quences.   It was, of course, the Ides of March prediction (pages 32-35). However, Caesar's

successors, the emperors of Rome, paid far more attention to the dire warnings of prophets, augurs,

psychics and astrologers, often consulting their own book of prophecy, the Sibylline Verses.

Tiberius was blessed with the services of an astrologer who was apparently never wrong. His

story is told in 'The Emperor's Dragon' (pages 36-37). The later

emperors, too, had cause to fear the future, as is revealed in 'The Fall

of Eagles' (pages 38-47).

Julius Caesar's failure to heed warnings of danger and his subsequent demise has inspired many artists, including Jean-Leon Gerome (1824-1904), who painted *The Death of Caesar* in 1867.

Tiberius, who ruled over Roman Empire from AD 13-37, was more noted for viciousness than acts of sacrifice, despite the piety displayed by his sculpted image.

THE RIDDLES OF THE GODS

Praying can bring one of the most profound senses of spiritual connection that perhaps any person can experience. Although very few people expect an answer from their chosen deity, since early times there have existed sacred places where an appeal to the divine is often followed by an answer of sorts – although the convoluted, even rhythmic, way in which the reply may be delivered may take a great deal of thought to decipher. Among the peoples of the ancient world, consulting an oracle was considered to be the highest form of divination. During a consultation, questions could be put directly to the gods and, if these remote, incomprehensible beings were in a benevolent mood, an answer would be given.

The Greek-speaking peoples, in particular, were addicted to oracular pronouncements. Even the great philosophers such as Plato and Socrates were firmly in favour of this system. In fact, in his blue-print for an ideal society – *The Republic* – Plato was content to place an oracle at the centre of the state to advise, guide and provide the sanction of divine beings.

The primary oracle sites of the Greek world were situated at Delphi, Dodona and Delos. However, many other sites existed in places such as Didyma, Livadia and Colophon. Even as far away as Baia and Cumae in Italy, and Siwa in the western deserts of Egypt, oracles were honoured and consulted.

It is interesting to note that the oracle sites seem to have been established at sacred locations which were one degree of latitude apart. Dodona lies at 39° 30 minutes, Delphi at 38° 30, Delos at 37° 30, and so on. This apparent geographical sophistication

The island of Delos was one of the three main oracle sites in Greece – there were others in places as far away as Baia and Cumae in Italy and Siwa in the western deserts of Egypt. Ancient oracle sites were situated at sacred locations only one degree of latitude apart.

becomes all the more amazing when it is matched with other oracular sites in Asia. These also seem to continue the system to the slopes of Mount Ararat in Armenia. Such precision of placement illustrates a knowledge of the earth that, according to modern experts, ancient people would not have possessed.

THE BLACK DOVE

The oracle of Dodona was the most venerated Greek shrine. Its patron deity was none other than Zeus himself, King of the Olympian gods. In the distant mountains of north-western Greece, a grove of oak trees stood on the slopes of Mount Tomaros. The wind rustling through the leaves of these sacred trees was said to bring messages and portents which would be interpreted by the sanctuary's priests. However, even though remoteness and a certain difficulty in reaching the site were part of the ritual, Dodona was a little too difficult and too remote to challenge the popularity of the celebrated Delphic oracle, situated some seventy miles from Athens. The historian Herodotus was told by Egyptian priests that the Dodonian oracle was founded by one of two female temple initiates who had been captured and sold into slavery by Phoenician pirates. The other eventually found her way to the western deserts in Libya where she became the first oracular priestess of Ammon at Siwa. However, Herodotus heard a different tale from the very lips of Promeneia, Timarete and Nicandra, the oracle priestesses of his day. According to them, Dodona was founded by a black dove which had flown from Thebes of the Hundred Gates in Upper Egypt. This miraculous bird had perched in the boughs of an oak tree. Speaking with a human voice, it had commanded the building of a temple to Zeus through which he could make his will known to men. Of these two versions, Herodotus preferred the less supernatural explanation, but suggested that the two accounts might not be incompatible. He thought that the exiled woman may have been called a dove due to what seemed her peculiar manner of speech, which made her sound like a bird to the highland Greeks, and that her dusky Egyptian skin was the reason she was remembered as a black dove. So, according to the best authority, it was Egyptian magic that was practised in the lonely highlands of Greece.

THE HOUSE OF AMMON

Even amongst the Greeks, the efficacy of the solitary Egyptian shrine of Siwa was unquestioned. Founded by the second 'black dove', this oracle lay some eight days' march across the pitiless sands of the western desert. Siwa was the home of the god Amun or, as the Greeks called him, Ammon. This ancient deity of the Nile-dwellers had become the paramount divinity of Egypt during the eighteenth dynasty. He was initially identified with the sun god Ra but, as Greek encroachment became more pervasive, King Ammon also became equated with the supreme deity of the Olympian gods. Thus, by the time of Classical civilization, he was known as Zeus-Ammon, a god whose most devout worshipper was Alexander the Great himself.

Although accounts vary, this oracle was said to operate by means of a divine boat whose movements and those of its bearers were interpreted as Zeus-Ammon's answer to questions. The priests who carried it would dance in the hot sun until, like the later Sioux natives of North America, they would fall into an ecstatic trance. The movements of the boat were then watched closely as its prow dipped and rose.

Oracle priestesses told Herodotus that the oracle most revered during his time at Dodona was founded by a black dove which had flown there from Egypt.

Questions would be called out from an assembled crowd and divinations of the god's answer would be interpreted from the movements of the vessel and of those who bore the immense burden.

THE BEAST GODS OF EGYPT

Since the ancient Egyptians worshipped many strange gods who, bizarrely to Greek eyes, often had the heads or attributes of animals, it is not surprising that these beasts were looked to for knowledge of the future. The movements of the jewelled sacred crocodiles were closely watched, as indeed were those of cats (sacred to Bast, a huntress goddess), apes (sacred to Thoth, god of wisdom), and serpents, which were thought to be generally holy.

Foremost among these animal gods was a huge ox known as the Apis Bull. This bull was held to be the incarnation of the soul of Osiris, god of fertility, the afterlife and the underworld. It was kept in a great temple in Memphis in Lower Egypt. Herodotus tells us that the Apis was known by certain markings and signs. It was the calf of a cow incapable of conceiving another offspring, and said to have been fertilized by lightning. It had to be black with a square patch of white on its forehead; on its back, the figure of an eagle must show; its tail had to have double hairs; and on its tongue there should appear the figure of a beetle. Once such an animal was discovered, it was the signal for tremendous rejoicing by the Egyptians, particularly as the bull was conveyed to the temple which would be its home.

The Apis Bull was widely renowned as an oracle. When it licked the garment of the astronomer

Eudoxus of Cnidus, it foretold his approaching death. The Bull also boded ill for Germanicus (the father of Caligula) by refusing to eat from his hand. Germanicus was later poisoned. The death of Cleopatra was signalled by the mournful bellowing of the distressed beast. However, the portents provided by the bull were not always so respectfully honoured. When the Persian King, Cambyses, led his Persian forces to occupy Egypt in 525 BC, the Egyptians showed their contempt for their conqueror by calling him 'The Mule'. The Persian ruler raged at this insult and swore that 'This mule shall eat their ox'. So saying, he took a spear and cast it at the Apis Bull, wounding the sacred beast in the thigh. With no further ceremony, Cambyses ordered that the bull be killed, dressed, and served for dinner. The Egyptians never forgave the Persians for this, and later supported Alexander the Great in their overthrow. As for Cambyses himself,

The most revered of Egypt's animal gods was the ox known as the Apis Bull, thought to be the incarnation of their god Osiris's soul, which gave them oracular signs.

he, too, had cause to regret his rash impiety because, while drunk, he attempted to sheath his sword but gashed himself in the thigh instead. There followed a virulent 'fever of the blood', from which the great Persian conqueror perished.

THE ISLAND OF MICE

An Egyptian influence was also thought to exist at Delos. This small island, of the Cycladic chain, housed the oracle of Apollo, god of prophecy, and of his mother and sister, Leto and Artemis. Apollo was said to have been born here, and the sanctity of the island was so great that death was not

This 16th century Italian engraving of Apollo with a dog's head (1589) probably refers to the Egyptian practice of venerating animals as oracles.

THE NESTS OF DIDYMA

At Didyma, too, Apollo was the patron deity – who was said to give his riddling predictions through the bubbling of a sacred spring, which burst forth in the presence of Alexander the Great. In the fashion of Delphi, Apollo's words were communicated at Didyma by means of an entranced prophetess who had inhaled drugged fumes from boiling cauldrons. It is this prophetess who figures in the following story. It seems that a number of refugees had fled from their own city, which had

allowed to gain a foothold upon it. If any visitor should have the misfortune to faint or to appear unwell in any way, then the islanders would unceremoniously dump their prone body into the sea. If there was even the slightest hint of sickness in a citizen, the stricken person would be moved immediately to another island to live or die according to the will of the gods.

Delos was also considered to be the primary home of Apollo, who was worshipped here as the god of mice. Mice played an important part in the Delian oracle, as the rodents scampered through a series of mazes, their twists and turns being interpreted as answers to questions.

fallen into the hands of the Persians. They hoped for the protection of the Histaeus, the tyrant of Miletus, on the Asiatic coast. This king gave his word that he would protect them, but sent to the oracle to obtain the consent of Apollo. The oracle's answer was not as enigmatic as was expected and told the king flatly that 'Foreign birds should be cast out of the nest'.

Instead of following this politically expedient advice the indignant tyrant instead went to Didyma and there collected eggs and fledgling birds from their nests around the sanctuary. When the prophetess heard of the king's odd activity, she immediately protested, 'How dare you take from Apollo those creatures who live under his protection!'

'The Road to Hell is open every day,
Smooth the descent, and easy is the way.'

VIRGIL

Histaeus answered, 'Apollo wishes to take from me creatures who live under mine.' This turned out to be a serious error, because the Persians, offended by the King's refusal to return his guests to their custody, reduced Miletus to rubble and sold its population into slavery. Thus, a proud and kind, but powerless king was considered to have brought war and ruin upon his people, and was humbled for not heeding the words of Apollo spoken through his priestess at Didyma.

THE VOICES OF THE DEAD

There is little doubt that drug-induced trances, combined with hypnotic techniques, were used by the prophets during ancient oracular rituals. However, at some oracles visitors who came to consult the gods were drugged by unscrupulous mediums to ensure their suggestibility.

The most notorious of these was the oracle at Livadia. Pausanias, a geographer and historian of the second century AD, has a disturbing account of this. He says that, after some days of fasting and drinking strange-smelling potions, the questioner was slipped down a chute into subterranean chambers in which he was terrified by serpents. Often he would stay underground for days, while whispers echoing around the cavern walls would reveal oblique answers to his questions. In a state of terror and sug-gestibility, he would see visions and believe himself

to be literally in the land of the dead, kingdom of Hades and Persephone. This shattering experience would lead the questioner to believe that he now knew the will of the underworld gods. Then he would be led out into the blinding light a changed man. This cunning stratagem did not always fool the more perceptive client, and visitor such as these would be quietly murdered 'while in the underworld' and never again appear in the land of the living to tell their tale.

The most eerie of these sinister sanctuaries was the Oracle of the Dead at Baia, near the modern city of Naples. The vast cave network carved into the solid rock there is an almost unknown wonder of the ancient world. Here, seances with unseen powers were held, and questioners were led deeper and deeper into the heart of the mountain until they came to an artificial 'River Styx' which they would literally believe were the waters that flow between the worlds of life and death. The description of the descent into Hell given in Book VI of Virgil's *Aeneid* is, in fact, a close approximation of a visit to the Baian oracle.

The Oracle of the Dead may have relied on volcanic gases much like the legendary 'mephitic fumes' that rose from the cleft at Delphi. The caverns lie on the shores of Lake Avernus, within the crater of an extinct volcano that was once considered to be one of the passages into the realm of Hades. The geographer Strabo (c. 63 BC-AD 23) wrote, 'The inhabitants affirm that birds flying over the lake fall into the water, being stifled by the vapours rising from it.' This portal to the powers of darkness was sealed up by General Agrippa, a close friend of Octavian Augustus, who for some reason known

Legend, though, tells a different tale. According to the poet Virgil, it was one of these sybils who told the Trojan hero Aeneas how to enter the underworld and emerge again safely. A later sibyl sold three prophetic scrolls revealing the fate of Rome to King Lucius Tarquinius Priscus (see The Fall of Eagles, page 38). According to the poet Ovid, these two sibyls were the same person. She was rumoured to have lived for seven generations because she had asked Apollo to grant her a life of as many years as there were particles in a handful of dust. The enigmatic god had seen fit to grant this request, but the sibyl discovered, to her cost, that she had forgotten to ask for eternal youth as well, and so lived on and on growing ever older until she was too weak to move. She was then placed in a suspended cage or bottle within the cave which became her constant home and prison. In this state, she became a sinister symbol of withered hope, for, whenever anyone asked her if there was anything that she desired, she simply replied, 'I want to die.'

only to himself loathed the place and swore that no one would ever use it again.

THE CAVERN OF CUMAE

Near Baia is the site of an oracle whose fame has lasted through the ages. This was the home of the sibyls of Cumae, a line of prophetesses who were said to speak with the voice of Apollo. The cavern of Cumae was excavated in 1932. From archaeological evidence, it appears that the sybil would sit in a niche at the back of the cave. Her replies were said to have been written on leaves laid upon the floor; when the supplicant entered, the wind of his passage would scatter the leaves into confusion, symbolizing our imperfect knowledge of the universe.

DIVINE INSPIRATION OR DEVILISH DECEIT?

Although the belief in the efficacy of oracles spanned, undoubtedly, for thousands of years, the possibility of long-term fraud should not be ignored. After all, a line of Pythia priestesses stretching back into mythical times – all possessed with the power of predicting the future – is possible, but is it likely? We do know that at least one false prophecy was delivered at Delphi, due to a corrupt Pythia who favoured the cause of a certain Spartan general. This, of course, is usually taken to be an exception rather than the rule, and both Pythia and Spartan paid with their lives, but prophetic vision could not possibly be guaranteed every time the oracle was consulted, no matter how many mind-altering drugs were administered. At Cumae, also, there is an inconsistency: the writer Varro (116-27 BC) hints that a sybil named Deiphobe was one of the accurate prophets there, which implies that, by omission, some of her predecessors were not.

The story of the doves of Dodona may hint at a cynical explanation. It seems that oracles could be kept informed about world events, such as the deaths of kings, the outcome of battles and the rise and fall of empires, by a network of carrier pigeons, doves or swallows. News of these events could then be passed on to the local population, suitably veiled, as the words of a god.

Furthermore, the very obscurity of the verses delivered by oracle priestesses would serve to cover their ignorance if they were asked a particularly difficult or personal question. Although this is an interesting suggestion – and before we conclude that all oracles were fraudulent – it should be pointed out that there is no actual evidence of widespread deceit. The truth, it seems, lies somewhere between the extremes of credulity and cynicism. Obviously some, perhaps most, of the oracle priestesses channelled accurate information involving predictive techniques. However, not all oracle centres could maintain the quality of true prophecy generation after generation. Perhaps sometimes a suitably talented priestess could not be found and, rather than declar-

ing the oracle sanctuary defunct, more unscrupulous priests would decide to introduce a fraud to further their own ambitions or those of their powerful patrons. It is this paradox incorporating political acumen and clairvoyant prediction that makes the oracle system one of the most fascinating and enigmatic mysteries the world has ever known.

THE ROOF OF THE WORLD

Oracular possession is not just a fragment of ancient history, however. There are places in the world today where human beings are apparently overcome by the force of divine power, and while under this influence, utter prophecies. The spiritualist movement of the West can be regarded as having an ancestry which stretches back to Delphi and beyond, although the beliefs of that movement are couched in Christian terms. The religions of the Caribbean and South America, too, involve trance possession. The mysteries of candomblé and voodoo encourage possession by 'loa' (divine horsemen) who are thought to 'mount' a

The last living example of how an oracle was used in the ancient world regarding State matters may be observed in Tibet's continuing tradition of consulting its State oracle.

human host much as a man would mount a steed. However, the Orient provides the last example of how an oracle is still used in affairs of state. In the Himalayan kingdom of Tibet – called the 'Roof of the World' – a spirit-being has spoken through mediums to warn and advise successive kings, and later, the Dalai Lamas, since before the coming of Buddhism in the seventh century AD.

In 1959 the Dalai Lama (sixth from left) escaped from the Chinese by following the State oracle's advice. A sudden sandstorm is said to have hidden him from the army.

In the light of modern Chinese claims to rule Tibet, by right as well as in fact, it is important to note that, historically, the two nations enjoyed a relationship similar to that of 'patron and priest'. The ruler of Tibet, the Dalai Lama, centuries ago allowed the nominal authority of the Chinese Emperor over Tibet, while he in turn acknowledged the spiritual and temporal primacy of the Dalai Lama. With Mao Tse Tung's assumption of power in China in 1949, however, this vague arrangement came to an end. This caused the lama rulers to look to their state oracle for guidance, which consisted of a succession of specially trained Buddhist monks who were said to be possessed by a devil called Pe-har. According to legend, this terrible being had been helped by one of the Buddha's disciples, and thereafter Pe-har promised to help and protect all those who follow the teachings of the Buddha.

Elaborate ceremonies surround any consultation of Pe-har. The oracle priest, with eyes pressed shut, is helped to his throne. Around him, monks chant sonorous invocations. When the medium's eyes open and seem about to burst from their sockets, the possession by Pe-har has begun. The priest turns red and his body becomes contorted with pain. He sweats profusely and gasps for air. His gestures grow wild until he calms, then he rises, bows three times, and begins to dance. Whirling around and around, again contorted with pain, he slows and questions are put to him. Only then does the oracle finally speak.

During the four centuries of the existence of the oracle, there have been a large number of successful predictions. His suggestions did not stop the British from decimating the Tibetan army in 1904, nor the Chinese from taking over in 1950. However, he did tell the Dalai Lama to leave Tibet in 1959, and the route he should take. The state oracle continues the consultations with the devil-king Pe-har, though not now on Tibetan soil. The oracle is firm that, one day, the Dalai Lama will return to his mountain kingdom.

THE VOICE OF APOLLO

At dawn on the seventh day of February, the Pythia of Delphi, attended by two priests, bathed in the Kastalian spring. Purified, she ascended to the sanctuary of the god Apollo, god of music and rationality, lord of light and truth. He was also known as 'Loxias the Riddler', for at Delphi, Apollo was primarily the god of prophecy. Above the massive portal, an inscription commanded 'Know thyself'. Pondering these words, the Pythia passed swiftly through the Hall of Offerings into the Adyton, a small dark chamber at the rear of the temple. There, she drank a draught of inspiration and chewed on sacred laurel leaves before settling precariously on a bronze tripod decorated with serpents, suspended over a deep cleft in the rock floor. As she inhaled the vapours that rose from the chasm beneath her, a branch of laurel was placed in her hand. When the branch trembled, it signified that the Pythia, oracle of Delphi, was ready to be possessed by the spirit of her god and reveal the fates of men.

The Centre of the World

Perched high on the slopes of Mount Parnassus, Delphi was a capital of sorts for the warring states of Greece. As far as the ancient Greeks were concerned, it was the centre of the world. It was here that the Omphalos or 'Navel Stone' stood. According to myth, Zeus, King of the Olympian gods, had freed two eagles – one at the ultimate west, the other at the furthest east. The eagles flew towards each other across the vast expanse of the earth to meet at Delphi, the centre of the world, where all questions could be answered and emissaries brought laws to be ratified by the sanction of the gods. It was also the place where the most celebrated oracle in the world had spoken since before recorded history. According to Greek mythology, a shepherd named Coratus was the first to discover the oracle's chasm in the sixteenth century BC. He soon found that, by breathing in the vapours that rose from its depths, he could see the future.

However, another tale told by Delphi's temple priests says the oracle was originally the earth-goddess Gaia, who spoke from a cave some seven miles from the present site. A monstrous dragon called Python guarded this cave. This beast was eventually slain by the youthful god Apollo after a terrible battle, and thrust into the rock-covered earth. Thus the ownership of the oracle now passed to the bright god, while the fumes rising from the decomposing dragon provided inspiration for a succession of mediums, each named the Pythia, to commemorate

The Temple of Apollo in Delphi, Greece, was the site of the famous Delphic oracle, who influenced much of Greek history through prophecy. The oracle would fall into a trance, which enabled her to foretell the future.

The Priestess of Delphi, 1890, by Henri Motte (1846-1922), portrays an oracle in the act of declaiming the future. She might shout or whisper, or speak in riddles, depending on how the god Apollo moved her.

Apollo's valour. The cleft in the rock is actually one of the most disputed points in the history of Delphi since no trace of it exists today. However, Greece is a country prone to earthquakes and landslides, so it is quite possible that this chasm was more than myth.

The Pythia's habit of chewing laurel leaves is mysterious since, far from sending one into a hallucinatory trance, the hydrocyanic acid released into the stomach would be likely to make one very sick indeed. It may be that this was a very necessary emetic if the Pythia's trance-inducing drink was in fact a potentially lethal potion such as, perhaps, snake venom.

THE VIRGINAL VOICE

At first consulted on only one day a year – 7 February, which is said to be Apollo's birthday – demand for the oracle grew over the centuries until the Pythia sat nine times between February and October on the seventh day of each month.

To ensure that the common people had access to the god, a special mass oracle was held annually on the steps of the Temple. Understandably, the pressure was so great that sometimes there were no less than three Pythias functioning in shifts. The women who took on the role of voice-piece for Apollo were originally youthful and aristocratic but, after a

Female oracles have captured artists' imaginations for centuries, as in this 1675 painting, *Sibyl of Delphi*, which shows a woman attired in what would have been a fanciful costume for the time.

scandalous episode in which a virginal Pythia ran off with a supplicant, only middle-aged peasant women of proven probity were considered for this most influential post. Indeed, so encompassing was the role of oracle that in no instance do we have a record of the name of any individual lady. They are all, without exception, always referred to simply as the Pythia. Although the mythical derivation of the name links it to the rotting carcass of Python (in ancient Greek, 'pythein' means 'to decay') – alternatively, the word 'pynthanomai' means 'to ask'.

If the role of the Pythia was onerous, it was hardly less so for those who wished to consult the god. Delphi is a difficult and almost inaccessible place to get to even today. In the ancient world, its remoteness required a perilous pilgrimage. On arrival, an audience with the Pythia was in no way guaranteed, even if one came with lavish gifts. Lots were drawn and if one happened to get through the first stage, there was always 'the ritual of the shivering goat' to be overcome. It was the custom to bring a goat to a sanctuary priest prior to the consultation. An urn of ice cold water was then thrown over the unfortunate animal. If it trembled, all was well, and the consultation could proceed; if it did not, then the poor pilgrim was turned away, presumably to return at some later date with a more amenable goat. A successful supplicant would then be purified in the Kastalian spring and brought to the sanctuary with the advice, 'Think good thoughts and well-omened words'. Once in the exalted presence of the Pythia, he could voice his question.

What happened next is still a matter for conjecture. For centuries, it was believed that the Pythia mumbled incomprehensible garbage, which the well-informed and politically astute sanctuary priest would then interpret while shrewdly guessing the outcome to any given question. This effectively made the whole rigmarole of Delphic ritual a fraud. This view owes much to the anti-pagan propaganda of the early church, which considered the Pythia's trance to be some sort of hellish sexual possession.

Mistranslation also plays a part in the confusion. The Greeks described the Pythia's trance as 'Mania', by which they meant divine possession. Unfortunately, this translated into Latin as 'Insania', a word too close to insanity for comfort. The ancient Greeks, though, had no such misgivings; in fact, they were quite convinced that the Pythia went into a trance and spoke clear, though often riddling, answers to direct questions, and the correct interpretation of this was left to the supplicant – sometimes with deadly consequences.

THE POWER OF THE PROPHECIES

One such supplicant was the famously wealthy King Croesus of Lydia, who, doubting the power of the oracles, sent emissaries to every oracle in the Greek world in 550 BC. To each, he addressed a simple question, 'What will I be doing in exactly one hundred days' time?'. Only the oracle of Delphi provided the correct answer: 'I know the number of the sands and the measure of the sea. I understand the dumb and hear him who does not speak. The savour of the hard-shelled tortoise boiled in brass with the flesh of lamb strikes on my senses.'

Croesus was very impressed because he had thought up the unlikely activity of boiling a tortoise and lamb together in a brass cauldron. As a measure of his esteem, he sent 3000 cattle, a huge golden

'I know the number of the sands and the measure of the sea. I understand the dumb and hear him who does not speak. The savour of the hard-shelled tortoise boiled in brass with the flesh of lamb strikes on my senses'

THE ORACLE OF DELPHI, 550 BC

bowl and his wife's jewellery to Delphi together with another question: 'Shall I make war on Persia?'. The oracle replied, 'If you cross the Halys River a great kingdom will be destroyed'.

Cheered erroneously by the Pythia's comment, Croesus at once embarked on a war which proved to be disastrous for his country. The Persians won, conquering Lydia and forcing Croesus to flee into exile. Eventually, Croesus made his way to Delphi where he angrily burst into the sanctuary, bemoaning his loss and blaming the gods and their mouthpiece the Pythia for everything. Calmly, the Pythia replied, 'Croesus has no right to complain. Apollo foretold that he would subvert a great empire. Had he desired to be truly informed he ought to have enquired whether his own or that of the Persians was meant.'

The Persian menace was to prove the impetus for another famous prophecy in 480 BC when the mighty hosts of Xerxes threatened Athens itself. The Athenian delegation to the oracle were horrified when she screamed, 'Why sit, you doomed ones? Fly to the world's end. The headlong god of war is

speeding in a Persian chariot. Rise. Haste from the sanctuary and bow your hearts to grief.' The ambassadors were horrified but refused to leave Delphi until Apollo was in a better mood.

They again sought audience the next day, and were greeted with more hopeful words: 'Zeus the All-seeing grants Athena's prayer that the wooden walls only shall not fall but preserve you and your children'. Since Athens had no walls of any description, the phrase 'wooden walls' was taken to mean a fleet of ships. After much debate, the population of the city was evacuated to the island of Salamis. Athens soon fell to the Persians, who destroyed the Parthenon and slaughtered those who had refused to go.

The Persians then turned their attention to the rich temple of Delphi itself. Their approach was terrifying and the priests packed up as many of the temple treasures as they could find. Throughout this panic, the Pythia remained unmoved and bade them stop their preparations for flight with the words: 'Apollo will protect his own'. And so it happened; the Persian force was swept away by a massive landslide less than a mile from the sanctuary.

THE VOICE IS STILLED AT DELPHI

A slow decline at Delphi began when Philip of Macedonia conquered Greece. Although the Pythia declared his son Alexander to be invincible, Philip was unimpressed. His view of oracles was jaded, to say the least; he may have been influenced by a story of a Spartan general who had bribed the Pythia to

Many female mediums served Apollo, the Greek god of music, truth and prophecy. He was the son of the king of the gods, Zeus, who freed from opposite points two eagles who flew across the world and met at Delphi, proving to the Greeks that Delphi was the centre of the world.

THE LAST ORACLE OF DELPHI

The last oracle given by a Pythia to the ruler of Greece, Julian the Apostate, stated:

❝ Tell the king, the fair-wrought house has fallen, no shelter has Apollo or sacred laurel leaves. The fountains now are silent. The Voice is stilled. ❞

condemn his rival in one of her prophecies. However, the supernatural aura of Delphi was not quite gone, for when the Roman Commander Sulla sacked the temple in 86 BC it is said that an eerie music was heard which frightened his soldiers. The materialistic Sulla laughed and said, 'Listen how Apollo, god of music, is happy to help Rome.' Needless to say, despite the ominous portents, the looting continued.

The Emperor Nero, too, helped himself to some of Delphi's treasures in AD 66. He wanted to refurbish a newly rebuilt, if a little fire-damaged, Rome. However, another Roman, the Emperor Hadrian proved to be a friend to Delphi and restored the shrine in AD 132. Another looting took place under Constantine, and later under the barbarian Goths.

By the time Julian the Apostate ascended the throne, there was little left of Delphi, although even this last pagan emperor sent his doctor Oribasius to seek an oracle. He found an old woman living amongst the tumbled ruins. Silently she bathed in the Kastalian spring and enacted the ancient rites before taking her place on the tripod to deliver the last oracle of the Pythia: 'Tell the king, the fair-wrought house has fallen, no shelter has Apollo or sacred laurel leaves. The fountains now are silent. The Voice is stilled.'

ALEXANDER AND THE ORACLES

Few heroes of the ancient world could equal the reputation of that of Alexander the Great. This almost legendary Macedonian king carried his wars to the very edge of the known world. He fought battles in India and Afghanistan, conquered the largest empire that the world had ever known and, died in Babylon in 323 BC, at the age of just thirty-three.

Even though his father, King Philip of Macedonia, a celebrated conqueror himself, had gone to great lengths to ensure that Alexander was brought up in a rational, civilized 'Athenian' manner, yet his son retained a strong mystical streak which derived from the influence of his witch-mother Olympias, whose Dionysian leanings have been described by the historian and novelist Mary Renault. Olympias was, by turns, loved, hated, worshipped and reviled by Alexander, and she was certainly a powerful factor in her son's life. It has even been suggested that he went to the ends of the earth primarily to get away from a mother who was known to dance naked, entwined with snakes, in orgiastic occult rites.

None the less, Olympias had conveyed to Alexander that he was in some measure divine. He devoutly believed that he was the descendant, if not the reincarnation, of the great Homeric hero Achilles, who fought and fell before the walls of Troy. From his mother he must have heard how an eagle had alighted on the roof of the palace at the moment of his birth, proving that Zeus, the king of the gods, favoured him above all others. His later successes bore out his mother's words, yet Alexander spent his life moving from one oracle to another for confirmation of the will of the gods, and reassurance of his standing. His father would not have approved. Philip of Macedonia was not a believer in the will of the gods and maintained a healthy scepticism about the power of oracles. After all, he had bribed enough of them to ensure that the pronouncements of the gods favoured his own political aspirations.

THE KNOT OF GORDIUS

After the murder of Philip of Macedonia, a crime Alexander and his mother were suspected of, the invasion of Asia Minor began and open war existed between Macedonia and the might of the Persian Empire. As he and his Macedonian army fought their way through Asia Minor in 336 BC, Alexander visited the vast Temple of Apollo, god of prophecy, at Didyma, which housed one of the most famous oracles of the Greek world. This oracle had been silent for one hundred years since the Persians had stolen the cult statue of the god. However, according to the Roman chronicler Plutarch, when Alexander set foot in the precincts, the sacred spring which delivered the words of the god suddenly bubbled up and began to flow

Olympias, mother of Alexander the Great, was a strong contributor to Alexander's desire for the approval of the gods, whose will he sought through oracles throughout his life.

This 16th century painting shows The Birth of Alexander the Great *(356-323 BC). Alexander's mother claimed that an eagle alighted on the palace roof at the moment that he was born, thus proving to her that Zeus favoured him.*

once more. The priestess of the oracle pronounced Alexander 'Lord of Asia'.

The next year, Alexander and his forces came to the ancient city of Gordion. There, in the Temple of Zeus which crowned the inner citadel, was a simple farm cart, which held the key to the mastery of the world. The cart had belonged to Gordius, founder of the city, who centuries before had left posterity with a riddle and a prophecy. It was said that the man who could unravel the incredibly complex knot which bound the yoke to the shaft would conquer the world. This task had baffled all of those who had attempted it before then.

Alexander examined the knot, to find that its ends were concealed within its twisting complexity. After some moments, Alexander turned his attention to the wooden pin which went through the knot. Some say he lifted this and the famous Gordian Knot fell apart. Others, including the chronicler Arrian, said that Alexander took his sword and, with the words, 'It doesn't matter how the knot is loosened', severed it with one blow. The prophetic happenings at Gordion were said to have concluded with a dramatic thunderstorm that same night, signalling the noisy approval of Zeus the cloud-gatherer, King of the Gods.

Fear of this favourite of the gods spread. For example, in the maritime city of Tyre – the scene of one of the bloodiest battles of Alexander's wars – the local cult statue of Apollo was chained to its plinth for fear that it would physically desert the beleaguered city and walk to Alexander's side.

Towards the end of 332 BC, the mighty King Alexander came eventually to Egypt where he was immediately acclaimed Pharaoh. The Egyptian people looked on him as a saviour since, under Persian rule, their culture had been suppressed and their gods dishonoured. Alexander was to make no such mistake and set off on a hazardous pilgrimage to one of the most prestigious oracles in the ancient world – that of Ammon, at the Siwa oasis. To Alexander and his fellow Greeks, this god was none other than their own Zeus in another guise.

THE ROAD TO SIWA

With a small force, Alexander undertook the gruelling eight-day journey to Siwa across a pitiless sea of sand. More than once, the favour of the gods was invoked as the men grew fearful. On one occasion, they ran out of water but were saved by a sudden, and totally unexpected, rainstorm. This was a natural phenomenon almost unknown in those parched lands. Unsurprisingly, Alexander saw this as an excellent omen. Finally, the party was led to the safety of the oasis of Siwa by two crows.

Without bathing or changing his dusty robes, as other men might have done, Alexander made straight for the sanctum of the god. He was greeted at the gate by a shaven priest who spoke in faltering Greek. According to Arrian, the priest wished to address the king as 'My son', as any cleric might, but, because of his imperfect knowledge of Greek, he actually called him 'Son of god'. Taking up the cue, the rest of the assembly shouted, 'Son of Zeus-Ammon, master of all lands, unconquered until he is united with the gods'.

This marble Roman bust of Alexander the Great shows how young he was when he died in 323 BC, having conquered the largest empire the world had ever known.

With this praise ringing in his ears, the great Alexander entered the temple to stand before the ram-headed image of the deity.

'Son of Zeus-Ammon, master of all lands, unconquered until he is united with the gods'

GREETING AS ALEXANDER ARRIVED IN SIWA

He stood in the gloom of the small inner sanctum and asked his questions. Unknown to Alexander, a temple priest was concealed within a false ceiling. We cannot know precisely what the king asked his god but his first query must have concerned his own divinity. The second question concerned a matter troubling the king. According to later writers, he asked, 'Has my father's murderer been punished?' The third question related to the future, 'Will it be given to me to be ruler of the world?' The biographer Arrian merely states that, 'The answers to all three questions gladdened Alexander's heart'. However, later writers go into greater detail. They claim that the oracle definitely pronounced Alexander a god. Not only that but, in answer to the question about his father's murderer, the oracle expressed puzzlement, saying that Alexander was the son of no mortal father but the offspring of Zeus-Ammon himself. The answer to the third question may have altered the course of world history, because the oracle confirmed that Alexander would indeed be master of the world.

This was a pivotal moment for the young Macedonian because Darius, Great King of Persia, had recently written to Alexander offering him the western portion of the empire if the youthful conqueror would come no further. This was a handsome proposition upon which one of the Macedonian generals, Parmenio, commented, 'If I were Alexander I would accept'. Alexander is said to have countered, 'If I were Parmenio, so would I'. The words of the oracle of Ammon may have given Alexander the confidence to reject Darius and press on to ultimate victory.

Now, in Egypt, Alexander wore ram's horns on his helmet to symbolize his devotion to Ammon. He was invested with the ancient rites of the Pharaoh and took his place amongst the dynasties of Ancient Egypt. It was probably at this time that a peculiar rumour spread amongst both the Greeks and Egyptians. The substance of this was that Alexander was actually the son of Nectanebo, Egypt's last native ruler, who had fled to Greece when the Persians had taken his kingdom. This exiled Pharaoh was said to have transformed himself into a ram-headed serpent and lain with Queen Olympias.

THE SPEAKING TREE

Almost five years after his encounter with the god Zeus-Ammon, Alexander found himself confronted with an oracle that was not so favourable. Legend has it that, during his invasion of India, a group of high-caste Brahmins took the great conqueror to the Speaking Tree. This towering growth was said to whisper in all the languages of mankind and to foretell the future.

Characteristically, the brave Alexander marched straight up to its mighty trunk. Loudly he spoke his question, 'Am I to conquer India, and be truly the master of the whole world?' The prophetic boughs creaked in answer, 'No, India will not fall beneath your sway, and you will die young.' In fury, the Macedonian king commanded that the tree be hacked down. It was not long after this that the Macedonian soldiers, who formed the backbone of his army, refused to go any further and demanded to go home. Heartbroken, Alexander reluctantly agreed.

THE CROWS OF BABYLON

During the long march westward, the aged Hindu seer Calanus, who now accompanied the retreating army, fell ill and announced that he would burn himself alive on a pyre in the Indian fashion. From the account of Alexander's admiral, Nearchus, we learn that, bidding Alexander farewell from the midst of the flames, Calanus cried, 'We will say our farewells in Babylon'. Pondering the import of these dark words, Alexander continued towards his capital.

Babylonian astrologers hastened to meet him with equally dire warnings. They said that the god Bel, patron of Babylon, had pronounced that it would be death for the king to enter the city. Consequently, Alexander refused to continue and withdrew to Borsippa some miles to the South to consult with the astrologers there. However, the notoriously sceptical general Anaxagoras urged Alexander to ignore the omens. So, in April, 323 BC, Alexander and his depleted force passed through the gates of his capital city of Babylon. The king and his advisors were appalled to see a flock of crows wheeling above the Ishtar Gate. It seemed that the birds which had led Alexander to his father Ammon no longer favoured him.

Now installed in the royal palace, Alexander may have been advised to forego the crown for one day and make another king in his place. After all, the god Bel had merely said that the king would die. He had not actually named Alexander specifically. So the grim 'ritual of the substitute king' began. A simple-minded young man was dressed in kingly finery,

crowned and acclaimed by the court. One day later, this unfortunate was dragged from the throne and executed. Now, surely, the prophecy of Bel had come to pass, for was not a king dead? Alas for Alexander, the gods were not so easily fooled. He soon contracted a fever, though some claim that he was

poisoned, and it soon became evident that he would die. As he gasped his last breaths, his generals and companions gathered around his bed. Now Alexander himself turned prophet. In answer to the question, 'To whom do you leave the empire?'

Seers warned Alexander he would die young, and in Babylon if he entered it. Disregarding them, he entered anyway, as Charles Brun's (1619-90) painting, *The Triumph of Alexander*, or *The Entrance of Alexander into Babylon*, shows.

Alexander weakly replied, 'The strongest.' History has proved him right. But even the strongest are weak at times, and that is the Achilles heel of everyone. Could Alexander have meant the gods are strongest?

THE IDES OF MARCH

When the great Julius Caesar met his gory end on 15 March 44 BC at the hands of Brutus and the Roman senators, he should not have been too shocked by the turn of events. He had previously been warned by Vitricius Spurinna, a reader of omens, who had cried, 'Beware the Ides of March'. That very morning, his wife Calpurnia had tried to dissuade him from attending as she had had a terrible nightmare in which she had seen her house crumbling before her eyes and her husband bloodied and dying at the feet of his now deceased old rival Pompey. Some months earlier, too, the first intimation of impending disaster had occurred when the tomb of Capys, founder of the city of Capua, was unearthed. A bronze plaque was discovered upon which were inscribed prophetic words: 'When once the tomb of Capys is brought to light, then a branch of the Julian House will be slain by one of his kindred'. As if these troubling prophecies were not enough, the Romans, who always had an eye for signs and wonders, noticed that wild birds had nested in the Forum, the very heart of the city.

However, none of these dark omens was enough to put Caesar off his plans. He was a man of boundless ambition and, though he had achieved the rank of dictator to the Roman people, he was determined to be declared king by the Roman senate, a move which they found impossible to stomach. When Caesar mounted the steps, he again encountered Spurinna who looked at him gravely. 'The Ides of

The Death of Julius Caesar, painted by Vincenzo Camuccini in 1793, depicts the murder of Caesar in the Senate. His assassination was foretold by ancient and contemporary prophets.

March are come,' quipped the balding dictator.

'Aye, but not yet gone,' countered the gloomy Spurinna, with foreboding.

THE FATAL BRANCH

History records that, no sooner had Julius Caesar stepped into the senate chamber, he was stabbed twenty-three times by his disgruntled 'friends, Romans and countrymen' to fall dead at the base of a statue of Pompey, his old enemy. Tradition tells that the killing blow was delivered by Marcus Brutus, a man rumoured to be Caesar's illegitimate son, and therefore a 'Branch of the Julian House'. These prophetic words apart, if Julius Caesar had paid more attention to the priestly functions of his high office, he may have received a warning from an impeccable source – namely, the Sibylline Books which were housed in the holiest temple and in the city guarded by the Vestal Virgins.

Centuries before the time of Caesar, Rome, then a small mud-brick city, was ruled by a line of tyrannical kings. It was to visit one of these petty monarchs, King Tarquinius Priscus, that a lady known as the Sibyl, a gifted oracle inspired by the god Apollo, left her cave at Cumae with nine scrolls and a peculiar sales pitch. Standing before the king, she said that she would sell the unopened scrolls for one million gold pieces. The king laughed and rejected her offer. At this, the Sibyl threw three of the scrolls into a fire. She then demanded two million gold pieces for the remaining six. Again she was rejected and a further three went into the flames.

The sweating king belatedly began to realize that the contents must be very valuable indeed, and so he grudgingly paid three million gold pieces for the surviving scrolls, and the Sibyl happily returned to her mysterious cave.

These scrolls were originally guarded by another line of Preistesses, the Vestal Virgins. These maidens were also the keepers of the sacred flame of the goddess Vesta, which was regarded as the 'hearth of Rome', and was never allowed to go out.

Many prophecies and omens foretold Caesar's death. The Romans noticed wild birds nesting in the centre of Rome, which indicated to them that their ruler would die soon.

In 80 BC, a fire in the temple destroyed the original prophecies, but the texts were reassembled later by eminent scholars of the time.

The remaining scrolls contained many verses which were confusing poetic forecasts of the future of the Roman State and its rulers. The verse that seems to refer to Julius Caesar is the first in a series called 'The Succession of the Hairy Ones'. These verses remained a closely guarded secret when the first emperors were in power.

'A hundred years of the Punic curse
and Rome will be slave to a hairy man,
a hairy man that is scant of hair.
Every man's woman and each woman's man.
The steed that he rides shall have toes for hooves.
He shall die at the hand of his son, no son,
and not on the field of war.'

This riddling poem becomes easier to understand when it is realized that the word 'Caesar' means 'hair'. Thus, the balding Julius was a 'hairy man who is scant of hair'. His sexual habits were a scandal in republican Rome; he was 'every man's woman and each woman's man', this line, however, could also reflect his mass popularity. In the Sibylline verses, an army was quite often symbolized by a horse and so the legions that bore Julius to power had 'toes instead of hooves'. Finally, the 'son, no son' who slew him was none other than his reputedly illegitimate son Brutus. A more apt final line to the verse might have been 'to the gain of his son, no son' – because his adopted son Octavian became the first Roman Emperor.

This bronze statue of Julius (Gaius) Caesar – Rome's last dictator prior to its series of emperors, and the father of its first Emperor Octavius – was made around 44 BC and stands in Acosta, Italy. Shakespeare made into a moral tale the story of his arrogance towards divine warnings and his betrayal by friends and colleagues.

THE FUTURE IN THE ENTRAILS

Gazing at the internal organs of a sacrificed animal to reveal the will of the gods and the course of the future was thought to have originated in the Stone Age, and was extensively practised in the ancient world by the Babylonians, the Greeks and the Romans. This form of divination is still practised in Borneo, Burma and Uganda.

The Etruscans, who were earlier inhabitants of Italy, were said to obsessed by it; the Roman writer, Cicero, himself a seeker of omens said, 'The whole Etruscan nation has gone mad on the subject of entrails'.

Lambs or sheep were the unfortunate beasts that were most usually sacrificed, although goats, pigs and oxen were often slaughtered, too. Julius Caesar claimed that the Druids of Britain read the entrails of human victims. However, it is assumed that this was the exception rather than the rule, and was more likely to have been political propaganda.

Fortune-telling by entrails is known as hepatoscopy, extispicy and augury. The most important organ to be examined was the liver, which in astrology is ruled by the planet Jupiter. In Roman mythology, Jupiter was the king of the gods, known as Zeus to the Greeks, Ammon to the Egyptians, Baal in Babylon and Thor in northern Europe. So, in all systems of belief from Sumeria to Scandinavia, the liver was considered to be the prime organ of importance, and quite often thought to be the seat of the soul.

The fact that a freshly slaughtered beast would have a shiny, reflective liver may have indicated that this organ acted as a mirror for the will of the king of the gods. Museums around the world contain many examples of clay models of livers, each divided into fifty-five areas, which were used as references by Babylonian diviners.

The spiral of the intestines themselves are the next in order of importance. Diviners would judge by the odd or even number of turns in the gut whether the omen was negative, if odd, or positive, if even.

THE EMPEROR'S DRAGON

Of all the rulers of the Roman Empire, none was more addicted to signs and omens than Tiberius. His paranoia was legendary and led him to commit many ruthless and cruel acts that ensured his place in the annals of infamy. Of him, the oracular Sibylline Books said, 'He shall be mud well mixed with blood, and a pillow shall be his end'. Above all, he feared the fulfilment of a prophecy which had been made by an astrologer named Thrassylus on the lovely island of Rhodes.

Tiberius, born in 42 BC, was the step-son of Octavian Augustus Caesar, successor to the assassinated Julius, and their relationship had always been strained. Despite the influence of Tiberius's mother, the disgraced prince had been exiled from Rome for many years. It was while staying at Lindos on Rhodes that the unlikeable Tiberius met Thrassylus, who by careful calculation and prophetic insight assured the future emperor that he would be restored to favour and recalled to Rome.

Now, Thrassylus has a unique reputation among astrologers. He is said never to have been wrong – even when he was lying. By some quirk of fate, this corrupt and infinitely bribable man's predictions always came true, no matter how unlikely they sounded at first. We cannot be totally sure that he actually believed Tiberius would be restored to the imperial court; however, Thrassylus restated the prophecy many times until Tiberius lost patience with him. One day, according to the Roman historian Tacitus, Thrassylus painfully climbed the steep steps to the high acropolis at Lindos only to find Tiberius seated at a table working on a horoscope chart surrounded by his fierce guards.

'Whose horoscope is that?' enquired Thrassylus.

'Why, yours,' replied Tiberius, 'and it seems that you are about to suffer a terrible fall.'

The acropolis of Lindos stands on 300-foot high cliffs and Thrassylus was understandably nervous. Thinking quickly, the sweating astrologer said, 'That would be a pity because, since our horoscopes are so similar, any fate that befalls me will also befall you within one year.' At this unexpected news, Tiberius changed his mind, but Thrassylus had not finished. 'Look at the ship approaching the harbour; it brings news which heralds your return to Rome in triumph.'

And so it happened. Tiberius did indeed return to

This glass cameo (42 BC-AD 32) bears the profile of the cruel and ruthless Emperor Tiberius (Claudius Nero), who ruled the Roman Empire after the death of Julius Caesar's son.

SYBILLINE PREDICTION

The following lines describe the smothering to death of Tiberius by his great-nephew Caligula, predicted centuries earlier by the Apollonian oracle Sibyl:

66 He shall be mud well mixed with blood, and a pillow shall be his end. 99

the court of his step-father – eventually to succeed him as emperor. He ensured, however, that Thrassylus was always nearby.

Another of Thrassylus's predictions resulted in the relocation of the entire imperial court. He predicted that Tiberius would die in Rome, so the Emperor afterwards simply refused to go there, building himself a sumptuous palace on the isle of Capri.

There, on another high terrace, Thrassylus met his end, according to the biographer Suetonius. While he was sharing a glass of wine with Tiberius, a lizard ran across the astrologer's hand. He looked up sadly and said, 'This is the omen I have dreaded, for it means my death. Beware, Tiberius, for your lizard will call you within one year.' At that, Thrassylus quietly passed away.

THE EMPEROR'S LIZARD

When Tiberius had been acclaimed Emperor, the King of Ceylon had sent him an enormous lizard as a gift. It was probably an iguana or a Komodo dragon. The emperor doted upon the ill-natured, ill-smelling beast. He kept it in a cage and fed it every day. As a mark of his affection, this hater of humanity called the creature by his own name, Tiberius.

Some months after Thrassylus's death it became imperative for the emperor to pay a visit to his capital. With immense pomp, the imperial court was again on the move. But, just as the walls of Rome came into view, Tiberius was horrified to discover that his beloved dragon was dead. It lay motionless on the floor of its cage, swarms of ants crawling all over its body.

The shock of this was too much for the ageing ruler, and

it is probable that he suffered a heart attack. Panic-stricken courtiers carried the prone Tiberius to a nearby villa while a messenger was sent to Rome.

Soon, the emperor's great-nephew Caligula arrived, demanding that he be left alone with his kinsman. As soon as he had secured the door, Caligula took the imperial signet ring from the unconscious Tiberius's finger and, coming out of the chamber, announced to the assembled senators and court that, with his dying breath, Tiberius had proclaimed him his heir. At this point, Tiberius himself made an unexpected and dramatic reappearance. Supporting himself against the door frame, he demanded his ring back. The apologetic Caligula lay him down on the bed and, as soon as he had again secured the door, smothered the old man.

Both Thrassylus and the Sibylline oracle had been right once more. Tiberius had indeed died as Thrassylus had predicted – not in the city of Rome, but in a house called the Villa Roma.

'Beware, Tiberius, for your lizard will call you within one year.'

THRASSYLUS, UPON HIS DEATH, TO TIBERIUS

Thrassylus accurately predicted that the death of Tiberius would be linked with that of his lizard – both died within a year of the other.

THE FALL OF EAGLES

On a cold December morning in the early days of the Roman Empire, during the reign of Tiberius Caesar, a young man of the imperial family went on a private religious mission to a cavern on Mount Gaurus. Although imperial by birth, this particular scion of the Caesars was not prominent or even publicly acknowledged by his more illustrious relatives. In fact, they were rather ashamed of him since his limp, nervous twitch and continual stammering made him something of an embarrassment. His name was Claudius.

Painfully limping, the young man descended the dim, tortuous passage into the cave to meet the great and mysterious sibyl of Cumae, spiritual descendant of that ancient divinely inspired Sibyl who had so cheated King Tarquinius Priscus. Entering, Claudius was confronted by an ancient woman who sat suspended in a cage hanging from the rocky roof. Naturally assuming that this was the celebrated oracle, he nervously began his address, 'Oh sib...sib...sibyl...,' he stammered.

But before he could continue, a mocking voice echoed through the cavern. 'Oh Clau... Clau... Claudius.'

Terrified, with bowed head, Claudius realized that the spectre in the cage was a mummified corpse and that the true sibyl, a much younger woman, had moved into the wan light. Still shaking, Claudius managed to stumble through the rest of his speech. 'I have come to ask you of the fate of Rome and of myself.' At once, the prophetic frenzy came over the oracle and the room was plunged into darkness. Calming, the sibyl spoke her riddling words:

'Who groans beneath the Punic Curse
And strangles in the strings of purse,
before she mends must sicken worse.
Her living mouth shall breed blue flies,
And maggots creep about her eyes.
No man shall mark the day she dies.
Ten years, fifty days and three,
Clau...Clau...Clau shall given be.
A gift that all desire but he.'

(trans. Robert Graves)

Claudius left the cave filled with dark foreboding for the future. He knew that it was Rome and her empire that 'groaned beneath the Punic Curse' because,

'Ten years,
fifty days
and three,
Clau...Clau
...Clau shall
given be.
A gift that
all desire
but he.'

SIBYL OF CUMAE
TO CLAUDIUS

The Torches of Nero, **painted in 1876 by Henryk Siemiradzki, portrays Nero (Roman Emperor, AD 37-68) burning Christians, his aim being to keep the populace under the control of the Roman Empire and himself.**

more than a century before, the Romans had sworn by the name of Apollo that they would maintain a perpetual friendship with the North African city of Carthage. Then, succumbing to jealousy, they had betrayed that trust and destroyed it in the Third Punic War. The 'strings of purse' referred to the greed and corruption that would eventually leave the city as rotten as a corpse. And yet, there was hope in the sibyl's prophecy, for 'No man shall mark the day she dies'. Even then, it seems, Rome – though sick and cursed – was thought of as eternal. But what was the 'gift that all desired but he'? Claudius would have to wait the allotted time of ten years and fifty-three days before that part of the prophecy was revealed.

In AD 41, after the assassination of the Emperor Gaius, better known as Caligula, many members of the ruling family were slaughtered by Republican legionnaries. Claudius managed to conceal himself behind a curtain in the palace, and escaped the first spate of murders. However, he was discovered by another troop of soldiers. Fearing, with the death of the emperor, that they would be unemployed, they thrust a laurel wreath on the head of Claudius and proclaimed him Caesar. The power of the Emperor of Rome was the gift that all men desired – all but the umambitious, timid and scholarly Claudius. So Claudius became the fifth Emperor of Rome, sixth in succession from the great Julius Caesar.

THE HAIRY ONES

The concept of imperial succession brings us back to that earlier Sibyl who delivered her prophetic books to Tarquinius Priscus (616-579 BC), for which she extorted a fabulous price from the neurotic monarch (see The Ides of March pages 32-35). These three scrolls were believed to foretell the history of Rome and were consulted, first by the senate, and later by the emperors, in times of crisis. One of the more controversial aspects of these prophetic writings is a fairly long series of verses called 'The Succession of the Hairy Ones', which, if they do pre-date the events of which they speak, count amongst the greatest predictions of all time. The word 'Caesar' means 'hair' or 'hairy', deriving from the fact that the ancient founder of the line was very hirsute. The first verse, which refers to Julius Caesar ('the hairy man who is scant of hair'), takes as its starting point the same Punic Curse mentioned above:

'A hundred years of the Punic Curse
And Rome shall be slave to a hairy man,
A hairy man who is scant of hair.
Every man's woman and each woman's man.
The steed that he rides shall have toes for hooves.
He shall die at the hand of his son, no son,
And not on the field of war.'

The dictator Gaius Julius Caesar was the first of his family to attain absolute power in Rome, even though he did not actually manage to make himself emperor. His scandalous reputation was a point of pride amongst his marching legions, who composed a scurrilous song to highlight their dictator's foibles:

'Home we bring, the bald whoremonger,
Romans lock your wives away.
All the bags of gold you sent him,
Went his Gaulish tarts to pay.'

Julius's right hand, Mark Anthony, even went so far as to accuse Octavian of gaining his position as heir by pandering to his uncle's many vices.

(For a more complete explanation of the first verse, see The Ides of March, pages 32-35.)

'The hairy one next to enslave the State
Shall be son, no son to this hairy last,
He shall have hair in a generous mop.
He shall give Rome marble in place of clay
And fetter her fast with unseen chains,
And shall die at the hand of his wife, no wife,
To the gain of his son, no son.'

The second verse skips over the period of the Second Triumvirate of co-rulers, Mark Anthony, Lepidus and Octavian, and the civil wars that followed. It concentrates on the victor, Octavian, who accepted the title of Augustus, and proclaimed himself first Emperor of Rome. Octavian Augustus (27 BC-AD 14) boasted that he had found Rome made of clay and left it made of marble just as the fourth line of the verse predicts. The 'unseen chains' with which he fettered Rome were the imperial system itself which he established. His 'wife, no wife' was an interesting character – a scandalous lady by the name of Livia, who, while pregnant with her second child, divorced her husband to marry Augustus. Theirs was a business partnership par excellence. There was never any sexual contact between them, their whole relationship being one of mutual political necessity.

Livia's cold heart became proverbial because when, after thirty years of marriage, Augustus threatened to disinherit her son, Tiberius, she began to poison her husband's food. The canny Augustus realized that an attempt was being made on his life and refused to eat anything but fruit picked with his own hands – specifically, figs from a tree in his private garden. Livia secretly made a small incision in each fruit to introduce her venom while it still hung from the branch. Augustus eventually succumbed to her murderous scheming, and Tiberius became Emperor, as the third verse of the prophecy foretold.

THE HAIRY THIRD
TO ENSLAVE THE STATE

'Shall be son, no son, of this hairy last.
He shall be mud well mixed with blood,
A hairy man that is scant of hair.
He shall give Rome victories and defeat
And die to the gain of his son, no son.
A pillow shall be his end.'

THE PUNIC CURSE

The Romans' failure to uphold their promise to Apollo led to the Punic Curse and to Rome's subsequent downfall after the sickening of its leaders – which Apollo's oracle reminded Claudius.

66 **Who groans beneath the Punic Curse**
And strangles in the strings of purse,
Before she mends must sicken worse...
No man shall mark the day she dies. 99

Tiberius was dominated by his scheming mother politically but had, in his younger days, been a successful general, winning several victories in Germany. The story of his association with the Arab astrologer Thrassylus and of his eventual end is told in The Emperor's Dragon on pages 36-37.

'The hairy fourth to enslave the State
Shall be son, no son of this hairy last.
A hairy man that is scant of hair,
He shall give Rome poisons and blasphemies
And die from a kick of his aged horse
That carried him as a child.'

The hairy fourth was the notorious Caligula, a ruler whose progressive paranoia and continuing mental instability made his name a byword for cruelty. It is said that his predecessor Tiberius thought that the only way that posterity was going to look kindly upon his career, was if he was replaced by someone even worse. His 'son, no son' Caligula fitted the bill perfectly. Apart from making his horse Incitatus a member of the senate to show his contempt for that august body, Caligula also declared himself a god and chopped the heads off sacred statues, replacing them with his own likeness. Thus he fulfilled the fourth line of the prophecy. His downfall came when a group of army officers led by Cassius Chaerea assassinated him in AD 41. It is said that as their blades penetrated his body, he remarked, 'Don't be silly... don't you know I'm a god?'

There are several correlations between the first and fourth verses of the oracle. In Caligula's case, the most notable being the identification of the army as 'an aged horse that carried him as a child'. In

Julius Caesar's verse, the army is described thus: 'The steed that he rides shall have toes for hooves'. The reason for this odd identification may lie in Caligula's true name, which, like his notable ancestor's was Gaius Julius Caesar.

'The hairy fifth to enslave the State
To enslave the State, though against his will,
Shall be that fool whom all despised.
He will have hair in a generous mop.
He shall give Rome water and winter bread
And die at the hand of his wife, no wife
To the gain of his son, no son.'

Poor scholarly Claudius was 'that fool whom all despised'. Still, his reign was a successful one. His conquest of Britain is not mentioned in the prophecy, but another great achievement is. That was the refurbishment of the Ostia, the port of Rome which had previously been unusable during the winter months, and also the building of an enormous aquaduct which brought fresh water into the over-populated city. This is the 'water and winter bread' of the prophecy. Claudius's 'wife, no wife', was his niece Agrippina, sister of his predecessor Caligula. Agrippina had the same scheming nature as Livia and bore a great resemblance to her great-grand-mother. This provided the perfect political match for the insecure emperor. As with Livia and Augustus, the marriage was an arrangement of State that did not involve consummation. Agrippina fed Claudius poisoned mushrooms from her own plate in AD 54. After this, she was heard to joke that truly mushrooms were the food of the gods because it was by means of a mushroom that Claudius became one.

This Indian sardonyx cameo bears the profiles of the Emperor Claudius and Agrippina the Younger, his niece, [left]; and his brother Germanicus and his wife Agrippina the Elder [right].

'The hairy sixth to enslave the State
Shall be son, no son of this hairy last.
He shall give Rome music and fire.
His hand shall be red with a parent's blood.
No hairy seventh to him succeeds
And bloodied will be his tomb.

The hairy sixth was Agrippina's son Nero, the last of the Julio-Claudian line. He was an unstable boy who fancied himself as a poet the equal of Homer, and as an athlete worthy of the laurels of victory. Nero was also prone to uncontrollable fits of rage. Apart from persecuting the Christians by turning them into human torches, he also kicked to death his pregnant wife Poppea during one of his violent bouts.

The early part of Nero's reign was completely dominated by his mother, who controlled him to such an extent that he felt that he had no freedom whatsoever. Eventually, the young emperor decided to drown her in a specially constructed collapsible pleasure barge that he duly presented her with. Agrippina was delighted with his gift and took a leisurely cruise on the Tiber river. At a prearranged location the whole vessel broke apart and Agrippina was plunged into the water. However, Agrippina was an excellent swimmer. Nero now took the direct approach and sent a centurion to kill her.

Agrippina faced death bravely and demanded that the soldier stab her in the womb that had borne so monstrous a son. Thus, Nero's hand was red with a parent's blood as in the fourth line of the prophecy.

But what of the third line? It is true that Nero considered himself a poet and musician of some renown, a view with which everyone around him naturally concurred. The actual extent of his talent is still the source of some debate, however, as is his alleged complicity in the burning of Rome. The notion of Nero fiddling while the city burned is erroneous; the fiddle was not then invented, and Nero happened to be at Actium when the blaze occurred. When he heard about it, he ordered that the gates of the imperial gardens be opened so that the fleeing multitude had somewhere to go. Later, during his lifetime, the blame for the arson was laid at the door of the newly formed Christian sect, and was the initial cause of their persecution.

Nero's own death came as the result of a revolt in 69 AD. After composing a lament, he attempted to fall on his sword, but didn't have the stomach for it. In desperation, he asked a slave to

A colossal Roman marble head of Nero, c. AD 65. Nero's egocentrism knew no bounds, which led to a revolt against him in AD 69.

do the deed for him and, with the words, 'What an artist the world has lost in me', the last of the Julio-Claudian Caesars died. However the story of the emperor's semi-suicide was not widely believed and a pretender claiming to be Nero arose in the east. In Rome, meanwhile, a riot ensued close to his tomb, which the mob believed was empty. A ruthless suppression of the throng was carried out by the praetorian guard and, as the Sibylline prophecy had foretold, Nero's tomb was spattered in blood.

THE ROLL OF THE DICE

Even though the Sibylline skip over the period of the Triumvirate, there were other prophecies which did not. The earliest of these was made by Julia, mother of Octavian, who, when pregnant, had a dream that she was about to give birth to the god Apollo. Since Octavian's rival, Mark Anthony, identified himself with Apollo's rival Dionysus, the stage was set for a shattering confrontation.

Mark Anthony was by now ruler of the eastern half of the Roman Empire. Like Julius Caesar before him, he had fallen in love with Queen Cleopatra VII of Egypt, whom he bigamously married in defiance of his matrimonial link to Octavian's sister, Octavia. However, Anthony's luck did not prosper and he complained that he dwelt in Octavian's shadow, which Plutarch described in the first century AD.

There were other portents which foretold the fall of Anthony: the city of Pisarum, founded by Anthony, was destroyed by an earthquake; a statue of Anthony was seen to sweat, though it was wiped dry again and again; the temple of Anthony's supposed ancestor Hercules was struck by lightning; and, at Athens, the image of Dionysus (Anthony's favourite god) fell from the Parthenon during a storm. Finally, a bad omen was perceived on Cleopatra's flagship *The Antonias.* Swallows nested under the stern, but another flock drove them out and killed their young. This was taken to foretell the end of the lovers' dreams of conquest and the extinction of their progeny.

However, Mark Anthony was optimistic, for there were obscure verses in some of the Sibylline oracles that hinted that Rome itself would be overcome by forces from the east. He and Cleopatra chose to interpret these as meaning that they would be victorious over Octavian and dominate the Roman Empire. However, their combined forces were ignominiously defeated at the Battle of Actium (32 BC). Both later committed suicide, Anthony in a traditional Roman manner, by throwing himself on his sword, and Cleopatra, by means of the venom of an asp. Unknown to the fated couple, the predicted domination of Rome from the east was not to occur for a further three hundred years.

THE FATAL HOUR

Although the 'Succession of the Hairy Ones' had come to an end in AD 69, many generals took advantage of the vacuum at the head of the state and made a grab for power. In one year, four military commanders 'assumed the purple' of an emperor, only to be assassinated by the next in line. Rome stabilized under the rule of Vespasian (AD 69-79) who was so successful that he became one of the few Emperors to die in bed. It is said that on his deathbed he mocked the pretensions of the hairy ones; his last words were, 'Oh dear, I seem to be becoming a god!'.

Vespasian was followed by his two sons, Titus and Domitian. Titus reigned for only two years, but under Domitian the Romans relived the days of terror under Nero. The Emperor Domitian had been jealous of both his father and elder brother. His surly, unpleasant character soon developed into a paranoia rivalling that of the long-dead Tiberius. His life became a vicious circle of suspicion followed by wanton cruelty, which in turn created plots against him, making him even more suspicious and cruel.

WHY ANTHONY LOST

Mark Anthony complained of living in Octavian's shadow, the reason for which the Greek biographer and philosopher explained in the first century AD:

Anthony kept in his house an Egyptian soothsayer skilled in the casting of horoscopes. This man, either to please Cleopatra or because he wished Anthony to know the truth, made no secret of his reading of Anthony's fortune. Although glorious and brilliant by any other standard, this fortune was constantly eclipsed by Octavian, so the soothsayer advised Anthony to stay away from his young colleague. 'Your guardian spirit', said the Egyptian, 'stands in awe of his. By itself it is proud and mettlesome, but in the presence of Octavian's spirit yours becomes daunted and submissive.' And the turn of events confirmed the soothsayer's words, for whenever the two men cast lots or threw dice, either for amusement or to make decisions, Anthony was the loser.

The historian Suetonius lived through the tyranny of Domitian and wrote of a prophecy that had a direct bearing on the emperor's death, which came in AD 96. It seems that Domitian once consulted a Germanic astrologer named Ascletarion to ascertain the time and circumstances of his own death so that he might avoid them. The astrologer, a man who obviously lacked the wit of the earlier Thrassylus, told the emperor exactly how and when he would die. The date was given, the place – the imperial bedroom, the time – the fifth hour, and the circumstances – by bloodshed. The malevolent emperor then asked how and when Ascletarion himself was destined to meet his end. The astrologer replied that he was fated to be savaged by wild animals and that his remains would never rest in a tomb.

Loved by Julius Caesar, Queen Cleopatra of Egypt – in *Der Tod der Kleopatra* (Gem lde, 1875/76), by Hans von Makart (1840-1884) – married Mark Anthony, whose failure to gain absolute control of the Roman Empire caused both to commit suicide.

'Then I will prove the futility of your prediction,' laughed the mad Domitian. He then ordered that the poor stargazer be burned and his ashes thrown into the river Tiber. The emperor's orders were carried out but, as Ascletarion's body burned, a sudden downpour extinguished the flames. It was then that a pack of ravenous wild dogs leapt upon the charred corpse and dismembered it.

However, if Domitian thought that he could escape his doom by killing the man who told him of it, he was sadly mistaken. The fated day grew ever closer and Domitian, more frightened now, rounded up more astrologers and soothsayers and put them to death as well. As the fifth hour approached, Domitian was in an agitated state. His constant scratching caused a pimple on his head to bleed, an occurrence that prompted the emperor to say, 'I hope that this is the only blood that needs to be shed.' He constantly asked the time, and was relieved to be told by an exasperated servant, tired of the emperor's repetitive question, that it was the sixth hour and the fatal time had passed. At that moment, he was told that one of his spies had returned with news of yet another treachery and was waiting in the imperial bedroom. Domitian could not wait to discover the names of the conspirators, so he hastened to the bedroom and the blade of his assassin. The killing blow was delivered precisely at the time and place that

Ascletarion had predicted, and Domitian's death brought widespread rejoicing throughout the Empire.

THE PROPHETIC PURGE

In the reign of the Emperor Valens (AD 375-378), a group of unnamed conspirators sought the identity of his successor through the art of alectryomancy: divination by means of a cockerel (see Parting the Veil, pages 182-187). In strictest secrecy, they met and divined the Greek Letters theta, epsilon, omicron and delta, corresponding to TH-E-O-D in the English alphabet. Since the emperor's favourite was someone called Theodorus, it seemed obvious that he was the one who would next assume absolute power. However, this was not to be, for Valens, as suspicious as any other Roman ruler, had poor blameless Theodorus put to death as soon as he got wind of the prophecy. Not content with this, the emperor embarked on a purge of everyone whose name began with the doom-laden letters THEOD just to be on the safe side. This included a Spanish general named Theodosius who was tried on a trumped-up charge and duly executed. However, this general had a son also named Theodosius who prudently stayed out of the way until Valens had been killed in battle with the Visigoths. It was at this point, in AD 379, that Theodosius was proclaimed Emperor.

THE TWO YOUNG FOOLS

Theodosius (AD 392-395) was a fervent Christian and it was at his command that the oracles, including those of Delphi and that of the sibyl of Cumae, were

Even with all of his power, the Emperor Domitian still could not avoid his fate – portrayed in *Domitian (Titus Flavius Domitianus)* by Kupferstich von Matth us Merian (1593-1650).

closed down. He also tore down pagan temples throughout the Empire, from Egypt to Britain. He decided that the Roman Empire was too vast and unwieldy for one man to rule alone, so on his deathbed he divided it in half, leaving it to his two sons, Arcadius and Honorius, as was predicted in the last of the Sibylline verses:

'When two young fools between them do divide,
Our world, the elder on the younger side
By banning bloodshed in his Hippodrome
Bloodshed redoubles, while in the elder Rome,
The younger, yielding to barbarian folk,
Sees his most trusty Council rise in smoke.'

Theodosius I (Roman Emperor, AD 379-395) destroyed the oracular system and pagan temples from Egypt to Britain – after suffering from the attempts of the Emperor Valens to avoid a prophecy.

The elder brother, Arcadius, took charge of the Eastern Empire from his capital of Constantinople, the 'younger Rome'. Thus he became 'the elder on the younger side'. Even though the Empire was by now nominally Christian, many traditional Roman passions had been retained, the foremost of these being gladiatorial combat. With religious ethics and sport now in conflict, the arena was set for trouble. This occurred when a zealous young monk named Telemachus leaped into the famous Hippodrome of Constantinople and stood between two fighting gladiators. Confused, the fighters turned to the emperor's box for instruction and, receiving no adequate reply, left the ring. The fickle crowd, denied their bloody entertainment, took out their wrath on the monk and stoned him to death.

The Emperor Arcadius, outraged by this impious action retaliated by banning the Games. This in its turn resulted in violent carnage throughout the city, which was so extreme it threatened to overturn the imperial throne itself. 'Bloodshed redoubled' indeed.

In 'the elder Rome,' the younger brother Honorius had troubles of his own. The power of a barbarian general named Stilicho had made the emperor a powerless puppet. To please his military master Honorius did away with much of Roman pomp and ceremony – this included publicly burning the three books of the Sibylline verses which had been carefully preserved for centuries. Thus, the emperor saw 'his most trusty Council rise in smoke.'

All that was left of Rome might now have devolved to Constantinople, the new Rome in the East. Again the Sibyl had been proven correct. But the last word should be reserved for Constantine the Great (AD 307-340), the emperor who had been the first to convert to Christianity and had founded his city to stand for the values of the new faith. As he lay dying, it is said that a look of horror appeared in his eyes and he repeated over and over 'thirteen, thirteen, thirteen.'

It was not until the reign of Constantine XIII that the Christian Roman Empire fell to the Turks. This happened in AD 1453. It is interesting to note that, if the numbers of that year are added together according to the rules of numerology (1+4+5+3) the result is thirteen.

CHAPTER TWO

THE DIVINE REVELATIONS

Through the ages, men and women have been inspired to carry out the will of the Divine on earth. It should not be forgotten that, without those who stood out from the crowd to speak of their own inspirations, many of today's great faiths would not exist, or at least not in their present form. Neither should the bravery of these souls be under-estimated. They often risked everything to tell the truth as they saw it and to reveal a divine plan for their people and the world.

Joseph accurately foresaw that the Pharaoh's dream of seven fat and seven thin cows heralded seven years of plenty, followed by seven of famine.

The Bible details many prophets, some of whom were law-givers and teachers, others who believed that God had given them the gift to divine the future. Of the latter, one of the most renowned is Joseph, son of Jacob. Sold into slavery in Egypt, Joseph rose from desperate straits to become virtual ruler of the country, all due to a prophetic dream. His amazing story is presented in 'Joseph and the Pharaoh's Dream' (pages 50-51).

Another renowned prophet was Daniel – he who survived the lions' den. Born into captivity much later than Joseph, his story is nevertheless similar, since it involves a king's troubled slumber and the meaning of his nightly visions. This prophet is justly remembered for this vision, as retold in 'The Revelations of Daniel' (pages 52-55).

St Malachy of Armagh was a twelfth-century cleric who foretold the reigns of all future popes, from his own time to the present and beyond.

An early seventeenth-century portrait of Anne Boleyn (1507-36) by Frans Pourbus the Younger. The second wife of Henry VIII was said to be a witch.

Even though it has been claimed that his prophecies were a sixteenth-century Jesuit forgery, they are still given credence within the Church. It is argued that if they were written some time during the 1500s, then the accuracy would have waned after that point. Judge for yourself whether this is the case in 'The Papal Prophecies' (pages 56-59).

Evidence of visionaries is found in every age, but surely none can be as famous as the legendary Joan of Arc (pages 60-63), who was inspired by angelic voices to seek out the true king of France and ensure that he was crowned. Another visionary, although not so famous as Joan, was Elizabeth Barton, a girl who was ruthlessly used for political purposes, and whose folly and bravery is documented in 'The Holy Maid of Kent' (pages 64-65).

Another testament of faith is provided in 'The Ghost Dance' (pages 66-69). The prophet here is Wovoka, the so-called 'Paiute Messiah' who gave the Native American peoples hope when all seemed lost. However, his new religion was tragically false and ultimately led to disaster.

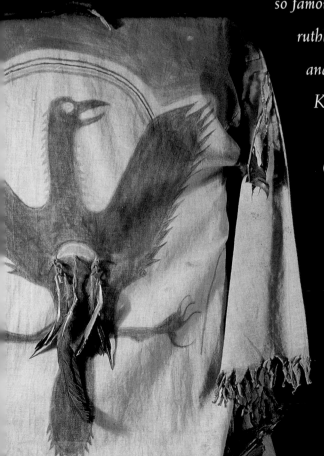

The mythic Thunderbird decorates this ceremonial 'Ghost Dance' shirt. The designs for such clothing came from Native Americans' dreams or trances

JOSEPH AND THE PHARAOH'S DREAM

The story of Joseph in the Book of Genesis reveals one of the first, possibly the original, prophet to have a notable influence on a ruler and a nation. The son of Jacob, Joseph wore the multi-coloured coat which was a mark of his father's favour. Apparently Joseph was a boastful boy who irritated his older brothers by telling them of his dreams, which he interpreted as meaning that their descendants would bow down to his. Infuriated beyond endurance, they lured the radiant boy into a trap and sold him into slavery in Egypt.

After many tribulations, including staving off the unwanted advances of his owner's wife and many years of imprisonment, Joseph made a remarkable comeback due to a troublesome dream that afflicted the Pharaoh.

THE BAKER AND THE BUTLER

Two of Joseph's fellow captives were the royal baker and butler who were under suspicion of theft from the royal estates. Though neither the butler nor the baker at first deigned to speak with the Hebrew slave, the pair were soon troubled by dreams which they found impossible to interpret.

Joseph's old skill rose to the occasion when he asked the butler to recount his nightly vision. The butler told of a vine bearing three bunches of grapes. In his dream, he had taken the grapes, pressed them into the Pharaoh's cup and passed it to the king. Joseph told the butler to rejoice, because in three days he would be released and the Pharaoh would lift up his head and restore him to his former office.

Not to be outdone, the baker then told his story. In his dream, the baker bore three white baskets on his head. In each were many sweetmeats for the Pharaoh, but then birds descended on the top most basket and ate all the delicacies. Upon hearing this, Joseph gravely told the baker that in three days the Pharaoh would hang him. And so it happened.

A DREAM OF FAMINE

Now, after the butler had been back at court for two years, he learned that the Pharaoh had experienced troubling dreams which none of his wise men could decipher. Remembering Joseph's skill, he suggested that the Hebrew be brought from prison and given the task of interpreting the Pharaoh's dream. On his arrival at court, Joseph insisted on hearing the dream from the king's own lips. The Pharaoh recounted that in his dream he stood upon the bank of the River Nile, out of which came seven fat cows which then grazed in a meadow. But then, seven starving cows, so thin that he could see their ribs, came forth and devoured the fat cows. Yet, even after such a filling meal, the seven cows did not look any better fed than they had in the first place. Then the Pharaoh spoke of another dream in which seven ears of corn were devoured by seven ears which were withered and blasted.

Without hesitation, Joseph declared that there would be seven years of plenty throughout Egypt followed by seven years of terrible famine. He then suggested that corn and foodstuffs should be stored through the first seven years to make up for the lack in the second. The Pharaoh was delighted and raised Joseph to the rank of Overseer to the Kingdom and gave him the task of organizing the food storage and distribution. Joseph was so successful in this task

A fresco by Raphael/Raffaello Santi (1483-1520), *Joseph Interpreting the Dreams of the Pharaoh*, portrays Joseph impressing the Pharaoh by explaining that the king's dreams foretold feast and famine.

that, during the time of famine, Egypt could actually export food to other, less fortunate, nations.

Although this story has all the elements of legend about it, there may be some basis of truth. During the Twelfth Dynasty of the Pharaohs, Egypt did indeed suffer from grievous famines that were caused by particularly high Nile floods. The worst of these occurred in the reign of Amenemhat III (1842–1797 BC). It was also at this time that Semitic peoples, such as the Hebrews, settled in the Delta region just as this tale of Joseph illustrates.

THE PHARAOH'S DREAM

The symbolism of the Pharoah's dream suggested seven abundant years and seven lean years in Egypt.

66 And, behold there came up out of the river seven well-favoured kine and fat-fleshed; and they fed in a meadow. And, behold, seven other kine came up after them out of the river, ill-favoured and lean-fleshed; and stood by the other kine upon the brink of the river. And the ill-favoured and lean-fleshed kine did eat up the seven well-favoured and fat kine. So Pharoah awoke. 99

GENESIS 41, VERSES 2-4

THE REVELATIONS OF DANIEL

In the traditions of Israel, only the names of Moses and Abraham were more revered than that of the great prophet Daniel. He was born at a much later period than either of the patriarchs of Judaism, probably in the sixth century BC, when the people of the Holy Land had been conquered and transported to the shores of the Tigris and Euphrates rivers by King Nebuchadnezzar II. By now, the Hebrews were captives in the great and corrupt city of Babylon, which occupied an area – if Herodotus is to be believed – of two hundred square miles, and whose walls enclosed such splendour that no civilization since has surpassed its opulence.

Nebuchadnezzar, like the Egyptian pharaoh long before him, was troubled by dreams. Nightly, his slumbers were disturbed by the image of a statue with a head of gold, breast and arms of silver, belly and thighs of brass, legs of iron and feet of iron and clay. The king dreamt that a stone was then cast at this image, breaking it into tiny pieces that were carried away by the wind. The stone that had smashed the statue then grew until it became a mountain and filled the whole earth.

Furious that his astrologers and priests were unable to interpret his dream, the king looked to Daniel for an explanation. The answer came to Daniel while he slept. He told the king that the head of gold represented Nebuchadnezzar himself, and that after him would come an inferior ruler, who was symbolized by the breast of silver, and so on through to iron – until finally there would be a king 'with feet of iron and clay'. After this interpretation, Daniel was made chief advisor to the king. Nebuchadnezzar, heartened by Daniel's words, now regarded himself as the greatest king that would ever be. Accordingly he declared himself a god and raised a colossal golden statue. He then commanded all his subjects to fall down and worship his image. All Hebrews, Daniel included, were therefore constrained by the First Commandment: 'Thou shalt not fall down before graven idols', and were unable to comply with the king's order. For this grave offence, three men were placed within a fiery furnace, but miraculously, saved by their god, they emerged unscathed.

Daniel interprets the dream of Nebuchadnezzar – to reward him for the accuracy of his interpretation, the king made Daniel chief over all the astrologers and wise men of Babylonia.

THE BIBLICAL PROPHETS

Israel, the Holy Land, is famous for the number of its prophets. They include Isaiah, Jeremiah, Amos, Ezekiel, Elijah and many, many others. However, unlike other peoples, the ancient Hebrews frowned on the practice of foretelling the future, seeing it as nothing more than pagan worship in another guise.

The primary role of the Hebrew prophet was not to predict future events, but to convince the people to maintain and adhere to the Law. This was, and indeed is, the Covenant of Moses which had been handed to him on Mount Sinai in the form of two stone tablets on which were inscribed the Ten Commandments.

Nevertheless both the Old and the New Testaments contain many examples of seers, both holy and occult. The wild-haired prophets of the desert, and later the Apostles, come under the former category; under the latter are the Witch of Endor (see page 175), the soothsayers of Egypt and Babylon, and the notorious conjurer Simon Magus, who tried to buy sacred power from the Apostles.

Most of the predictions in the Bible refer either to the woes that will befall the holy city of Jerusalem and its people, or they prophesy the coming of the long-awaited Messiah. In Christian terms, since the Messiah has already been here, they are now taken to refer to the Second Coming.

Two hundred years before the birth of Jesus, the prophet Isaiah foresaw that far-away Babylon would grow into the 'Lady of Kingdoms' and overwhelm his people. Later, writers such as St John of Patmos described this 'Lady of Kingdoms' in an unflattering light: the Whore of Babylon. She, or rather the city, became the very symbol of corruption:

'Behold, the days come that all that is in thine house, and that which thy fathers have laid up in store until this day shall be carried to Babylon; nothing shall be left saith the Lord.

And of thy sons ... they shall be eunuchs in the palace of the king of Babylon.'

Isaiah 39. 6-7

In late twentieth-century terms, the words of Ezekiel have struck a chord with the inhabitants of the modern state of Israel which was founded in 1948:

'And they shall say, This land that was desolate is become like the garden of Eden; and the waste and desolate and ruined cities are become fenced and are inhabited.'

Ezekiel 36.35

Approximately twenty years before the Babylonian invasion, the prophet Jeremiah agreed with his predecessor:

'And this whole land shall be a desolation, and an astonishment. And these nations shall serve the king of Babylon seventy years.'

Jeremiah 25.11

However, Jeremiah foresaw the eventual end of the powerful empire too:

'And Babylon shall become heaps, a dwelling place for dragons, an astonishment and a hissing, without an inhabitant.'

Jeremiah 51.37

The prophet Daniel, who spent most of his life in the 'City of Sin', foretold the coming of a great goat or ram which is taken to represent Alexander the Great:

'Therefore the he-goat waxed very great: and when he was strong, the great horn was broken; and for it came up four notable ones toward the four winds of heaven.'

Daniel 8.8

The ram was the symbol of Greco-Egyptian god Zeus-Ammon, whom Alexander believed was his celestial father. He did die 'when he was strong', at Babylon in 332 BC. Four of his generals – Ptolemy, Antiochus, Seleucus and Cassander – then violently divided Alexander's mighty dominion.

Nebuchadnezzar was succeeded by his son, the decadent Belshazzar, the 'king of silver', who also favoured Daniel. One evening when the king was feasting with a thousand of his nobles, a most extraordinary event occurred. A disembodied hand appeared and wrote mysterious characters on the wall of the chamber. Dumbfounded, Belshazzar called for his soothsayers, but not one of them could interpret the message. Now Daniel emerged and spoke. Addressing the king boldly, the prophet offered to

THE FALL OF BABYLON

At that moment, a clamour arose from the mighty walls of Babylon as an invading army of Persians, led by King Darius I, forced their way into the under-defended city. Before the night was done, King Belshazzar lay dead, Babylon had fallen, and Darius, son of Ahasuerus, ruler of the Persians and Medes, was in control. Daniel, who was not unhappy at this turn of events, prospered under Persian rule; he was made a prince and a governor by King Darius, who had become the 'king of brass', as Daniel had predicted. However, Daniel was later thrown into a den of lions for being too forthright with the new king. The Biblical story tells how an angel held shut the mouths of the lions, so they were disinclined to harm him. Remorsefully, Darius released the prophet and restored him to his former position as royal advisor.

The 'king of iron' turned out to be Xerxes the Conqueror, whose reign saw constant war in Greece and Asia Minor. It was this Xerxes who allowed the captive Hebrews to go back to Jerusalem and he paid for the Temple of Solomon to be rebuilt. It is assumed that Daniel, who by this time was well advanced in years, returned with them.

The reputation of the prophet Daniel does not rest on these incidents alone. He also received five symbolic visions which came to him in the form of dreams. These complex portents set out the fate of his own race and are collectively known as the 'Revelations of Daniel', interpreted by some to be a tragic prophecy of the end of the world.

read the supernatural inscription. Scanning the words with ease, the prophet pronounced, 'God hath numbered thy kingdom, and finished it. Thou art weighed in the balance and found wanting. Thy kingdom is divided and is given to the Medes and the Persians.'

THE PAPAL PROPHECIES

One medieval prophet whose clairvoyant insights were ascribed to divine favour was St Malachy, otherwise known as Malachy O'Morgair. He was a native of the old Irish kingdom of Armagh who died in AD 1148. Chroniclers of the time described him as 'meek, humble, modest, obedient and obliging to all'.

In his youth, he so far out-stripped his fellow students in learning, and his masters in virtue, that he came to the attention of Imar, an irascible hermit monk who undertook Malachy's spiritual education. Imar put the boy through a harsh regime of physical, mental and religious exercise.

Malachy became noted for his abilities to heal miraculously all but the most hopeless cases. On some occassions, he did not even need to see the patient and could heal remotely. When King David of Scotland appealed for the saint's help for his dying son, Malachy merely told him that the boy was again well, and this turned out to be the case.

Malachy also seems to have been an insomniac, since it is said that he completely 'vanquished sleep'. This trait must have given him a lot of contemplative time and perhaps it is to this sleeplessness that we can attribute his uncanny powers of precognition. His famous papal prophecies were probably made in 1139 while he was on a pilgrimage to Rome. He committed to parchment a list of Latin phrases which were coded messages concerning the succession of future pontiffs.

MALACHY'S PROPHETIC PHRASES

Malachy is accredited with foretelling the destinies of a total of 112 Roman Catholic popes, from Celestine II up to and beyond Pope John Paul II. It is a sobering fact that Malachy's predictions, obscure though they are, have been accurate until now. Pope John Paul II is the one-hundred-and-tenth Pope in this sequence. Each prophetic phrase is usually no longer than four words – and refers to a family name, a birth place, heraldic designs or previous ranks held within the Church. As is usual with such

Malachy O'Morgair's coded messages about future popes include Pope Leo XIII, whose coat of arms was a blazing comet and who he called 'Light in Heaven'.

The destinies of 112 Roman Catholic popes were accurately foretold by St Malachy, the last two of whom are still to come.

oracles, they contain puns, cryptic clues and word play.

For instance, the phrase that corresponds to the twelfthth-century Pope Adrian IV is 'De Ruro Albo', or 'From the Alban Country'. Adrian or, to give him his birth name, Nicholas Breakspear, was the only Englishman ever to succeed to the papal throne. England, of course, is sometimes poetically described as Albion. Furthermore, earlier in his career, Nicholas had held the post of Abbot of St Albans.

The accession of Pope Pius III in 1458 was foretold as 'De Parvo Homine', or 'From a Little Man'. The Pope's family name was Piccolomini, which is Italian for 'Little Man'. Similarly, Alexander IV was called 'Signum Ostiensis'. He had previously been Cardinal of Ostia. One example of heraldic word play is in the phrase that corresponds to Pope Leo XIII. Malachy called him 'Lumenum Caelo', or 'Light in Heaven'. This pope's coat of arms was a blazing comet.

Moving up to the twentieth-century, Pope Benedict XV, who reigned from 1914 to 1922, was described as 'Religio Depopulata', or 'Religion Laid Waste'. This was an apt description for a pontiff who presided over the horrors of the First World War, the Russian Revolution and the collapse of European empires.

More recently, the accession of Pope John Paul I was the one-hundred-and-ninth in Malachy's sequence. This pope's phrase was 'De Mediate Lunae,' or 'From the Half Moon'. He was elected in August, 1978, on a half moon and his reign only lasted thirty-three days, just over one lunar cycle.

The present Pope John Paul II is described by Malachy as 'De Labore Solis', or 'The Labour of the Sun'. He is the first non-Italian pope in 456 years, and is a native of the Polish city of Krakow. It was here that the astronomer Copernicus formulated his then heretical theory that the earth, far from being the centre of the universe, was in fact in solar orbit, or in Copernicus's words 'laboured about the sun'.

THE FUTURE POPES

So what of the future of the Catholic Church? Malachy rarely gives the length of reign allotted to any particular pontiff, so perhaps it is disturbing to note that there are only two remaining phrases in the succession sequence. The first of these, predicting

Named by St Malachy as 'Labour of the Sun', Pope John Paul II arrives in his native Krakow, Poland – where Copernicus introduced the idea that the earth orbits the sun.

John Paul's immediate successor, is 'Gloria Olivae', or 'Glory of the Olive'. This may be a reference to the Benedictine Order of Monks, who are also known as the Olivetans. This prophecy has a darker side since there is a suspicion that a Benedictine will lead the fight against the Anti-Christ. The olive has also been interpreted as the symbol of the Jews – perhaps we will have a pope of Jewish origin? Another possibility is connected with the desire of the present pontiff to hold a ceremony of thanksgiving on the Mount of Olives in Jerusalem on New Year's Day, 2000.

The pope to succeed 'The Glory of the Olive', will be 'Petrus Romanus', or Peter of Rome, the final pope. He is a pontiff who merits more than a brief phrase. Malachy said, 'In the final persecution of the Roman Church, there will reign Peter the Roman, who will feed his flock among many tribulations, after which the seven-hilled city will be destroyed and the dreadful judge will judge the people'.

St Malachy was not alone in foretelling the fall of Rome and the papacy. In 1909, Pope Pius X experienced a mystical vision which terrified him. 'Will it be myself or one of my successors?' he wrote. What is certain is that the pope will leave Rome and, in leaving the Vatican, he will have to walk over the dead bodies of his priests'.

THE PROPHECIES OF ST MALACHY

Celestine II (1143-1144)
Ex Castro Tiberis ❖ From a Castle on the Tiber
Pope Celestine's real name was Guido de Castello. He was from Castello, which lies on the shores of the Tiber.

Eugene III (1145-1153)
Ex Magnitudine Montis ❖ From the Greatness of the Mount
Pope Eugene was born at the castle of Grammont (Great Mount) and his family name was Montemagno (Big Mountain).

Innocent III (1198-1216)
Comes Signatus ❖ Signed Count
This pope was descended from a family of noble counts surnamed Signy or Segny.

Gregory IX (1227-1241)
Avis Ostiensis ❖ Bird of Ostia
Once Cardinal of Ostia, this pope had an imperial eagle as his crest.

Urban IV (1261-1264)
Heirusalem Campaniae ❖ Jerusalem of Champagne
A native of Troyes in Champagne, Urban later became Patriarch of Jerusalem.

Nicholas IV (1288-1292)
Ex Eremo Celsus ❖ Elevated Hermit
Nicholas had reluctantly accepted elevation to pope after being a hermit for many years.

Clement V (1305-1314)
De Fessis Aquitanicus ❖ Ribbon of Aquitaine
Previously Archbishop of Bordeaux in Aquitaine, his shield bears three ribbons or 'fesses'.

John XXII (1316-1334)
De Sutore Osseo ❖ The Cobbler of Osseo
Born with the family name of Ossa, his father was a shoemaker.

Nicholas V (1328-1330)
Corvus Schismaticus ❖ Schismatic Crow
Nicholas was an antipope who reigned concurrently with his rival John XXII during the Great Schism. The prophetic phrase may refer to the fable about the crow who stole the peacock's feathers.

Benedict XII (1334-1342)
Frigidus Abbas ❖ Cold Monk
Pope Benedict had been a priest at the monastery of Frontfroid (Cold Front).

Callixtus III (1455-1458)
Bos Pascens ❖ Grazing Ox
Callixtus was a member of the notorious Borgia family, whose crest was a golden bull grazing. Some have commented that it should have been a Golden Calf.

Alexander VI (1492-1503)
Bos Albanus in Portu ❖ White Ox in the Gate
Another Borgia possessing the bull motif pushed, bribed and possibly murdered his way to the papal throne.

Pius III (1503)
De Parvo Homine ❖ Of Little Man
Pope Pius reigned for only twenty-six days and had the family name of Piccolomini which means 'Little Man'. This pope was a Borgia puppet.

Julius II (1503-1513)
Fructis Jovis Juvabit ❖ Fruit of the Young Jove
Pope Julius's coat of arms was a sapling oak tree. The oak had long been considered the tree of Jupiter or Jove.

Clement XIII (1758-1769)
Rosa Umbriae ❖ Rose of Umbria
Previously this pope was Cardinal of Umbria.

Pius VI (1775-1799)
Peregrinus Apostolicus ❖ Apostolic Wanderer
This pope was driven into exile by revolutionary wars.

Gregory XVI (1831-18460
De Balneis Etruria ❖ From the Baths of Etruria
He was a member of the order of St Romuald based in Etruria.

Pius IX (1846-1878)
Crux de Cruce ❖ Cross of Crosses
The cross this pontiff had to bear was loss of his power to the House of Savoy whose symbol was a cross during the unification of Italy.

John XXIII (1958-1963)
Pastor et Nauta ❖ Pastor and Navigator
Previously Patriarch of the most nautical of cities, Venice, Pope John navigated the church through difficult times.

Paul VI (1963-1978)
Flors Florum ❖ Flower of Flowers
Born in Florence, the 'Flower of Cities', Pope Paul's coat of arms included three fleur-de-lys, traditionally held to be the most perfect of blooms.

JOAN OF ARC AND THE VOICES OF THE FUTURE

On 30 May, 1431, the boyish frame of Jeanne d'Arc was led to the stake at the English-held town of Rouen. Accused on over seventy counts of witchcraft, this teenage girl was reputed to have terrorized her enemies and inspired the beleaguered French nation after one hundred years of war.

Jeanne, better known as Joan of Arc, was born to a poor family in disputed territory at Domrémy in Lorraine, France, in 1412. Little is known of her early life, save that she had two brothers.

It was at the tender age of thirteen that Joan first heard her 'voices'. She claimed that she not only heard, but often saw, the heavenly forms of St Michael the Archangel, St Catherine of Alexandria and St Margaret of Antioch (a chivalrous figure in her own lifetime who was said to have been eaten by a dragon).

At the prompting of these saints, Joan set off to find the Dauphin Charles, the rightful king of France. Charles had been deprived of his kingdom by the alliance of the English

Joan of Arc was burned at the stake in the English-held town of Rouen, France, on 30 May, 1431. Legend claims that her heart was found intact amongst the ashes.

and Burgundians, who had seen to it that the infant king of England, Henry VI, had been accepted as monarch of France. It should be noted that, then as now, it is not easy to have a quiet conversation with a monarch, even an outlawed one, if one is an unknown peasant from the back of beyond. Yet Joan managed it, possibly due to the connivance of certain factions at court who saw the advantage of having a heavenly messenger on their side.

It was Joan's intention that the Dauphin Charles should give her an army – to raise what became the long-drawn-out siege of Orleans – and that she should escort the dauphin to Rheims for his coronation. Charles was sceptical of her claims, and as a test placed a nobleman on his throne so he could mingle with the throng un-observed. Unflinchingly, Joan immediately bowed low to the simply-dressed Charles. Impressed, the prince decided to outfit Joan to her specifications, in plate armour with a knightly banner of her own. But the dauphin was unwilling to put an inexperienced girl in charge of an armed force, so he provided hardened generals to conduct the battle. Nevertheless, just six months after leaving her humble home, Joan found herself at the head of an army.

Joan of Arc (illustration above by Howard Pyle in *Harper's Monthly Magazine*, December, 1904) claimed that she conversed with angelic beings who led her to defend the rightful French king, the Dauphin Charles, against the English and the Burgundians.

VOICES OF VICTORY

The year 1428 saw the relief of Orleans, followed by a series of French victories that devastated English morale. Yet ordinary French soldiers were convinced that as long as they had 'La Pucelle d'Orléans' or 'The Maid of Orleans' to lead them, they could never fail. The serenely confident Joan also had ultimate belief in her convictions. Aided by her 'voices' she predicted battles, ambushes and the enemy's strategy.

In February of 1429 she sadly informed the com-mander Robert de Baudricourt that the French had been defeated some two hundred miles away. It took two days for this information to be confirmed. The English commander, the Duke of Bedford, raged: 'She is a disciple and lyme of the fiend, called the Pucelle, that used fals enchantments and sorcerie.' The capture of Joan of Arc became an urgent priority. However, it was not the English who seized her, but the forces of Burgundy. The Burgundians then offered their captive to the highest bidder. Ungratefully, the Dauphin Charles did not see fit to ransom 'La Pucelle', and the English came up with 10,000 francs for 'the purchase of Joan the Maid, who is said to be a sorcerer'.

The outcome of her trial was a foregone conclusion, yet her self- assurance did not waver as she stood in the dock. The eminent bishops who were her judges heard that she was in league with the devil, practised witchcraft and had bartered her soul for earthly power. Part of the price for this, it was claimed, was that she always wore men's attire. And, indeed, Joan refused to dress in any other way. On three separate occasions, Joan was forced to undergo tests to prove first her gender, and then her virginity.

THE INSPIRATION OF ANGELS

Joan did not deny that, as a child, she had danced about 'the fairy's tree' at Domrémy, or that she daily held conversation with her angelic friends. However, the court was disinclined to believe that her supernatural allies were of heavenly origin, preferring a more diabolical explanation. Then, stories of her clairvoyant powers were examined.

'Is it true,' she was asked, 'that your battle sword was found behind the altar of St Catherine's Church in Fierbois, even though no one knew of it beforehand?'

'It is so,' replied the Maid.

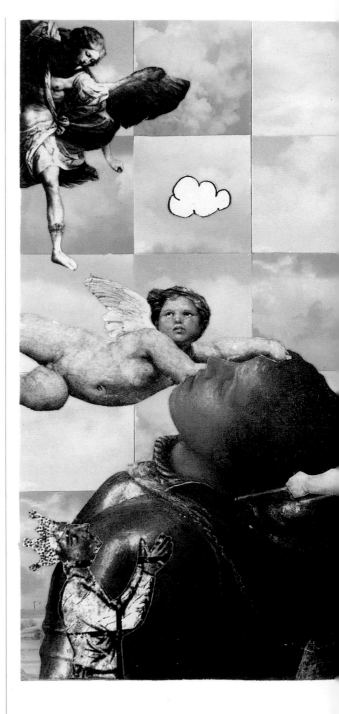

Then the eminent bishops asked if she was aware that such powers were forbidden by the Church. Joan replied that she was only a simple girl without learning, but that she knew the things her voices told her were right – thus, Joan of Arc condemned herself by denying the authority of the

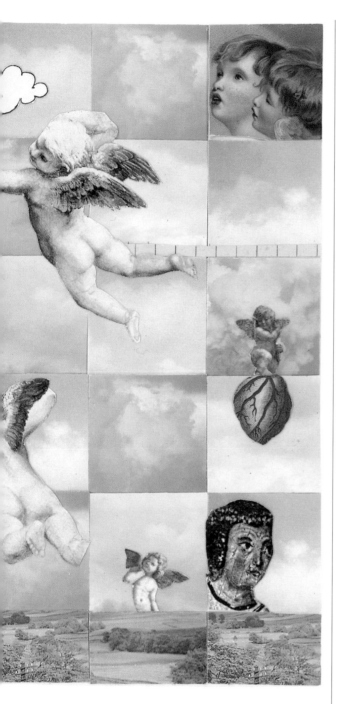

Despite being maligned as 'being in league with the devil' in a court more formidable than a battlefield for a poor ignorant girl like Joan, the 'Maid of Orleans' maintained that the supernatural voices she heard were of divine origin. Some said that she both found her sword and knew the results of far-away conflicts by means of them.

So what are we to make of St Joan, who was finally canonized in 1921 as patron saint of soldiers? At her trial, she exhibited no prophetic powers nor gave any real indication of heavenly favour, revealing herself to be a simple girl with obstinate convictions, yet there is little doubt that she was convinced of the rightness of her mission. A mission that ruthless men had appropriated and equally ruthlessly abandoned as the bloody politics of the era demanded.

Raymond Balze's idealized representation of Joan of Arc, reproduced in *Wallon's Life*, indicates the mythical stature that she acquired in France, when her mere presence in battle made enemies quake.

Church. Certain clerics were of the opinion that her life should be spared and that she should spend her sentence in a convent. However, the Duke of Bedford refused to listen to any such suggestions of lenience and demanded that the defendant be burned alive at the stake.

THE HOLY MAID OF KENT

Elizabeth Barton was born in the English village of Aldington in 1506. She worked as a domestic servant and her life seemed destined to be unremarkable. However, her mundane existence was shattered when she became seriously ill in 1525.

Falling into a violent fever, Elizabeth began to see visions, and her ramblings soon became the talk of the village. It swiftly became apparent that, in her trances, Elizabeth could see the future. Her almost miraculous recovery did not halt her visions, and soon she was known as an accurate oracle. Since suspicion of witchcraft was a very real danger, her family put Elizabeth into the care of a local clergyman, Richard Maister, who soon became convinced that her gifts were of heavenly rather than diabolic origin. Maister wrote to Archbishop Wareham at Canterbury, who sent two monks to investigate.

One of these, the politically astute Edward Bocking, immediately saw a chance to revive the standing of the Catholic Church in England by means of Elizabeth's prophecies. Bocking lost no time in instilling a sense of holy mission in the girl and had soon moved her to the Convent of the Holy Sepulchre at Canterbury where she continued to pour out her divine revelations. Elizabeth had been convinced that her gifts came to her directly from the Virgin Mary herself. Meanwhile, Bocking ensured that Elizabeth Barton's reputation grew and she was soon known as the Holy Maid of Kent.

> 'Hither am I come to die and I have not only been the cause of all those persons which at this time here suffer'
>
> ELIZABETH BARTON

During this time, the still reasonably athletic King Henry VIII was in the middle of his first, but by no means last, marital crisis. His wife of many years, Catharine of Aragon, had failed to produce a much-needed male heir, so Henry sought divorce. The Catholic Church took an even dimmer view of such matters than it does today, so a collision between Church and State was inevitable. Public opinion was essential to both sides, so when the Maid of Kent spoke, everybody listened.

She said that a vile root with three branches existed in England and that as long as it lived, the country would suffer under tyranny. The vile root was immediately interpreted as being the king himself, with the three branches being the Dukes of Norfolk and Suffolk and the first minister Cardinal Wolsey, all of whom were in disfavour with Rome. It was fortunate for the Maid that the Church had the upper hand at this time, otherwise the irate king might have taken action against it.

In 1527, Henry again petitioned the pope to end his marriage. On cue, the Holy Maid of Kent toed the ecclesiastical line. 'I speak in the name and authority of God,' she thundered, 'If this king does not desist in this impious action, he will die within seven months and his daughter, Mary, a true friend to Rome, will rule in his stead.' This prophecy caused considerable disquiet in the country, yet the king still did nothing.

The controversy came to a head in 1533 when Henry broke with Rome, declared his union with Queen Catharine null and void, and his daughter

Mary illegitimate and ineligible for the throne. He then married his mistress Anne Boleyn. The people of England remembered the words of the Maid and waited for their monarch to die. Seven months passed and His Majesty seemed in the rudest of health and happy with his new queen. No disaster struck the House of Tudor and many began to doubt the motives of the so called 'Holy Maid'.

In November 1533, Elizabeth Barton, her mentors Richard Maister and Edward Bocking, and several others were arrested and tried for treason. Considering the severity of the crime, the court's sentence was comparatively light. Elizabeth was to renounce her claims of divine inspiration at St Paul's Cross and then to be imprisoned. The wrathful king was not satisfied with this, however, and commanded that all should be executed.

TO THE GALLOWS

On 21 April, 1534, Elizabeth Barton and her confederates were dragged on hurdles through the streets of London to the Tyburn gallows. As she stood on the grim scaffold, the Holy Maid of Kent made her last statement. 'Hither am I come to die and I have not only been the cause of all those persons which at this time here suffer. And yet, to say the truth, I am not so much to be blamed, considering that it was well known unto these learned men that I was a poor wench, without learning;

but because the things which fell from me were profitable unto them, therefore they much praised me and bare me in hand that it was the Holy Ghost which said them, and not I. And then I, being puffed up with their praises, fell within a certain pride and foolish fancy which have brought me to this.'

The Maid may have had the last laugh, as she had predicted that one day the king's blood would be licked by dogs. After Henry's death, his body lay overnight on a table at Syon House. Eventually his bloated body split and the household dogs were found to be licking the spillage, thus fulfilling her prophecy.

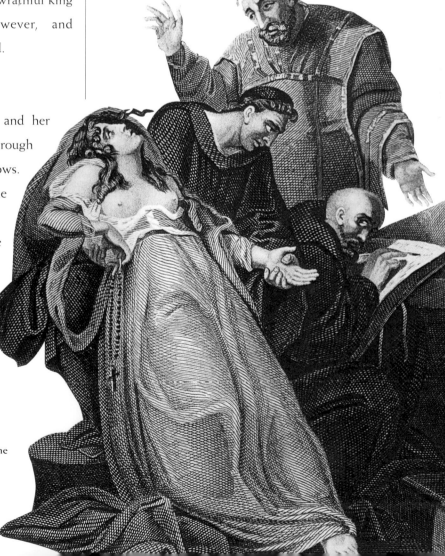

While she swooned in trance, clergymen noted the prophecies of the Holy Maid of Kent which they publicized to further their own political ends.

THE GHOST DANCE

In the last decade of the nineteenth century, while the USA stood poised on the brink of world power, a Native American mystic united the depleted tribes of his people in one last, and ultimately futile, effort to defeat the white man.

Wovoka, son of Numitaivo, was born in 1858 among the Walker river Paiute tribe, who inhabited the arid desert around the Great Salt Lake between the Rockies and the Sierra Nevada. From a very early age, Wovoka seemed marked out as one touched by destiny. His grandfather Wodziwob had been a famous shaman and his father was known to have received dream visions.

Wovoka was not to spend his life within his own culture because, when he was orphaned at the age of fourteen, he was adopted into white society. Taken in by rancher David Wilson of Mason Valley, Nevada, Wovoka abandoned his Paiute name for a while, calling himself Jack Wilson. For many years, this complex boy lived a strange life.

The Arapaho tribe's buckskin 'Ghost Dance' shirt features birds, stars and a turtle, which had mystical significance for Native Americans, who wore the shirts for the Ghost Dance rite – meant to bring back the spirits of their dead.

Outwardly Christian and immersed in small-town life, he never forgot his Paiute heritage. This mixture of influences affected him profoundly and his mystical leanings were enriched by the mingling of the two cultures. On his return to the Paiute people, and despite his youth, Wovoka was soon to become a leading medicine man of his tribe.

At the age of thirty-one, Wovoka was stricken with scarlet fever. As he lay insensible, the sun dimmed into a total eclipse. Terrified Paiutes roused the ill man and begged him to pray. Wovoka mumbled a few words, then sank into unconsciousness again.

He awoke several days later to claim that he had been with God. His resurrection proved that he was the reincarnation of Jesus Christ and would

RIGHT: The grandson of a famous shaman, Wovoka was the last medicine man to unite the Native American tribes in one last attempt in 1890 to drive the white man away via his 'Ghost Dance'.

lead not just his own people but all Native Americans to freedom from the bondage of the White Man. Wovoka predicted that, in 1890, all those who had died in the struggle for freedom would rise again and drive the white men back to the sea.

This prophecy spread through the Indian nations, who were by now disheartened by their many defeats and in need of a message of hope. To fulfil their desires, Wovoka instituted the Ghost Dance cult to help the spirits of their fallen brethren to return. Soon, the so-called 'Ghost Shirts' were proudly worn by warriors across the Midwest. By the power of the 'Great Spirit' as channelled by Wovoka, these garments were said to make their wearers invulnerable to bullets. As far as the White Man was concerned, the tribes were confederating to make trouble again. The scene was now set for tragedy.

The dawning of 1890 saw the culmination of years of double-dealing, broken treaties and sense-

less violence between the Native Americans and the White Man. The buffalo was almost extinct and the Native American way of life had been altered forever. In response to this, the Ghost Dance spread across the plains, capturing the hearts of the

The warriors' belief that 'Ghost Shirts' would protect them from bullets turned to dust when 350 unarmed Native Americans were gunned down at Wounded Knee Creek.

SITTING BULL

Sitting Bull, or Tatanka Yotanka, had in his youth undergone a gruelling initiation ceremony practised among his people, the Hunkpapa Sioux. Sharpened stakes were driven through the flesh between the shoulder bones and attached to rawhide ropes. These bonds were then attached to the branches of a tree, lifting the body until just the tips of the toes touched the ground. Then the warrior began to dance, to twist and turn, every move causing agonizing pain.

Few warriors were able to stand the torture for more than a few hours. Yet Sitting Bull danced this dance of pain for three days, until he entered a visionary state. In trance he saw what the coming of the white man would do to his people. It is from this act that Tatanka Yotanka gained his unyielding determination, which later helped him defeat George Armstrong Custer and his Eighth Cavalry at the Battle of the Little Big Horn in 1876.

Shosone, Cheyenne, Sioux, Arapaho, Kiowa, Wichita and Pawnee. In vast numbers, warriors would dance for five consecutive nights hand-in-hand, circling slowly to the left whilst intoning the names of those who had died in massacres, of starvation, of disease, on forced marches, in prison or of alcoholic despair. Even the ageing Sitting Bull had been caught up in the fervour and his martyrdom in the cause of Wovoka at Grand River by a detachment of Cavalry did much to drive the message of the Paiute prophet deep into the hearts of Native Americans everywhere.

On the night of 28 December, 1890, 350 unarmed Sioux men, women and children gathered for a Ghost Dance at Wounded Knee Creek. The dance continue throughout the entire night, but at dawn, a unit of the 7th cavalry opened fire on the people, mowing the participants down. Wovoka's vision had been false. The Ghost Shirts did not stop

United States cavalry, known as 'Casey's Scouts' leaving the scene of the massacre at Wounded Knee Creek, South Dakota.

the bullets of their enemies.

As quickly as it had begun, the Ghost Dance cult came to an end. The unfortunate Wovoka appeared to have suffered a complete breakdown. He finally renounced his Paiute name and again became Jack Wilson. He died in 1932 and was buried at the Walker Lake Reservation, a relic of a world that no longer existed.

WOVOKA'S VISION

The Native Americans' desperate battle for survival is conveyed by Wovoka's words on his Ghost Dance:

66 The Ghost Dance will raise our dead braves, and the white men will be driven from our land and then we will see the great herds of buffalo return, and all will be as it once was. 99

CHAPTER 3 THREE

THE POLITICS
OF PROPHECY

*U*nsurprisingly, many powerful rulers have at times turned to astrologers, soothsayers and prophets for help — as theirs is a role that throughout history has had more than its share of loneliness and suspicion. Unfortunately the comfort they sought was often short-lived...

An ancient prophecy made by a forgotten race was so potent in its influence that it hastened the fall of the mighty Aztec Empire and the birth of a new and even more bloody age, as the Emperor Montezuma discovered to his cost in 'The Plumed Serpent', (pages 72-75).

A mighty crusading order of warrior monks came to a bloody end by the connivance of a king and a pope. The fate of this order's last Grand Master, Jacques de Molay echoed down through French history as did his prophecy and his curse. This tale of bitter conflict is told in 'The Vengeance of the Templars' (pages 76-79).

In Britain, the treacherous world of Tudor courtly politics was the domain of

A sixteenth-century English metal plate engraved with a depiction of a holy city seen in a vision by Elizabethan mystic Dr John Dee.

Napoleon Bonaparte by (Paul) Hippolyte Delarouche (1797-1856). Napoleon's wife, Josephine, was told as a child that she would one day become 'Queen of the West'.

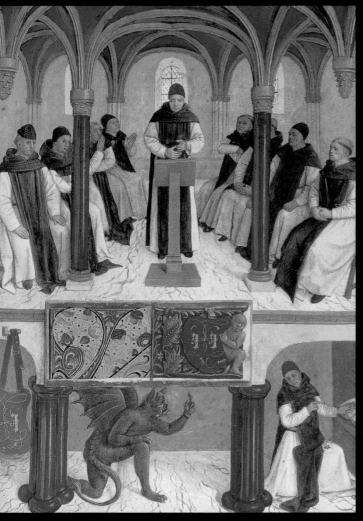

Jean Fouquet's fifteenth-century painting shows St. Bernard, Abbot of Clairvaux and Knights Templar advocate (1090-1153), being tempted by a devil.

Dr John Dee, whose reputation was such that the writer Ian Fleming based the character James Bond, the ultimate spy, on him, as 007 was Dee's assigned 'code number', which protected him as advisor to Queen Elizabeth I. His story of courtly intrigue is revealed in 'Dr Dee and the destiny of a Queen' (pages 80-83). However grand the doctor's reputation might have been, the same cannot be said of his dubious associate Edward Kelly, 'The Crop Eared Rogue', whose shadowy activities are investigated on pages 84-87.

Queen Catherine de Medici of France was an adept poisoner and mistress of political intrigue, whose success as a ruler was largely attributed to the foreknowledge provided by her astrologers Luca Gauricus and Michel de Nostradamus. 'The Field of Honour' (pages 88-89), tells how the death of her husband King Henri was predicted by two of the most talented prognosticators in history.

The unfortunate King Charles I, however, lacked the acumen of the wily Catherine, and his demise was predicted in the seventeenth century by the enigmatic William Lilly, 'the English Merlin', whose fascinating story is told in 'The White King and the flames of Gemini' (pages 90-93).

A happier fate was foretold for two girls on the Carribean island of Martinique. The prophecy behind their ascension to power is revealed in 'Queen of the West, Queen of the East' (pages 94-95).

THE PLUMED SERPENT

In the year that was called One Reed, according to the old Mayan calendar, the great ruler of the Aztec Empire, the mighty Montezuma II, grimly awaited the fulfilment of a prophecy that would bring about the end of an age, reduce his vast dominions to rubble and finish his life.

In ancient texts, later interpreted by Spanish clerics of the sixteenth century, it had been prophesied that the white god Quetzalcóatl, the Plumed Serpent, would return to the land when the year One Reed came. The influence of this god had been as a great civilizer of the people, and to him, many of the Mexican people attributed the foundation of their culture. According to myth, Quetzalcóatl had

been cast out of the Empire after his duel with the god of magic and prophecy, Tezcatlipoca, the Smoking Mirror. Quetzalcóatl was said to have fled eastward, promising eventually to return with fire and rage to take his revenge.

THE RETURN OF THE WHITE GOD

With a very heavy heart, the Emperor Montezuma bowed before the idol of Tezcatlipoca. Deeply he inhaled the smoke which brought visions from a golden bowl between the image's knees. Vainly he sought comfort from the signs he perceived in the black obsidian mirror, set in the navel of the statue, to descry the ominous warnings of his god. He had witnessed numerous fires in the sky, and received reports of strange, distorted, unnatural births of children and beasts.

So he was troubled, but not surprised, when news came from the east that white men dressed in metal, like the scales of serpents, with plumes of feathers upon their heads, had arrived within the boundaries of his domain. Alarmingly, these strangers rode upon huge deer and possessed weapons that could spit fire, the like of which no one had ever seen before.

The leader of these men was called Hernando Cortés, but Montezuma was convinced that he was actually the white god Quetzalcóatl come back to his kingdom again. In desperation, the emperor ordered many sacrifices to beg higher powers for assistance. But the cruel gods of the Aztecs were silent, even

Ancient Aztec and Toltec texts foretold that Quetzacóatl, the plumed white serpent god who established their civilization, would one day reappear in Mexico to take revenge for having been cast out.

though the innumerable steps of the pyramids of the sun and the moon were soon slick with human blood.

Inexorably, the invaders approached the capital Tenochtitlán. Montezuma sent envoys to assure the returning god that he would be honoured above all others if only he would go home again. To sweeten his words, much gold and many precious objects were sent, but these only fired the strangers with a passion to continue. Cortés was heard to remark, 'We Spaniards have a strange disease which can only be cured by gold'.

Without a hint of resistance from the Aztec people, Cortés and his meagre army entered the capital of Tenochtitlán to be warmly, if warily, welcomed by the emperor. With all the deference due to a returning god, Montezuma showed Cortés the sights – the architectural wonders and the gory horrors – of his city.

Cortés was amazed by the cleanliness and order of the capital, which greatly contrasted with the filth and squalor of the finest cities of Europe. But he was sickened by the bloody slaughter which formed a large part of Aztec religion. He quickly realized the Aztecs would obey their absolute ruler Montezuma without question, and so the Spanish forces seized the emperor and used him as a puppet to work their will.

It was only when the invading Spaniards had captured Montezuma and occupied Tenochtitlán on 13 August, 1521, that the Aztecs began to resist. By then, it was too late, and Cortés and his small force of less than one thousand men armed with muskets, shielded by armour and possessing swords of steel, defeated a hugely superior army. The

Montezuma was convinced that Cortés was the 'plumed serpent'. The seventeenth-century painting by Miguel and Juan Gonzalez, *The Conquest of Mexico: the Visit of Cortes to Montezuma*, depicts his entourage's initial reception by the Aztecs.

prophet-emperor Montezuma was slain. However, it is not known if the conquistadors had killed him, or his own Aztec people, who were frustrated with rage. It is known that, as Montezuma was stoned to death, he stood impassively, speaking not a single word but accepting his fate as divinely ordained.

Thus ended the Aztec Empire. European rule in the New World, and the age of change, had begun.

THE MAYAN CALENDAR

The ancient Mayan peoples had a genius for mathematics and astronomy. Over many centuries the Mayan priest-kings developed these disciplines into the most accurate calendar system the world has seen. The secret of their calendar's accuracy lies in their having not one system of time-keeping but two. The first is similar to ours, consisting of a year of three hundred and five days. This was used for mundane purposes such as planting and reaping, and of course, keeping a count of one's age. The second calendar system was sacred, having a year of two hundred and seventy days, and was based on the cycle of the planet Venus, which the peoples of ancient Mexico identified with their god, the Plumed Serpent, Quetzacóatl. This sacred system was used to plan ceremonials, sacrifices and astrological pronouncements. In this calendar, twenty zodiac signs were used, each one governing one day.

1 Alligator	11 Monkey
2 Wind	12 Grass
3 House	13 Reed
4 Lizard	14 Ocelot
5 Serpent	15 Eagle
6 Skull	16 Vulture
7 Deer	17 Motion
8 Rabbit	18 Knife
9 Water	19 Rain
10 Dog	20 Flower

These signs were then grouped into thirteen-day periods, the first day acting as a 'ruler' of the rest appearing in that group. So, the period of the Alligator would begin with 1 Alligator, to be followed by 2 Wind, then 3 House and so on. The period of the Serpent would begin with 1 Serpent, followed by 2 Skull, then 3 Deer. The two calendars would only coincide once every 52 years. An elaborate ceremony ushered in the new era, and was called 'Tying the Bundle'. However, when 52 of these bundles had passed, this marked the beginning of 'the Change of the Age'. The calendar system was therefore used as a form of divination.

The Conquest of Mexico by Cortes shows how Aztec attempts at peace with people they thought to be gods failed miserably after Cortés discovered how much gold they had.

CONQVISTA DE MEXICO POR CORTES. N. 7

THE VENGEANCE OF THE TEMPLARS

In March, 1314, a man who had been influential among the monarchs of Europe, and Grand Master of one of the most powerful sects in Christendom, was led to his execution in Paris. His name was Jacques de Molay and the story of his downfall involves some of the most tantalizing mysteries of medieval times.

The Knights Templar had been founded more than 300 years before, during the tumultuous days of the First Crusade. Their story begins with Hugh le Payan and eight other knights who arrived at the precarious court of Baldwin I, King of Jerusalem, in AD 1100. These knights, each from a noble family, had taken monkish vows of poverty, chastity and obedience, but they also took arms against the enemies of the Church with the avowed aim of protecting pilgrims and travellers to the Holy Land against 'infidels, thieves and attackers'. Their militant vows ensured that they would fight to the death and never retreat unless they were outnumbered three to one. To the Islamic Saracen, it was as if a tribe of fearless wild men had come amongst them.

Establishing themselves in the ruins of King Solomon's

Jacques Bernard de Molay, who cursed King Philippe and Pope Clement V, and thirteen generations of their progeny, upon his death at their hands.

Temple on the Mount, they were known as the Poor Knights of Jesus Christ. The seal of their order won ecclesiastical approval because it expressed their humility by showing two poor men mounted on a single horse. Yet whatever their view of poverty, they were not to remain poor for long. In Europe, the knights won the support of the famed Abbot Bernard of Clairvaux, the world's most respected theologian. Due to his unreserved admiration of the order, recruits to the knights became a flood by the 1130s and, soon after, the Poor Knights became known as the Knights of the Temple of Solomon, or the Knights Templar.

St Bernard aside, there were those who were deeply suspicious of the order's motives, even at that early stage. The fact that the knights conducted their ceremonies in strictest secrecy did not endear them to their crusading fellows, and soon rumours began to spread that these knights were not quite as orthodox as they would have everyone believe. It was said that their original Christian zeal had been tainted by exposure to Judaism and Islam in the Holy Land, that they had renounced Christ and worshipped an idol in the shape of a human head which they called Baphomet, and that unnatural vices were practised amongst them. These knights were also said to be masters of the occult arts, understanding the secrets of astrology, alchemy and numerology. Even their early tenure of the Temple ruins was now called into question, since it

A POPE FOR A KING

Eventually the crusades failed and the Knights took up residence throughout Europe, where they remained a powerful influence for some centuries. The rumours of their occult practices continued, but it was not the taint of heresy that caused their downfall. Due to their enormous wealth, the Knights had set up a novel system which we would recognize today as banking. Over the years, the order had made loans to merchants, adventurers and kings, earning considerable profit from the exercise. Now they were back in Europe providing an unspoken challenge to the papacy, which regarded the order as a separate and rather worrying armed 'church' holding influence over monarchs simply because they held the bank balance. This was a simply intolerable situation, and one that

The Abbot of Clairvaux – seen here preaching during the Second Crusade in the presence of King Louis VII of France at Vezeley in 1146 – admired the Poor Knights of Jesus Christ.

was known that the original eight knights had excavated the site and apparently discovered hidden treasure of a most remarkable kind. This last rumour was seen to be a self-evident fact since, at their own considerable expense, the knights built many strong castles to protect the frontiers of the fragile Crusader kingdom.

Philippe le Bel, King of France, was determined to remedy, but first he had to find a compliant pope. His first step was to kidnap and murder Pope Boniface VIII. This pope's successor, Benedict XI, was also disinclined to act, so Philippe had him poisoned. After this, the College of Cardinals was unwilling to elect one of its members to the fatal office, so the church remained without a head for some time. Eventually, the French king invited the whole conclave of cardinals to the dedication of a new

'I call upon you King Philippe and you Pope Clement to stand with me before the throne of God before the year is out. And my curse shall be upon your line until the thirteenth generation, until one shall come to his end at this place.'

JACQUES DE MOLAY

Jacques de Molay was burned at the stake for heresy in 1314 with his second in command because the King feared the Templars' influence.

cathedral. Once the unsuspecting prelates were within, the king ordered that the doors be locked. The cardinals protested, but the king demanded that they use their captivity to elect a pope. If they did not, he would stop feeding them, and if this was not inducement enough, he would be quite prepared to remove the roof. Faced with these rather unpleasant possibilities, the cardinals decided to elect their oldest and most ailing member. This was the Archbishop of Bordeaux, a man so feeble that he had been carried into the church on a litter. No one expected him to survive long but, as soon as his unanimous election was announced, the moribund cleric nimbly leapt from his bed, crying that God had seen fit to perform a miracle! The new pope took the name Clement V and expressed his debt to King Philippe by conspiring with him to undo the mighty Templars.

With the Church now on his side, Philippe acted decisively. On Friday, 13 October, 1307, a highly organized and unified action took place throughout France. All of the Templars were arrested, their chapels and strongholds were seized, their goods were confiscated and the Grand Master Jacques de Molay was put in chains. However, the vast wealth of the Templars still eluded the rapacious king, so torture was employed to loosen the tongues of his unfortunate captives.

THE CURSE OF THE GRAND MASTER

In their torments, many Templars spoke of strange rites and blasphemies which became the prosecutor's main arguments at the trial of de Molay. It was claimed that the Templars did not venerate Christ at all, but repudiated him and spat and stamped on a crucifix, that they worshipped the mysterious idol called Baphomet, and that they indulged in ritual homosexuality. Unweaned babes were supposed to have been sacrificed in foul black magic ceremonies. It was even suggested that the deaths of the two previous popes should be laid at their door.

Bravely, Jacques de Molay countered all the charges, but on certain matters he would not speak, even under the duress of the vilest torments. So it was that in March, 1314, de Molay and his second in command were roasted to death under the vengeful gaze of both king and pope. But as the agonies engulfed the Grand Master, he shouted out 'I call upon you, King Philippe, and you, Pope Clement, to stand with me before the throne of God before the year is out. And my curse shall be upon your line until the thirteenth generation, until one shall come to his end at this place.' So saying, de Molay mercifully died.

As he had prophesied, both Pope Clement and the king were dead within one year. The latter was fatally wounded during a wild boar hunt. The eyes of his corpse could not be closed; and the look of horror in them was said to be so terrifying that a bandage was wrapped around his head to spare onlookers.

Thirteen generations of accursed French kings passed after the death of King Philippe, the last being Louis XVI, who was overthrown by the French Revolution. After being imprisoned with his family in a Parisian fortress known as the Temple – once the home of Jacques de Molay – King Louis was guillotined on the very same spot where de Molay was burned. As he died, someone shouted, 'Jacques de Molay, you have been avenged.'

Just as predicted, the last French king under de Molay's curse was guillotined on the same spot where the chief of the Knights Templar was burned.

DR DEE AND THE DESTINY OF A QUEEN

The forbidding walls of the Tower of London have concealed many tragedies over the centuries, but its dungeons were never so full as in the days of 'Bloody Mary', Queen Mary I (1553-1558). It was within that grim fortress in the heart of the bustling city that Dr John Dee, one of the most remarkable men of the sixteenth century, was imprisoned and condemned to death for the crime of casting a horoscope.

The dark and secretive world of Tudor politics was a dangerous setting for a prophet of any sort, and much more so for Dr Dee, a person whose erudition and insight made him a powerful ally and, equally, a dangerous enemy.

By the time Queen Mary had occupied the throne for not quite two years she had already put down two rebellions. The first had been a plot hatched by the Duke of Northumberland which had placed the crown on the head of her ill-fated cousin, Jane Grey, for the brief period of nine days. Then came another revolt, this time led by Sir Thomas Wyatt, who wished to make Mary's half-sister, the Princess Elizabeth, Queen.

The reason for this unrest was Queen Mary's desire to return England to the Catholic faith. As part of this scheme, she had married Philip of Spain in 1554, and set about burning as many heretic Protestants as her agents could seize hold of. This was the perilous scenario that was soon to embroil the retiring John Dee in mortal danger.

John Dee was a Welshman, the son of a minor court official, born on 13 July, 1527. At an early age

Dr John Dee (1527-1608), an erudite Welsh mystic, alchemist, mathematician and geographer, was Queen Elizabeth I's astrologer. He attracted great notoriety as a sorcerer.

he showed an amazing capacity for academic study. He attended the then newly founded University of Cambridge, and it soon became evident that he was something of a child prodigy. Later, he studied mathematics, geography, Latin, Greek, astrology, alchemy, philosophy and theology. He gained himself the title of 'Doctor', which in those days meant little more than 'the learned'.

By 1554, Dee was resident at Mortlake and was considered the most knowledgeable man in the kingdom. He was also widely thought to be a wizard, with powers comparable to those of Merlin. So it was that Robert Dudley, son of the now decapitated Duke of Northumberland, came to Dee with a commission. Dudley had hopes of marrying the imprisoned Princess Elizabeth, but since she, too, was likely to lose her head, it did not seem to be a match with a future. Dee set to work without delay. He took down the princess's place, time and date of birth and calculated her horoscope. To his astonishment, this map of the heavens revealed that, far from meeting her end at the hands of an executioner, Elizabeth would inherit the crown. To confirm his findings, Dee then secretly calculated a chart for Queen Mary herself, thus technically committing high treason.

> 'Behold, these things and their mysteries shall be known unto you...'
>
> *DE HEPTARCHIA MYSTICA,* **DR DEE**

THE SHADOW OF THE TOWER

By ancient law, it was forbidden even to speculate about the royal succession, much less to seek to predict it. The gossip soon got about that Mary's days were numbered. This must have struck the queen very deeply indeed, for if her half-sister was to succeed her, it meant that not only would she die but that she would also die childless. The furious Mary had Dee arrested and thrown into the Tower to await execution. Within days, both the innocent Princess Elizabeth and her impatient suitor Dudley had passed through Traitor's Gate into the grim fortress too.

While incarcerated, John Dee shared a cell with a kindly old man named Barthlet Green, who was charged with heresy, which in this case meant he disagreed with the queen's religious policies. When Barthlet was later burned at the stake, the smoke entered the cell window, nearly choking to death the distressed Dee in the process.

In time, Mary came to realize that her dreams of having a son were to be unfulfilled. Thus she acknowledged Elizabeth as her heir and released her from prison.

Dee also left the Tower in 1555. Admitting that it had been too close for comfort, he resolved to be more cautious in future. However, the people of London were ominously silent as Dee walked through the gate, because they believed that the ills of the realm were a direct result of imprisoning such a powerful magician.

ASTROLOGER ROYAL

When Mary died a lonely and embittered woman in 1558, Elizabeth rode into London in triumph. Dee was again approached by Robert Dudley, who asked him to choose a propitious date for her coronation. Again, Dee set to work, looking for a time which would indicate a long and prosperous reign, a time of

Dee made this wax disc, placing it under the table while using his crystal ball, to 'hear magic signs and words which counterbalance the effects of evil spirits'.

ELIZABETH'S CORONATION CHART

When Dr John Dee was commissioned to pick a suitable day for the coronation of Elizabeth I, he was faced with a mammoth undertaking. He not only had to pick a time that was propitious for the young monarch, but since the prevalent belief was that the 'Monarch and the land are one' he also had to choose a time that would be auspicious for the nation as a whole.

Since Dee had stated that 'Astrologie is an art mathematicall', he set about the task as a series of mathematical formulae and eventually chose Sunday 15 January, 1559, for the ceremony. The planetary positions of this date were both in harmony with the personal horoscope of the queen and the national horoscope, which was based on the coronation of William the Conqueror on Christmas Day, 1066.

However, one factor was amiss in his chart. Try as he might, Dee could not find a suitable time that would provide Elizabeth with a happy marriage and, more importantly, heirs of her blood. His problem was the planet Saturn – in astrological thinking, this creates a harsh restrictive influence, which damages any area of the horoscope in which it is found. In the case of the coronation chart, Dee found that if the sun – which represents rulership and royalty – was to be at the highest, most beneficial point of the horoscope, then Saturn must occupy the sector of relationships.

Despite the awkward ringed planet, the day was a success, although certain foreign ambassadors disapproved of Elizabeth's charm and casual manner as she moved among even the most humble of her subjects. It is also interesting to note that Elizabeth's sun sign was Virgo, the sign of the virgin.

Queen Elizabeth I Being Carried in Procession, c. 1600, attributed to Robert Peake. Dr Dee was amazed when his astrological chart for Princess Elizabeth showed that she would become Queen.

exploration and artistry, a golden age that would be remembered forever. He eventually suggested noon on 15 January, 1559. Accordingly, the crown was placed on the young monarch's head at that very moment. Dr John Dee continued to enjoy the favour of 'Good Queen Bess' who made him Astrologer Royal, and was consulted by her on many occasions throughout her forty-four year reign. Robert Dudley also thought highly of Dee, even though he never managed to wed Elizabeth or her

ill-fated cousin, Mary, Queen of Scots. There is a postscript to the story of Elizabeth's coronation chart because, although it indicated fame, glory and a sort of immortality, it did not mention marriage. The position of the cold planet Saturn in her House of Relationships indicated unequal partnerships, either because of differences in age (always a sore point with the queen), or rank. Therefore, Dr John Dee may also be responsible for the enduring legend of the 'Virgin Queen'.

THE CROP-EARED ROGUE

Although Dr John Dee, Astrologer Royal to Queen Elizabeth I, was widely regarded as the most knowledgeable man in the kingdom, his wisdom in choosing personal associates might be called into question. Dee's reputation was severely scrutinized when in 1582 he decided to employ a talented, but totally amoral, young man to work for him as a scryer, or crystal-gazer. His name was Edward Kelly (1555-1595). In time, however, many of Kelly's divinatory statements proved to be surprisingly accurate, possessing a truthfulness not entirely reflected in his personal character. His ready tongue and unscrupulous morals left much to be desired.

A seventeenth-century engraving portraying Dr Dee's medium Edward Kelly, who was an amoral rogue as well as a talented scryer (crystal-gazer).

THE DARK MIRROR OF THE AZTECS

Previously, Dee had completed a horoscope for King Philip of Spain, who rewarded him with the gift of a 'Magic Mirror' which had been used previously as the navel of a statue of the bloodthirsty Aztec god Tezcatlipoca. However, despite the good doctor's proficiency in alchemy and astrology, he did not possess the occult talent of scrying to any great degree, and so was forced into the company of Edward Kelly: crystal gazer, hedge sorcerer, con man, fake necromancer, dubious alchemist and general cheat. Kelly, whose real name was probably Talbot, was Irish, Welsh or from Worcester (the story changed in the telling), and had been subjected to the severing of one ear as punishment for his mendacity. Through him, Dee made contact with the realms of spirits and angels by way of the dark obsidian glass of the 'Magic Mirror', eventually achieving a communion with one of the most prestigious of the heavenly host, the Archangel Uriel himself.

All in all, Kelly was an unlikely medium for such a celestial entity as the Archangel Uriel. Kelly, it seems, was more used to the macabre company of the restless dead. In his book *Ancient Funeral Monuments*, seventeenth-century writer John Weever relates a morbid tale of necromancy performed by Kelly and a companion named Paul Waring in the churchyard of Walton-le-Dale in Lancaster. It is claimed that these two dug up a corpse of a man recently buried and 'by incantation conjured this cadaver to speak and utter strange predictions'. Though these strange predictions were not recorded, knowing Kelly's unsavoury reputation, they were likely to concern the whereabouts of buried treasure.

However, there is no hint of these black arts when Kelly was in Dee's service. On the contrary, Kelly and Dee would sit in a darkened room intoning pious verses while gazing into the inky surface of the Mirror until contact with the angelic realm had been made. Then, the entranced Kelly would reply to Dee's questions. On 5 May, 1583, Dee asked the

Edward Kelly was renowned for his ability to contact other spirit realms and beings, as portrayed in this painting in which he summons a corpse from the grave.

'Provision of foreign powers against the welfare of this land which they shall shortly put into practice ... the death of the Queen of Scots is not long unto it.'

archangel, 'As concerning the vision which yesterday was presented to the sight of E. K. as he sat at supper with me in my hall – I mean the appearing of the very great sea and many ships thereon, and the cutting off of the head of a woman by a tall, black man – what are we to imagine thereof?'

Uriel, replying through the mediumship of Kelly, spoke, 'Provision of foreign powers against the welfare of this land: which they shall shortly put into practice. The other, the death of the Queen of Scots: it is not long unto it.'

However, it was to be five more years before the head of the unfortunate Mary rolled from the block, and a further year before the Spanish Armada sailed into English waters. Dee had informed Queen Elizabeth long before these events, and sufficient new ships had been constructed for Drake and his sea-hawks to defeat the threat of invasion.

THE 'SMOKING MIRROR' AND THE SHEW STONE

The village of Mortlake was overwhelmed by the visit of the entire royal court in 1575. The reason for this regal invasion was the desire of Queen Elizabeth I to see the magical glass in the possession of Dr John Dee. But Dee had recently suffered a bereavement, and since it was not the custom for the monarch to enter a house of mourning, the mirror was brought to the village green for Her Majesty's inspection.

This almost-circular, black obsidian mirror had been a gift to Dr Dee from King Philip of Spain, who had received it as a tribute from a conquistador. It seems likely that the mirror had once been the famous 'Smoking Mirror' of Tezcatlipoca which the Aztec ruler, Montezuma, had once consulted.

Had Queen Elizabeth deigned to visit her astrologer some years later, she would have seen another wondrous sight. This was an egg-like irregular orb of slightly pinkish crystal which Dee called 'The Shew Stone'. It was with this crystal that his fly-by-night associate, Edward Kelly, was said to have made contact with the higher angelic realms. Indeed, Kelly claimed

that the stone had been handed to him by the Archangel Uriel in person. This exalted being apparently took the form of a child, and floated outside the window of the Mortlake house before giving the crystal egg to the occupants.

This unlikely tale aside, Dee intended the crystal to be used to make two-way contact with spiritual planes. For more mundane, predictive purposes, Edward Kelly gazed into a polished piece of 'cannel cole', which was probably a reflective surface of jet, or even anthracite. Both the black mirror and the Shew Stone are now on display in the British Museum in London, with various objects that were once the possessions of Dr Dee.

The dark obsidian mirror used by Dr Dee to contact angelic realms is thought to have been part of the treasure taken from the Aztecs in Mexico by Cortés.

THE ROGUE'S END

The spiritual realms were not always to Edward Kelly's taste. After the angels had instructed him to marry, the fly-by-night necromancer, acting under pressure from Dee, reluctantly wed Joan Cooper of Chipping Norton. It was a disaster, prompting Kelly to suggest some wife-swapping with the horrified Dee. It is extremely unlikely that the suggestion was acted upon.

Kelly's end came while on a spying mission in Germany. Both Dee and his erstwhile assistant were guests of the Emperor Rudolph the Mad. On the pretext of attempting to turn lead into gold, Dee and Kelly had picked up a great deal of secret government information useful to Elizabeth of England. Dee had the good sense to head home before they were found

out, but Kelly, greedy to the end, persisted. Eventually, he was imprisoned in the castle of Zerner in Bohemia. At Dee's urging, Queen Elizabeth half-heartedly petitioned the insane emperor for his release. Mad Rudolph would have none of it, and still clung to the notion that Kelly could make his dreams of untold riches come true. In any event, Kelly entered the realm of spirits permanently when he fell from a castle turret while attempting to escape. The full truth will never be known. Did Edward Kelly expire as the result of a daring, but risky, escape plot, or was the cause the wrath of a disappointed and unstable emperor?

Despite Kelly's work contacting angels for her, Queen Elizabeth baulked at asking the mad Emperor Rudolph to release Kelly, who later fell mysteriously to his death.

THE FIELD OF HONOUR

In 1555, the vigorous, powerful and charismatic French king, Henri II, received a disturbing letter from an aged Italian astrologer named Luca Gaurica, who had Latinized his name in the fashion of the time to Lucas Gauricus. The letter warned the King not to go into battle in the summer of his forty-second year. His death would occur in single combat in an enclosed space through an injury to the head. Initially the king gave scant regard to the letter. He was only thirty-seven years old, and the prophecy appeard no more threatening than everyday life in the sixteenth century; secondly, an honourable death in open combat was preferable to any other, possibly ignoble, end. The reason the king paid any attention to this message was that Gauricus was the most famous astrologer of his age. In previous years he had gained a considerable reputation as a prophet for kings, princes and noblemen throughout Europe.

Henri's predecessor had also received a warning from Gauricus to the effect that he would be defeated at the Battle of Pavia. Furthermore, the Lord Constable of France, the Duc de Bourbon, had met his end on the very walls of Rome in 1527 exactly in accordance with the words of Gauricus.

A SECOND WARNING

While these predictions had ensured the Italian's fame, some of his clients were not pleased with Gauricus's prophecies of doom. The Duke of Milan had gone so far as to torture the astrologer in a particularly gruesome fashion for daring to foresee his death. Gauricus had been lucky to escape with his life, even at the price of the mobility of his arms.

The jousting tournament which ended Henri II's life, depicted in the 1559 engraving by Hogenberg, *The Killing of Henry II of France (1519-59) at a Tournament for the Wedding of Philip II of Spain with Elizabeth.*

Henri chose to ignore Gauricus's prediction, but his wife, the enigmatic Queen Catherine de Medici, took him far more seriously. She stored the information away for future reference, while the court of France continued as if nothing had happened. In time, Gauricus's words might have been forgotten had not confirmation of his prediction come from an obscure town in the South of France. Michel de Nostredame, better known as Nostradamus, had published the first of his books of prophecies called *The Centuries* (see pages 152-161). Verse 35 of Book 1 seemed to repeat the ominous warning of Lucas Gauricus:

A CRUEL DEATH

In the summer of King Henri's forty-second year, all France celebrated the double weddings of the king's daughters to the Duke of Savoy and the king of Spain. A tournament was held as part of the festivities, and Henri took to the field in his golden armour with its distinctively barred helm and lion crest. He was challenged by Count Montgomery, Captain of the Scottish Guard and proud bearer of the Lion of Scots banner. The king was happy to ride against him. They engaged twice with no conclusive result. On the third pass, however, Montgomery's lance splintered, shattering the king's barred helm and piercing him through the eyes. So grievous was this wound that a blacksmith actually had to stand on the king's face for leverage while the lance was removed. Montgomery fled the scene while poor Henri lingered for ten further days in excruciating pain. Now, forewarned by the prophecies of Gauricas and Nostradamus, Queen Catherine swiftly acted to seize power and place her young son on the throne with the minimum of disruption.

On the strength of this successful prophecy, Nostradamus's reputation was elevated to unsurpassed heights, making him a worthy successor to Lucas Gauricus as the most famous astrologer in the world. Even today, the prophecies of Nostradamus are seriously contemplated and reinterpreted time and again.

'Le lyon jeune le vieux surmontera
En champ bellique par singulier duel:
Dans gage d'or les yeux lui crevera:
Deux classes une, puis mourir, mort cruelle.'

'The young lion will overcome the old
on the field of war in single fight:
He will put out his eyes in a
golden cage of gold:
Two passes one, then to die a cruel death.'

Henri II, King of France (1519-1559), by Thevet, 1584. Henri's wife, Catherine de Medici, was forewarned of her husband's death.

Queen Catherine summoned Nostradamus to attend her in Paris, ostensibly to calculate horoscopes for her children, although still she took no overt action concerning her husband.

THE WHITE KING AND
THE FLAMES OF GEMINI

The Great Fire of London was one of the most devastating events in the long history of the city. Starting in Pudding Lane at 1.30 am on Sunday, 2 September, 1666, it swiftly swept through the mainly wooden buildings at tremendous speed, consuming everything in an area one and a half miles long and half a mile wide. Thirteen thousand and two hundred houses, eighty-seven churches and St Paul's Cathedral were incinerated yet, incredibly, there was no loss of life.

Human nature demanded a scapegoat. Since the distraught baker in whose shop the blaze had started seemed a poor target, and there were no convenient foreign arsonists to be found, the vengeful authorities turned their fury on William Lilly, the most famous astrologer in England, who was known as *Merlinus Anglicus*, the English Merlin. William Lilly was a well-known media celebrity of his day, so his arrest unsurprisingly caused a public sensation.

The Great Fire of London, 1666, the Dutch School, 17th century. A fire in a bakery set off the blaze that devastated most of London in 1666, since most of the buildings were made of wood.

from AD 677. This was called *The Prophecy of the White King*. It foretold a battle fought on a moor near a river. The royal army would be defeated and this would be a good thing since much misery and war would be caused by a king who, either because of his frequent wearing of white apparel, or extreme delight in that colour, would be dubbed the White King by his people. The prophecy proclaimed that 'the White and noble king shall dye'.

This pallid monarch was immediately recognizable as Charles I, who had indeed worn white at his

PROPHECY OF THE WHITE KING

Lilly had been a distinguished prophet for many years. His counsel had been sought by both Royalists and Roundheads. It was said that he had been consulted by King Charles I and his arch-enemy Oliver Cromwell. It was Lilly who had predicted the fall of the Royalists and the eventual death of King Charles. In a pamphlet published in 1644, Lilly had proclaimed a prophecy which he said had been translated into Latin from ancient Welsh and dated

This image in a book by Lilly of the Gemini Twins (London's astrological sign) falling into a fire drew him into a battle with the courts that eventually ruined his career.

coronation instead of the traditional purple. The battle was that of Marston Moor, which lies on the River Ouse. It was also noted that later, when the king was a prisoner, he was kept on the Isle of Wight, and, at his execution in 1649, he went to the block in a simple white shirt.

Thereafter William Lilly was held in high esteem by the victorious parliament, who granted him several estates seized from exiled royalists. The death of Cromwell and the restoration of the monarchy under Charles II saw a downturn in Lilly's fortunes, and his properties were confiscated by the Crown. As a supporter of the old republican regime, he was in disfavour with the new royalists, so he was not short of enemies to point the finger at him when London went up in flames.

A BURNING CITY

The real cause of Lilly's arrest and imprisonment lay in a pamphlet which he had published the year before the fire. In it, Lilly had included an illustration of the Gemini Twins, the zodiacal sign of London, plunging headfirst into a city in flames. This was seen as foreknowledge of the event and even suggestive of a republican plot to regain power. It was with considerable difficulty that Lilly persuaded his hostile judges that his graphic prediction derived from the astrological arts rather than any intent of arson. Eventually the court grudgingly admitted lack of evidence and freed the terrified astrologer. However, the accusation stuck to Lilly for the rest of his life and he could never again claim the prominence he had once enjoyed. He prudently distanced himself from the city and died aged seventy-nine in 1681.

William Lilly (Ashmolean Museum, Oxford) was a respected seer known as 'the English Merlin', whose counsel was sought by both the Royalists and the Roundheads, and both King Charles I and his enemy Oliver Cromwell.

His political allegiance aside, it seems unfair that Lilly should have been singled out, since the Great Fire had been predicted by others, too. Humphrey Smith, a Quaker, had expressed similar views three years before the event: 'And as for the city and her suburbs, a fire was kindled therein, and the burning thereof was exceedingly great, but neither did the burning hurt them… this vision was shewn to me by the Lord'.

One hundred years previously, the notorious Mother Shipton had also foreseen the burning city (see pages 102-105). Nostradamus was also credited with such a prophecy, as indeed was the original Welsh Merlin of Arthurian legend. This was but cold comfort to his English imitator, who lived out the remainder of his life in obscurity.

The fall of Merlinus Anglicus marked the end of an era. No longer would rulers of any political note openly consort with soothsayers without attracting adverse comment.

PREDICTIONS OF FIRE

Lilly was not the only person to predict the Great Fire – Humphrey Smith, a Quaker, had recounted a similar story three years before the event.

66 And as for the city and her suburbs, a fire was kindled therein, and the burning thereof was exceedingly great, but neither did the burning hurt them … this vision was shewn to me by the Lord. 99

MERLIN THE MAGICIAN

The original Merlin of Arthurian legend was not always regarded primarily as a magician. According to Geoffrey of Monmouth (AD1100-1154) in his *History of the Kings of Britain*, Merlin was looked upon as a prophet whose father was a sub-lunar spirit or, possibly, even the Devil himself.

When King Vortigern of Britain desired the sacrifice of a boy who 'had no mortal father', so that the defensive tower he was building would stop falling down, the child Merlin was brought for the purpose. However, Merlin, like many a 'wonder-child' before him, confounded the king's Druids and made a prophecy of his own.

Merlin saw a vision involving two dragons, one red dragon and one white, doing harsh battle. Backwards and forwards they went, sometimes the white dragon having the upper hand, and at other times the red. Merlin prophesied that the white dragon represented both Vortigern himself and his invading Saxon (English) allies. The red dragon, however, represented the Celtic Britons, who would eventually win the contest.

Another tradition appears in Geoffrey of Monmouth's *Vita Merlini* (The Life of Merlin) in which Merlin, after the death of his friends and kin, is driven mad and retreats to the woods, taking with him a pig and a wolf as his only companions. There he uttered many prophecies and generally bemoaned his fate.

Gerald of Wales (AD 1145–1223) suggested that there may have even have been two Merlins – Merlin Ambrosius, who is associated with King Arthur and the town of Carmarthen, and Merlin the Mad, who lived in misery in the wilds of Scotland as the last prophet of druidic tradition. The Mad Merlin is said to have been reconciled with the Christian faith by St Kentigern, and suffered three 'deaths' in one day shortly afterwards.

QUEEN OF THE WEST AND QUEEN OF THE EAST

In the late eighteenth century, unrest in France and its empire was the cause of a sense of unease in Europe. Its rulers – royalty, nobles and churchmen – were uncaring and wealthy beyond the dreams of avarice. The poor, however, were wretched and resentful. Revolution was in the air, and soon things would never be the same again. The decline of the old aristocracy into decadence was matched by the rise of the middle class, a new elite who sometimes came from the most unlikely of places, like the Caribbean island of Martinique.

It was here that two young cousins, playing in the glorious sunshine, came upon an old slave woman who offered to tell their fortunes. One can imagine their amusement when the crone told the elder girl that she would be a queen of the West, while the younger would be a queen of the East. Nothing less likely could be anticipated.

Mistress of an Empire

The elder girl eventually joined the ranks of the French aristocracy by marrying the Comte de Bauharnais in 1779. However, this was an unsuccessful match, as his life ended on the guillotine, which she narrowly missed herself. Later, the young woman met an up-and-coming military officer whose self-confidence, strategic skill and awesome ambition marked him as a man of potential. They were married in 1796. His name was Napoleon Bonaparte, hers was Josephine. In 1804, Napoleon – now master of Europe – crowned his wife Josephine, Empress of the French, and Queen of Italy and Navarre.

The younger girl, Josephine's cousin, Aimée Dubucq de Rivery, had been sent from Martinique to a convent in France to continue her education but as the threat of revolution grew nearer, it was thought prudent to return her to her Caribbean home. Fate intervened in the form of Algerian pirates who stormed the ship and took Aimée prisoner. She was a particularly beautiful girl with golden hair, large blue eyes and a perfectly formed mouth – the pirates decided to sell her as a slave in Algiers. The ruler of that city was overwhelmed by her loveliness and, as he wished to win the Sultan of Turkey's favour, he purchased and sent her as a gift to the supreme monarch of the Moslem world in Constantinople.

Thus Aimée exchanged the repressive atmosphere of a French convent for the opulent, exotic luxuries of the Seraglio, the palace of the Grand Turk. The lovely Aimée – now renamed Naksh, 'The Beautiful' – soon became the favourite concubine in the harem of the fifty-nine-year-old Sultan Abdul Hamid. Within one year, she had borne him a son, who was destined to be the Sultan Mahmud.

Power Behind the Eastern Throne

Aimée, now the Sultana Naksh, had the foresight to realize that the Sultan's days were numbered; not wishing to suffer the often fatal consequences of being the concubine of a deceased ruler, she went to great lengths to win over his immediate heir, the lonely, dreamy Prince Selim. Her immense charm and beauty soon inveigled the prince into her bed, with the result that her influence grew stronger upon the death of her husband rather than diminishing. Now Aimée dared to appear outside the harem, the

The Consecration of the Emperor Napoleon and Coronation of the Empress Josephine, 2nd December 1804, by Jacques Louis David (1748-1835). As a girl, it is unlikely Josephine ever thought to marry an emperor.

first concubine ever to do so — impressing all with her dramatic style, a trait she shared with Josephine, although, in contrast to her cousin, Aimée dressed very plainly, mainly in black as befitted a widow. A slave would follow closely behind her, bearing her immense fortune in jewellery on a tray to display her wealth, and her personal barge was gilded and decorated in mother-of-pearl, with a large number of thin gold chains attached to artificial, jointed, golden fish which appeared to surround the vessel in a decorative shoal. Under her guidance, the Sultan Selim opened the secretive Turkish Empire to Western influences, and especially to the French. However, Selim had little luck as a ruler. His love of Aimée remained his one security in a troubled reign that ended when he was strangled by eunuch assassins in 1808, and was succeeded by his cousin Mustafa until he, too, was soon assassinated and Aimée's son Mahmud ascended the throne. Aimée retained her immense influence over the Empire by ruling through her son, known to history as Mahmud the Reformer.

The Sultana Naksh died in 1815, having effectively ruled the Turkish Empire for thirty-three years through the reigns of four sultans, and outliving Josephine by one year. The cousins never met as adults but must have marvelled at the old woman's accurate prophecy so many years earlier.

Aimée Dubucq de Rivery, born in 1766, was the mother of Sultan Mahmud, and the cousin of Josephine Bonaparte.

95

CHAPTER FOUR

THE DOOM SAYERS

Prophets who wail and gnash their teeth have always received a hearing from the general public. For some strange reason, these gloomy predictors seem to be more popular than those of a more optimistic turn of mind. Perhaps this has something to do with the belief of every generation that 'things used to be better', and that 'everything is going to wrack and ruin', and not forgetting 'I don't know how it's all going to end'. The following prophets of doom are some of the world's most famous, and infamous, predictors. One does hope that they had a better motive for their pessimistic prophecies than just being able to say 'I told you so!' If, that is, they lived long enough.

Robert Nixon appeared to have little motive at all — apart from his obsession with eating. This retarded youth could only speak coherently when uttering predictions, including one about his own death from neglect. His unfortunate story

A woodcut called *Old Mother Shipton Casting a Horoscope* is indicative of the fascination surrounding the woman who was dubbed the Yorkshire witch.

Pope Urban VIII's heavenly altercations were diabolical, given that Italian astronomer Galilei Galileo was quizzed over his beliefs, as depicted in *Galilei Before the Inquisition*.

unfolds in 'Robert Nixon, The Cheshire Idiot' (pages 98-101).

Ursula Southeil, better known as Mother Shipton, was a wizened crone with a great line in doom and disaster. Her encounter with the emissary of Cardinal Wolsey testifies to this. However, her literally dreadful poem concerning the disastrous end of the world is the foundation of her fame in the modern age, and is recounted in 'The Prophecies of Mother Shipton' (pages 102-105).

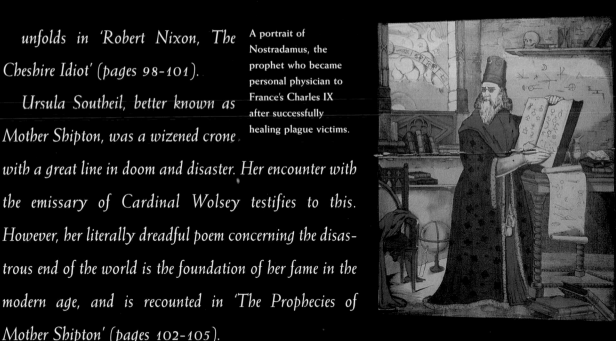

A portrait of Nostradamus, the prophet who became personal physician to France's Charles IX after successfully healing plague victims.

No treatment of the prophets of doom would be complete without that old pessimist Michel de

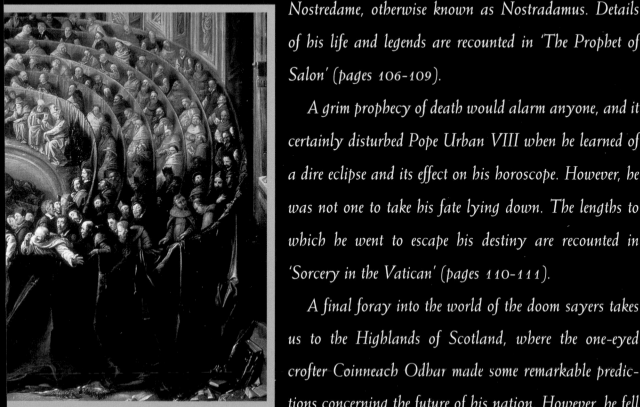

Nostredame, otherwise known as Nostradamus. Details of his life and legends are recounted in 'The Prophet of Salon' (pages 106-109).

A grim prophecy of death would alarm anyone, and it certainly disturbed Pope Urban VIII when he learned of a dire eclipse and its effect on his horoscope. However, he was not one to take his fate lying down. The lengths to which he went to escape his destiny are recounted in 'Sorcery in the Vatican' (pages 110-111).

A final foray into the world of the doom sayers takes us to the Highlands of Scotland, where the one-eyed crofter Coinneach Odhar made some remarkable predictions concerning the future of his nation. However, he fell foul of the Countess of Seaforth and pronounced doom for her family line. Coinneach's remarkable tale and terrible end are to be found in 'The Brahan Seer' (pages 112-115).

THE CHESHIRE IDIOT

Visitors to the manor house owned by the prominent Cholmondeley family in 1485 were surprised that such a noble household would employ a gangling boy whose odd appearance, which consisted of a disproportionately large head and huge vacant eyes, hardly fitted him for polite society. The boy's only enthusiasm was for eating, and he would gorge himself with vast quantities of food whenever he could. In fact, as he had been known to consume an entire leg of mutton in a single meal, he had to be watched continuously just in case he devoured a whole banquet at one sitting and caused his stomach to burst. Added to these unfortunate traits, the lads was a simpleton, incapable of performing complex tasks.

He did, however, have one unlikely advantage that made him an extremely valuable addition to the household: he was a prophet.

To describe poor Robert Nixon as an illiterate farm boy would be to understate the case considerably. He showed little desire to communicate at all, providing grunts for 'yes' and 'no'. But though he was mentally retarded, physically unprepossessing, and generally incoherent, he was capable of lengthy periods of lucidity in which he spoke with both assurance and

Robert Nixon was known as the Cheshire Idiot because he was regarded as a simpleton, except for rare moments when he seemed to take on another well-spoken and clairvoyant persona.

certainty about people, places and a future which he could not possibly comprehend.

THE RELUCTANT PROPHET

Born in 1467 to a poor family who admitted that Robert was too dim-witted to learn anything, the lad was set to guiding a plough as soon as he could reach the handles. For years it was assumed that he was unable to speak, so it was with total astonishment that his family heard that young Robert had accurately predicted the death of a neighbour's ox.

It was this prediction that brought Robert to the attention of Lord Cholmondeley, who took the boy into his house. Robert, however, was seized by an uncharacteristic display of emotion, and protested by howling, 'They will lock me up and starve me!'

His parents ignored his pleas, however, and Robert left unwillingly for his new life.

Cholmondeley had need of a prophet, for the times were troubled and rebellion was in the air. Robert, in the meantime, was not settling well into the ways of a great house, and his capacity for causing disarray and chaos soon set him apart from the rest of the household. Before long, he was once again sent to plough the fields, just to keep him out of the way. One day, while out working, Robert stopped and gazed intently at the sky, seemingly lost in another world and impervious to the shouts and taunts of his fellow workers.

He then said, 'I have seen things I cannot tell you, and which man never saw before.'

Robert proceeded to lecture the peasants for two hours on European history. Lord Cholmondeley was called and he too heard the 'idiot' speak of many things, including the Great Plague, the burning of London in 1666, the beheading of Charles I, the Restoration, the reign of William of Orange, the French Revolution and the Napoleonic Wars. Nixon flatly stated, 'When a raven shall build its nest in a stone lion's mouth on top of a church in Cheshire, a king of England shall be driven

The storming of the Bastille, 14th July 1789 – the French Revolution was one of the many significant events in European history that Robert Nixon predicted.

out of his kingdom and return nevermore. And as token of the truth of this, a wall of Mr (sic) Cholmondeley shall fall.'

Robert pointed at the wall, at which Cholmondeley laughed, 'The boy is truly mad. This wall will never fall down.' It crumbled the very next day. A close inspection of it offered no explanation. The prophecy of the raven came true in 1688 when King James II was obliged to flee the country after the so-called Glorious Revolution.

Robert continued prophesying. He predicted a mill stream would run dry, for instance, which it did shortly afterwards. He also stated that an heir to the Cholmondeleys would be born in a snowstorm when an eagle alighted on the roof of their house. This occurred in 1684, just as the family line was weakest, and appeared in grave danger of dying out. It was all the more remarkable since eagles were extremely rare in England in those days.

On 22 August, 1485, Robert once again stopped working. This time, he leapt about in an agitated fashion, brandishing his whip like a sword, crying out the names 'Henry' and 'Richard'. 'Up with all arms,' he shouted. 'Now, over the ditch and the

LEFT: When Henry VII (1457-1509) – seen here with his ministers Empson and Dudley – heard that Robert Nixon had predicted his victory over Richard III at the Battle of Bosworth, he acquired him from the prominent Cholmondeley family, hoping to make use of his prophetic skills.

ABOVE: Nixon's gluttony led to his death. As he himself foresaw, he was locked up and starved to death by one of the king's men, His Majesty's cook, who 'forgot' him for two weeks.

'When a raven shall build its nest in a stone lion's mouth on top of a church in Cheshire, a king of England shall be driven out of his kingdom and return nevermore.'

ROBERT NIXON

battle is won.' Robert then seemed to notice the astonishment of his colleagues and smiled, 'The battle is over. Henry has won.'

Two days later, news arrived that King Richard III had been defeated and killed at the Battle of Bosworth. The Earl of Richmond was the victor and had been proclaimed king as Henry VII.

When the new king's guards arrived with orders to bring the idiot to their master, Robert Nixon became more and more agitated. He ran frantically about screaming that the king's men would starve him to death. However, much to Nixon's relief, the first Tudor monarch treated Robert kindly and even assigned a scribe to accompany him at all times.

Robert's plough-boy days were over, but, as he had predicted, so, soon, was his life. His old habits died hard, and Robert took to stealing food from the palace kitchens. An exasperated cook eventually locked the boy in a cupboard while a farewell banquet was being prepared for the king's departure on a hunting trip. Unfortunately, in the feverish hustle and bustle of the court, the cook forgot about him.

Two weeks later, the king returned and had occasion to command the presence of his prophet. Only then did the cook remember the ever-hungry Robert Nixon. It was too late. As Robert had predicted, he had been starved to death by the king's men.

There is one prophecy made by Robert Nixon that remains to be fulfilled. In answer to the king's question about a possible invasion, the Cheshire Idiot replied that the kingdom would be safe until soldiers came 'with snow on their helmets bringing plague, famine and murder in the skirts of their garments'.

THE PROPHECIES OF MOTHER SHIPTON

Along with those of Nostradamus, the prophecies of Mother Shipton have had a chilling influence on people throughout the ages. Yet her life is so poorly documented that it is difficult to discern any hard facts. There is even some doubt as to whether this notoriously prophetic woman ever existed at all.

However, she was probably born of very humble stock around 1488 near Knareborough in Yorkshire. Her life cannot have been a happy one. As an infant, she was rumoured to be the daughter of the devil himself, and from an early age she was said to be hairy and hideous with a huge bulbous nose. Age did nothing to improve her appearance. By the time she was an old lady, her hunch-backed, crooked form emerging from her cave wearing a long black cloak and tall conical hat was everyone's idea of a stereotypical witch.

Mother Shipton has been tentatively identified with Janet Ursula Southiel, whose vile appearance was put down to a diabolical conception. She, like Merlin before her, was thought to have been the offspring of a virgin and a devil, and brought into the world at the height of a furious thunderstorm.

Placed in a convent at an early age, poor Ursula was the butt of many jokes. But these soon stopped because the cruel children who plagued her were subsequently pinched and bruised by unseen presences. It was assumed that these were relatives on her father's side of the family. Ursula didn't last long in a religious environment and left of her own accord. In short, she was a medieval dropout.

She later married the presumably short-sighted Tom Shipton, moved into a lean-to shack set against the entrance to a cave and began to supplement their meagre income by telling fortunes, usually in terms more obscure than the later Nostradamus himself. Most of her prophecies were about her own times – the wars between England and France, King Henry VIII's religious difficulties and his turnover of wives.

THE WITCH AND THE CARDINAL

The first prediction of any note that is attributed to her concerns the powerful Cardinal Wolsey, Archbishop of York and Chancellor to the king. Wolsey had already been the subject of another prophecy which predicted that 'Kingston would be the Cardinal's death'. The rattled Wolsey had gone to such lengths to avoid Kingston-upon-Thames that he had given the king the neighbouring palace of Hampton Court. ('Kingston' turned out to be one Walter Kingston – a messenger ordering the cardinal's arrest as he lay on his deathbed.)

Wolsey was naturally curious about Ursula and sent three of his men in disguise to her hovel to ask her what he should do concerning his troubles with the increasingly irritable king. Shipton immediately saw through the disguises and delivered a terrible prediction of an imminent fall from power for the cardinal. Angrily, one of the men roared, 'When His Eminence comes North, he will have you burned.'

Calmly, Mother Shipton replied, 'I'll wager that His Eminence will burn first.'

Some months later, the cardinal did in fact fall from grace and, fearing the king's displeasure, he fled to Yorkshire and the sanctuary of his cathedral. Legend has it that, when he encountered the

ABOVE: Mother Shipton's Cave in Knaresborough, North Yorkshire, where the prophetess was born in 1488, and is said to have lived with her husband, is now a tourist spot.

LEFT: This engraving after Sir William Ouseley, 1804, of Mother Shipton (1488-1561), born Ursula Southiel, shows how the seeress was perceived as a witch during and after her life.

'I'll wager that His Eminence will burn first'.

MOTHER SHIPTON

hag-like Mother Shipton on the wayside, the old woman prophesied that, though he would see the city of York, he would not reach it.

Wolsey brooded on the disturbing prophecy for some time and eventually dispatched a servant to persuade the witch to revise her prediction. When this messenger reached the cave, Mother Shipton was said to have cackled wildly and, to prove the efficacy of her powers, threw a linen handkerchief into a fire. To the servant's bemusement, the cloth did not burn and he returned to the cardinal with the news that Shipton was indeed a witch. Cardinal Wolsey determined to have her consigned to the flames as soon as the opportunity arose.

However, fortunately for Mother Shipton, the dire events she had predicted for the cardinal occurred not long afterwards. Wolsey did see York, as she had foretold, but from a castle tower at Cawood, some eight miles away. A message then arrived from the king commanding the cardinal to return to London. He sadly turned south again but on the way to the capital, contracted a fever so agonizing that he felt as though his flesh was melting from his bones. He died soon after at Leicester, having been stripped of all his titles and lands.

THE END OF THE WORLD

The cardinal's painful death contrasted with that of Mother Shipton, who passed away peacefully in 1561 or thereabouts, leaving behind her a mysterious box which can only be opened in the presence of two Anglican bishops. As yet, no high-ranking clergyman has claimed the honour.

Some eighty years after Mother Shipton's demise, a book of her prophecies was 'discovered' by an

enterprising printer who immediately published them, earning himself a nice profit in the process. These predictions proved to be stunningly accurate accounts of the beheading of Mary Queen of Scots, the sinking of the Spanish Armada, the voyages of Drake and Raleigh, the introduction of tobacco, the succession of King James I, and the dreadful events of the Gunpowder Plot of 1605. All of these had occurred, though, by the time her visions had entered the public domain. Undoubtedly her greatest prophecy, and the one upon which her reputation

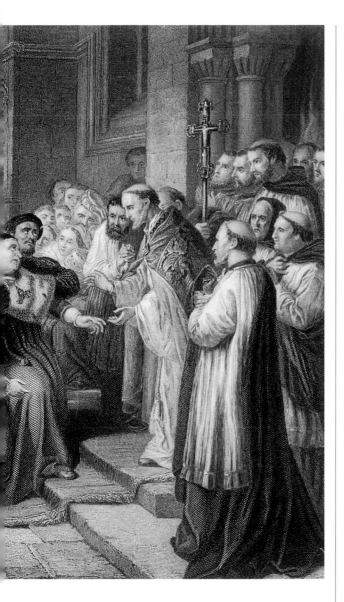

Cardinal Wolsey at Leicester Abbey, c. 1530, where he died
of a fever after having been stripped of all his titles and
lands. As Mother Shipton predicted, he died before her.

rests, comes in the form of an atrocious piece of
doggerel which has come down to us. In verse form,
it predicted the advent of cars, telegraphs, railways,
aeroplanes and even submarines, and concluded that
the world would end in 1881.

Of course the world did not end during the reign
of Queen Victoria, even though there were plenty of
people who were ready to believe that it would.
Nevertheless, there have been subsequent versions,
and interpretations of these prophetic verses, most
notably: 'The world to an end shall come in nineteen

hundred and twenty-one', or possibly 'Nineteen hundred and ninety-one'.

Unfortunately we cannot give Mother Shipton
the credit for her prophetic verses – since this
belongs to a certain Charles Hindley, who confessed
to the forgery in 1862. However, reputations are
even stranger than prophecies, and a wax effigy of
the prophetic witch, Mother Shipton, stood in
Westminster Abbey as an object of veneration for
centuries, while the cave which was said to be her
home is even now a popular tourist attraction.

THE PROPHET OF SALON

Michel de Nostredame, or Nostradamus, was born at noon on 14 December, 1503, at Saint Remy in Provence. His background was Jewish, of the tribe of Issachar, but he was brought up as a Christian by parents who had been forced to convert from Judaism under penalty of death. The main influences in his life were those of his two grandfathers, who were physicians, determined that their talented descendant should follow in their footsteps. After an early education in the classics, astrology, Hebrew,

Nostradamus (1503-1566) – the Latinized name for Michel de Nostredame – was a French physician and astrologer known during his time as the Prophet of Salon, which was his home. He was personal physician to Charles IX.

Latin and Greek, Michel went to Avignon to study medicine. Biographers tell us that he was adept enough at grammar, philosophy and rhetoric, but dangerously unconventional when it came to treating illness. Nostradamus washed between seeing patients, did not believe in bleeding as a treatment and had the curious notion that tying off a severed limb with catgut would be more effective than searing the wound with pitch.

However, Michel won great renown in treating the Black Death and did not seem to be afraid of the infection, although his reputation suffered when he was unable to save his wife and child from the dreaded plague.

His grief at their passing may have led him to an almost fatal error in those bigoted times by inadvertently revealing his Jewish origins. It is said that, when passing some stonemasons at work on a carving of the Virgin Mary, Nostradamus was heard to mutter the second Commandment: 'Thou shalt not fall down before graven idols'.

It was not long before this report reached the ears of the Inquisition, who were already suspicious of the remarkable survival rates of Michel's patients. Diabolical sorcery could be the only explanation for such medical miracles. Fortunately, in 1532, Nostradamus got wind of his imminent arrest and thought this an opportune moment to travel.

His wanderings took him all over southern Europe, and it is about this period of his life that several well-known stories are told. While he was in Italy, he encountered a swineherd named Felice Peretti. As the fellow passed, Nostradamus fell to his knees, addressing the astonished Peretti as 'Your Holiness'. Peretti was to be elevated to the papal throne in 1585 as

Pope Sixtus V, fifteen years after the prophet's death.

Another, more prosaic, incident has also found its way into legend. While Nostradamus was visiting a certain Monsieur de Florinville, the two took a walk. They saw two suckling pigs, one white, the other black, and de Florinville jokingly asked the fates of the two animals. Nostradamus replied, 'We will eat the black one and a wolf will eat the white.' De Florinville, wishing to make a joke at the expense of his guest, later

When his host one evening tried to fool Nostradamus by preparing for dinner a white pig which the prophet had predicted would be eaten by a wolf, the subterfuge only proved Nostradamus right again.

instructed his cook to kill the white pig and present it at dinner. That evening the main course was suckling pig. Laughing, de Florinville addressed Nostradamus, 'Well sir, we are now eating the white pig and a wolf cannot touch it here.'

'I do not believe it,' replied the prophet, 'it is definitely the black one that is before us.'

To settle the matter, de Florinville summoned the cook, who immediately confessed: 'All was done as my master commanded. The white pig was killed and roasted. However, while I was away on an errand, a small wolf cub who is being tamed in the household seized the flesh as it rotated on the spit. I feared a beating so killed the black pig and served that instead, and it lies before you now.'

A ROYAL SUMMONS

Though these stories have an apocryphal flavour, they do serve to show the awe in which Nostradamus was held. His fame spread to Paris and it was to the capital that he was summoned by the infamous Catherine de Medici, Queen of France. Queen Catherine was much taken with the mystical doctor from Provence, and called on him to predict the destinies of her children. Legend has it that Nostradamus produced a magic mirror and, with the aid of the angel Anael, showed Catherine visions of her offspring each wearing a kingly crown.

Legend aside, it is certain that Nostradamus calculated horoscopes for each of the royal children, predicting that they would all be kings. The Queen was well pleased, for her ambitions reached further than the borders of France. However, her eldest son, François, was destined to reign for just one year, to be succeeded by her second son, Charles, who died young after reigning for fourteen years. The third, Henri, managed fifteen years, his early death ending the Valois line. The fourth was the Duc Alençon, who just missed out on a crown by failing to win Elizabeth of England (who referred to him as 'The Frog'), but did manage to net the Netherlands as Lord Protector.

One royal child of whom Nostradamus took particular note was young Henri of Navarre. Because he was not one of the Queen's children, Nostradamus thought it prudent to conceal his insights from her. He bribed a servant to allow him into the boy's room as he left his bath. After observing the lad for some time from behind a curtain, the prophet made himself known and, bowing low, said, 'If God gives you grace to live, you will be

A tapestry (c. 1519-1589) showing Catherine de Medici with Charles IX and Henri III, two of her four sons – all of whom were foreseen correctly by Nostradamus to wear crowns. Only Duc Alençon failed to become a king.

King of France and Navarre.' This well-known story suggests that Nostradamus, in addition to the many other occult arts at his disposal, also practised molescopy, the study of the moles on the body which were said to be the physical equivalent of stars. It would seem that Henri's moles were indeed favourably configured because in due course he was to become the pragmatic King Henri IV, who was not above blithely changing religion to win a crown with the words 'Paris is well worth a Mass'.

THE COMMON TOUCH

There is one further, rather charming anecdote about Nostradamus. One evening, as he sat outside his house at Salon, the daughter of a local farmer passed him on the way to the woods – ostensibly to collect firewood. 'Good evening, Monsieur de Nostredame', she said. 'Good evening, my girl,' replied the great man. Later, on her return, she again said, 'Good evening, Monsieur de Nostredame.' The prophet gave her a knowing look, 'Good evening, young woman'. Obviously nothing was beneath his notice.

Nostradamus's fame as a healer and occultist spread throughout France. He produced two collections of cryptic predictions, whose meaning has been the subject of controversy for four centuries.

SORCERY IN THE VATICAN

The eternal city of Rome was buzzing with rumour in January, 1628, and expectations ran high that soon there would be a conclave to elect a new pope. For over two years now, a prediction of the pontiff's death had been a cause of concern to some and the butt of jests in the city taverns to others. However, as might be expected, the pontiff himself was not so amused by the prospect.

THE ASTROLOGER POPE

The pope at this time was Urban VIII, a prince of the house of Barberini. A cultured, elegant man, a patron of the arts and a consummate and cynical politician, Urban did not consider himself to be head of the Church, or even Christ's representative on earth, but rather a classical prince steeped in renaissance virtue and philosophical learning. Headstrong and arrogant, it was he who imprisoned Galileo for twenty years for daring to state that the earth moved. It was he who had all the birds in the Vatican gardens poisoned because their incessant twittering got on his nerves. And it was Pope Urban who commanded the demolition of much of historical and imperial Rome to make way for his own building programme. At the time it was quipped, 'What the barbarians did not do, the Barberini did!'

Pope Urban VIII may have been a half-hearted theologian, but he was a devoted believer in astrology, even though it had been condemned by Pope Sixtus V in 1586. Urban had learned the rules of this ancient art in his youth and was quite content to continue casting horoscopes even after he had bribed his way to the papacy. It was with some glee that he revealed the future death dates of several cardinals. In turn, they had the pontiff's own horoscope calculated and passed around with the intention of beating Urban at his own game and, hopefully, frightening him to death in the bargain. It was an unexpected bonus to the plotters to discover a particularly threatening eclipse of the moon looming over Urban's fortunes. The interpretation of this eclipse became the basis of the prediction of the pope's imminent death.

The concerned but determined pope summoned a heretical monk named Tommaso Campanella to the Vatican. This fifty-nine-year-old renegade monk had spent more than half of his life in one prison or another, and would have more usually expected to fall into the hands of the Inquisition rather than take up residence at the papal court. Campanella had experienced hardship and torture for his views in the past and, on one occasion, only escaped execution by pretending that he was mad. The pope now put his trust in a man who explored forbidden knowledge and did not hesitate to put this dubious learning to use in occult rites. Quite simply, Campanella's job was to keep the pope alive in defiance of the influence of the stars and planets.

THE EMERALD TABLET

One of the basic tenets of astrology is found in the so-called 'Emerald Tablet of Hermes Trismegistus', which was erroneously believed at the time to have been written by the greatest sage of Ancient Egypt. Part of this mysterious document – said by Neoplatonists to have been written by a legendary figure called Hermes, who authored certain works on alchemy, astrology, and magic – states a simple concept: 'As above, so below'. This was, and is, taken to mean that the planets, signs of the zodiac and celestial houses influence everything on earth for good or ill.

Tommaso Campanella, took a further radical, but logical step beyond this and this was the principal cause of his clash with ecclesiastical orthodoxy. He was convinced that, just as that which is above influences that which is below by certain magical practices, that which is below could alter that which is above and in effect, change fate itself. More importantly to the Church, however, was that this implied the mind of God himself could be changed by human will. It was this shocking theory that Pope Urban VIII enthusiastically embraced.

From late 1627, pope and sorcerer regularly spent time together. On these occasions, a neglected part of the palace was used, and servants, guards and priests were kept at bay. It was said that pontiff and heretic were engaged in raising spirits and placating the angelic and infernal powers which governed the course of the heavens.

THE RITE OF THE LITTLE SKY

In a sealed room with walls draped in white silk, the magician and the pope sprinkled libations of rose vinegar and burned fragrant incense. The floor was symbolically decorated with the circle of the zodiac, with movable lamps standing for each of the planets.

This gold coin from Avignon, France, was used in the reign of Pope Urban VIII (1568-1644) who had greater faith in astrology than religion.

The largest and most ornate of these were made of gold and silver, respectively, to represent the sun and the moon. These two lamps were not only vital to Campanella's attempt to prevent the lunar eclipse from happening, but also to create a personal sky for Urban, over which the true heavens might have no power.

So successful did the pope consider this magical rite to be that he recommended it, and the services of Tommaso Campanella, when one of his nephew's horoscopes was similarly afflicted in 1630. Later Campanella himself was forced to use his rite of the 'Little Sky' in 1639 when a dire threat was detected in his birth chart. However, his luck did not run to a third occasion, and he suddenly expired at the age of seventy.

A French monk who had met Campanella just before his death remarked, 'He has nothing to teach about the sciences but is very learned in music...but when I questioned him I found that he does not know what an octave is. But he still has a good memory and a fertile imagination.' So much for Tommaso Campanella!

Pope Urban VIII lived until 1644. His faith in the efficacy of astrology never wavered, although he was never quite convinced by religion. On the death of Cardinal Richelieu, Regent of France, Urban couldn't resist commenting, 'If there is a God, then Richelieu will have much to answer for. If not, he's done very well.' The same sentiment might have applied to him.

THE BRAHAN SEER

From ancient times, the Celtic peoples of the British Isles have been firm believers in the power to foretell the future – the second sight. Dr Samuel Johnson, a man who had little good to say about anyone who didn't happen to be English, made this observation in his book, *A Journey to the Western Isles of Scotland*: 'The second sight is an impression made either by the mind upon the eye or the eye upon the mind, by which things distant or future are perceived and seen as if they were present.'

THE ONE-EYED CROFTER

To this day, there are those in the so-called Celtic fringes of Europe who possess this uncanny ability, often unwillingly because the visions that the 'sight' reveals are often traumatic. Belief in this disturbing faculty is most associated with the bleak Highlands and islands of Scotland. The most famous, or indeed infamous, of those who could part the veil of the future was a one-eyed crofter named Coinneach Odhar. He was a native of the Isle of Lewis in the Hebrides and is better known as the Brahan Seer.

Born in extremely humble circumstances at some unknown point in the seventeenth century, Coinneach left his island home to find employment as a turf cutter on the estate of the Earl of Seaforth near Inverness. Once settled there, his reputation for uncannily accurate forecasting ensured that he would soon come to the attention of his aristocratic employer.

Some of the pronouncements that Odhar made to Lord Seaforth painted a chilling picture for Scotland. With his good eye, he would gaze intently through a pebble with a smooth hole in it. Through this, he claimed he could see what was to come to pass. Not only did he declare that 'horrid black rains' would cause desolation in Scotland, but he predicted the depopulation of the Highlands, with the people of his rugged land scattered to the four corners of the earth and replaced by flocks of sheep in their homeland. This has been interpreted to be the notorious highland clearances which banished the crofters from their land in the late eighteenth century. The simple fact was that raising sheep was far more profitable to absentee landlords than being burdened by poor tenants. The black rain of which Odhar spoke may well be the North Sea oil which has been an economic boost to Scotland on the one hand, but an ecological menace on the other.

Odhar made many other predictions concerning the fate of the Highlands. When he made the following prophecy, he was publicly mocked: 'Strange as it may seem to you this day, the time will come, and it is not far off, when full-rigged ships will be seen sailing eastward and westward by the back of Tomnahurich.' The construction of the Caledonian Canal 150 years later in 1822 saw the fulfilment of his bizarre prediction.

He foresaw changes that the Industrial Revolution would bring: 'Long strings of carriages without horses shall run between Dingwall and Inverness' – a pretty accurate description of a railway line, made a century earlier than Watt's invention. Odhar also said that 'Fire and water shall run in streams through all the streets and lanes of Inverness' – a clear vision of piped water and gas lighting.

Visions of those with second sight, like the 'Brahan Seer', may contain images and impressions similar to a collage which the clairvoyant must describe in his own words.

BEST BLOOD OF THE HIGHLANDS

On another occasion, the seer was walking across his master's field towards a water mill. Squinting at the idle wheel, he sadly said, 'The day will come when thy wheel shall be turned for three successive days with water red with human blood; for on thy lade's bank a fierce battle shall be fought in which much blood will be spilt.' Although Odhar's vision was clear, the details surrounding the event foreseen were not, and was not until Odhar actually visited the Moor of Culloden that the truth was revealed:

'The bleak moor, shall, ere many generations have passed away, be stained with the best blood of the Highlands. Glad am I that I will not see that day, for it will be a fearful period; heads will be lopped off by the score, and no mercy will be shown or quarter given on either side.'

More than eighty years later, in 1746, Culloden was indeed drenched in gore as the rebellious clans, led by the Stuart Bonnie Prince Charlie, fell before the onslaught of the redcoats under the command of a Hanoverian Duke. It was a ferocious massacre in which 6000 clansmen died, ending the hopes of the rash adventurer Prince Charlie.

HOW FARES MY LORD?

Anyone who possessed, or indeed possesses, the gift of second sight would admit that it can be more of a curse than a blessing, because it involves a commitment to tell the truth no matter how unpleasant or inconvenient that truth may be. Coinnach Odhar knew that his end was nigh when his master, Lord Seaforth, left for France on a diplomatic mission. His absence was so extended that Lady Seaforth summoned the seer. In the presence of her armed

Clear visions appeared to Odhar, who, while visiting the Moor of Culloden, foresaw the The Battle of Culloden of 1746.

retainers, she asked Odhar whether her husband was safe and well. The seer raised his pebble to his eye and laughed loudly, 'Fear not for your lord, for he is safe and sound, well and hearty, merry and happy'.

Lady Seaforth demanded to know the details of her husband's life, but Odhar was reluctant to divulge the information. Finally the Countess threatened him, and only then did he say, 'He is in a gay gilded room, grandly decked out in velvets, with silks and cloth of gold, and on his knees before a fair lady, his arm round her waist and her hand pressed to his lips.' In fury, Lady Seaforth accused Odhar of lying and of 'defaming a mighty chief in the midst of his vassals.' Odhar waited as the countess condemned him to death. Holding his stone to his eye the Brahan Seer pronounced his final prophecy which was to become famous. It is known as the Doom of the Seaforths.

THE BATTLE OF CULLODEN PROPHESY

Eighty years before it happened, the Brahan Seer foresaw what one of the bloodiest uprisings in Scottish History at the Moor of Culloden, and stated:

66 The bleak moor shall, ere many generations have passed away, be stained with the best blood of the Highlands. Glad am I that I will not see that day, for it will be a tearful period; heads will be lopped off by the score, and no mercy will be shown or quarter given on either side 99

THE DOOM OF THE SEAFORTHS

'I see into the far future, and I read the doom of the race of my oppressor. The long descended line of Seaforth will, ere many generations have passed, end in extinction and sorrow. I see a chief, the last of his house, both deaf and dumb. He will be the father of four fair sons, all of whom he will follow to the tomb. After lamenting over the last and most promising of his sons, he himself shall sink into the grave, and the remnant of his possessions shall pass to a white-coifed lassie from the east, and she is to kill her sister. And as a sign by which it may be known that these things are coming to pass, there shall be four great lairds [landowners] in the days of the last deaf and dumb Seaforth – Gairloch, Chisholm, Grant and Ramsay – of whom one shall be buck-toothed, another hare-lipped, another half-witted and the fourth a stammerer.'

Unable to tolerate any more, the countess ordered that Coinneach Odhar, the Brahan Seer, be taken to the bleak shore at Chanonry Point, there to be thrust head first into a nail-studded barrel of boiling tar. The prophet seemed resigned to this dreadful fate and endured his execution with no further word.

His doom-laden prophecy was dreaded by the Seaforths for generations, until at last it came true. A mute and deaf man fathered four sons who predeceased him. The foreknowledge of the tragedy tortured him all his life, especially as his property-owning neighbours, Gairloch, Chisholm, Grant and Raasay were buck-toothed, hare-lipped, half-witted and stammered respectively. He died in 1815 before his eldest daughter returned from India to inherit his land. In 1823, she accidentally killed her younger sister while driving a carriage, thus fulfilling the final prophecy of the Brahan Seer.

CHAPTER *5* FIVE

THE AGE
OF PROGRESS

A fter the Industrial Revolution of the late-eighteenth century, new ways of thinking dominated the world — but such advances did little to remove prophets from the scene. One of the greatest cities in the infant United States was the domain of Marie Lavaux, a woman who used all her wit and intelligence to set herself up as a prophetess of great influence, and who is remembered today as 'The Voodoo Queen of New Orleans' (pages 118-121).

The 'Mad Monk', Grigori Efimovich Rasputin, was a far more sinister influence on the imperial court of St. Petersburg than ever the Voodoo Queen was on her city. His story is told in 'Rasputin and the Prophecy of Death' (pages 122-125).

Edgar Cayce saw images of the future as he slept, so is known as 'The Sleeping Prophet' (pages 126-127), while Count Louis Hamon, in his guise as 'Cheiro the Society Palmist' (pages 128-131), met everyone who was anyone — a far cry from his humble origins in rural Ireland. Another larger-than-life character, Aleister Crowley [right] was to become known as 'The Beast Himself' (pages 132-135).

This Portuguese relic shows the three child-prophets who saw a vision of a 'beautiful lady' whom they said was the Virgin Mary.

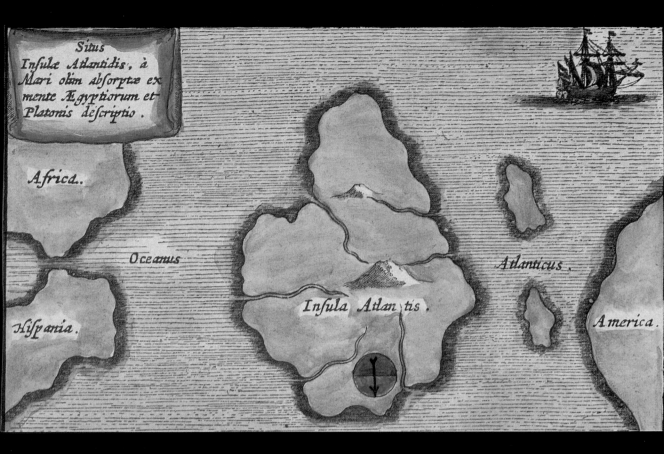

Situs Insulæ Atlantidis, à Mari olim absorptæ ex mente Ægyptiorum et Platonis descriptio.

Africa.

Oceanus

Hispania.

Insula Atlantis.

Atlanticus.

America.

A 1664 map of the legendary sunken island of Atlantis, by Athanasius Kircher. In the twentieth century, Edgar Cayce prophesied the re-emergence of Atlantis.

The murders committed by the 'Whitechapel murderer' have haunted the imagination since their occurrence in 1888 – the medium Robert James Lees claimed to have discovered his true identity in 'The Eyes of the Ripper' (pages 136-139). A decade later, aspiring author Morgan Robertson wrote a novel entitled 'The Wreck of the Titan' (pages 140-141), detailing the Titanic disaster with surprising accuracy – fourteen years before the event. Of the religious prophets who have flourished in the Age of Progress, none has caused so much consternation as 'The Lady of Fatima' (pages 142-143).

Many rulers have gained comfort from the ancient art of astrology. The Nazi hierarchy was obsessed with, and frustrated by, its possibilities (see 'Stargazers Under the Swastika' (pages 144-147). The Age of Progress concludes with 'Jeanne Dixon and the Day in Dallas', (pages 148-149), the tale of a psychic housewife who foresaw John F. Kennedy's assassination eleven years before the tragedy took place in 1963.

THE VOODOO QUEEN OF NEW ORLEANS

On a dark night in 1830, a heavy-set man, sweating profusely, stumbled through the narrow, foetid alleys of New Orleans, Louisiana.

Anxiously, he surveyed every darkened doorway, looking for some sign that the woman he was seeking lived there. Suddenly, a door opened, the light from within momentarily blinding him.

'You come lookin' for the Bosswoman?' a husky female voice asked.

'Yes, yes,' the man stammered.

'Then you've found her sure enough,' she laughed, as the man fearfully entered her home.

Sobbing with a combination of relief and nervousness, the man told his story in fits and starts. The cigar-chewing woman listened patiently as a tale of murder and injustice spilled from his lips.

The caller was a wealthy gentleman whose son stood accused of murder on the flimsiest evidence. Recourse to lawyers brought no comfort, and the frantic father, desperately in search of some slight hope, had come to request the assistance of the legendary sorceress Madame Marie Lavaux – the Voodoo Queen of New Orleans.

Politely, the enigmatic woman heard the man out. Then she asked what she could expect for her services.

Still disbelieving, the man replied, 'If you can get my son out of jail, I'll give you the deeds to a house on the Rue St. Anne.'

Without hesitation, Madame Lavaux said 'Done! Your son will be free very soon; never fear.'

On the day of the boy's trial, Marie visited the St Louis Cathedral and prayed for the entire morning while holding three guinea peppers in her mouth. She then went to the courthouse, and found no difficulty in persuading the janitor to give her access to the judge's chambers, where she positioned the peppers beneath His Honour's cushions. Having successfully performed this magical rite, Marie retired to a coffee house to wait.

A few hours later, she saw her client with a young man who could only be his now-released son. The gentleman now looked at Marie Lavaux with stark fear as he handed over the deeds to the property that she had been promised. A tale of magic? Perhaps. However, it is more likely that the news that Marie Lavaux was involved in the case was enough to terrify the best-protected of witnesses. Be that as it may, when the Voodoo Queen moved into her new establishment, all of New Orleans flocked to her door.

A FREEWOMAN OF SUBSTANCE

The Voodoo Queen, Marie Lavaux, was a figure of mystery from the outset, the facts surrounding her birth and death the subject of much speculation. Some say she was born in Haiti in 1794, or possibly in New Orleans in 1796, others say that she arrived in New Orleans after a slave revolt in Haiti in 1809. In the terms of old Louisiana, she was a 'freewoman of colour', possibly the daughter of a plantation owner and a slave. Her death is also a puzzle. Some say she died in her sixties, others that she was in her eighties, and some that she never died at all!

Her influence on the life of the city was all-encompassing. Slaves were frightened of her, and they could be bullied or bribed to cooperate with her schemes. It is claimed that, with the connivance of house servants, voodoo dolls would be left on the

Marie Laveau (Lavaux), the Queen of the Voodoos at New Orleans, in the Last Year of Her Life, **by E. W. Kemble in The Century, April, 1886. The Voodoo Queen was supposed to have been over 100 years old when she died.**

positions of power. Marie became a personal friend of the Marquis de Lafayette, General Jean Humbert, future president, General Andrew Jackson, and the pirate Jean Lafitte, and told their fortunes readily.

Marie did not reserve her talents for the powerful, though. She had a reputation of being kind to the needy and would often visit prisoners on death row, bringing them gumbo, a traditional seafood soup. She may have laced the gumbo with herbs to soothe physical and mental pain. Legend claims that she cheated the hangman by poisoning at least one condemned man to ease his agony.

During an epidemic of Yellow Plague in 1850, Marie showed her true nature and took a prominent role in health care. After all, if the Voodoo Queen suppported the white man's medicine, then it must be beneficial. Her influence probably saved the majority of the poor population of the city.

Marie Lavaux was a complex and enigmatic character who saw no contradiction between her faith as a Roman Catholic and her role as the chief Voodoo Priestess of the city. She firmly held to both religions with an unparalleled tenacity.

In her later years, Marie seemed to be able to appear in two places at once. This certainly added to her considerable occult reputation. The probable explanation for this supposedly paranormal power was that her daughter, also named Marie, resembled her to an uncanny degree, and it is this Marie who took over as 'Bosswoman' when her mother died,

pillows of prominent men. Frightened by this, these worthies would then run to Marie to have the supposed spell lifted – a service for which they paid most handsomely. Governors, politicians, judges and businessmen who wanted curses to be laid or removed came to her, and she made a good income this way. Marie also was famous for the efficacy of her love potions, and probably operated a bawdy house on the side, which, of course, was not just a lucrative business in its own right but a very useful source of information and blackmail material.

With all of her undoubted talents, she was a person to be reckoned with, and was appreciated by many in

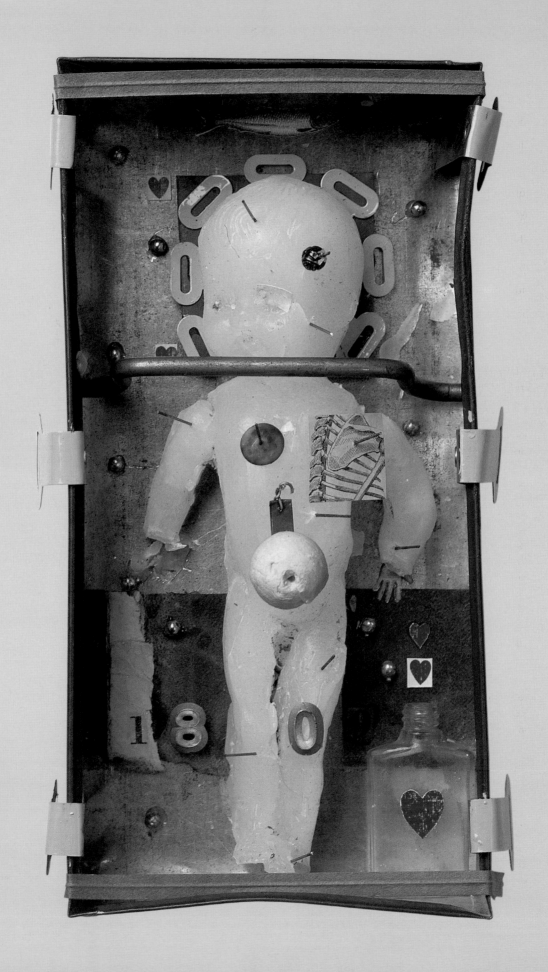

hence the confusion over the date of her death. Since she died, the spirit of Marie Lavaux is said to rise on St John's Eve, 23 June, and, to this day, her tomb is still revered by Voodoo cultists.

The figure of Marie Lavaux remains an enigma to this day. Was she a true prophet and sorceress or merely a shrewd businesswoman, adept at gaining information about her wealthy clients? Either way, Marie Lavaux's cunning and tenacity guaranteed her place as the first 'woman of colour' to achieve any sort of prominence in the Western World.

LEFT: Marie Lavaux would persuade servants to leave voodoo dolls on the pillows of prominent members of society, who would then pay her to undo their much-feared magic spells.

RIGHT: Andrew Jackson (1767-1845), the seventh President of the United States, who was nicknamed 'Old Hickory', was one of Madame Lavaux's most influential friends.

THE DIVINE HORSEMEN

Even though it is a commonly held belief that voodoo is a particularly sinister form of black magic, involving the creation of the 'walking dead', also known as 'zombies', it is in fact a religion which is practised throughout the Caribbean and its surrounding lands.

Voodoo has a number of variant forms such as Candomblé and Santeria in Brazil, Obeah in Jamaica and, most famously, Voudoun on the island of Haiti.

Rarely has there been any belief system which has been more tolerant than voodoo – a mixture of various West African tribal religions which arrived in the Caribbean in the seventeenth and eighteenth centuries.

Voodoo rituals are highly energetic, with vigorous dancing and loud chants. Often the participants enter an ecstatic trance which allows them to be possessed by a spirit called the 'Loa'. This is described as 'being mounted by the Divine Horsemen'.

Possession is not regarded as in any way a negative state – in fact, it is much sought-after because it is seen as a direct communication with the divine, and it is at these times of possession that the gods can speak directly

and often utter prophecies via their human mediums. Each Loa has his or her own character and attributes. At the manifestation of a powerful god such as Ogoun, lord of fire and war, the god is immediately offered a cigar and a bottle of rum, and to celebrate the arrival of the compassionate and beautiful Erzulie, goddess of love, cosmetics, perfumes and, of course, a mirror in which she can admire herself will be offered.

It could be argued that voodoo is one of the most up-to-date religions, since its gods have habitually been dressed in contemporary clothing. The best example of this is Baron Samedi, the god of death and graveyards, who was often portrayed as wearing top hat and tails.

Of course voodoo does have its darker side – the ecstatic rituals not only appeal to the gods but to other supernatural entities like the 'baka' – evil spirits who work their wickedness on humanity.

There are also numerous accounts of cursing and so-called 'devil dolls', the use of which is alleged to have fatal consequences. However, this is nowadays attributed to the power of suggestion rather than to any supernatural agency.

RASPUTIN AND THE PROPHECY OF DEATH

Russia can be perceived as a country of intense contrasts. Historically it has always been a despotism, ruled by dictators who could be almost casually benevolent, and sometimes ruled by tyrants with little humanity to speak of.

Nicholas II, the last Tsar of this vast empire, was one of the former type. Though totally convinced of his divine right to govern, and utterly opposed to any dilution of his imperial authority, Nicholas was a rather weak man, always striving to live up to the stern example of his father. He could really have benefitted from a sensible wife to add reason to his rule, but unfortunately the Tsarina Alexandra was rather neurotic, suspicious of any suggestion of reform and prone to religious mania. She was therefore of very little assistance to her husband.

Tsarina Alexandra's extreme religious fervour was to become more painfully obvious after the birth of their fourth child, and only son, Alexei. The baby was soon discovered to be suffering from haemophilia, a hereditary disease which prevents the clotting of blood. Since the boy was to be the next Tsar, this tragic fact had to be kept secret from the disgruntled, downtrodden masses. Every attempt was made to cure, or at least alleviate, the boy's condition. The Tsarina spent most of her time in fervent prayer, while the Tsar himself summoned skilled physicians to tend to his son.

Increasingly, the imperial family isolated themselves from society, while the decadent court of St Petersburg became a breeding ground for intrigue and gossip. In 1905, a wandering Siberian peasant with a reputation as a miracle worker was brought to the unhealthy, claustrophobic court as a curiosity. His name was Grigory Efimovich Rasputin.

THE MAD MONK

Rasputin has been remembered as one of the most sinister figures to stalk the pages of history. Yet many of the more lurid claims about 'the mad monk' are pure invention, or at least a twisting of the facts.

It is true that he was a drunkard, often downing three or more bottles of vodka a day. This massive alcohol intake certainly does not seem to have affected his libido, since his appetite for sexual excess was legendary. Paradoxically, Rasputin was indeed a holy man, or at least one whose particular brand of faith was devout. He

Grigori Efimovich Rasputin (1871-1916) was a Siberian peasant mystic known for his healing abilities, who inveigled his way into Russia's imperial family.

Rasputin exerted great power over the family of Tsar Nicholas II of Russia during the First World War. The Tsarina regarded him as a saint.

may have been influenced by one of the semi-heretical strands of Russian mysticism which clearly reasoned that, since God loves a repentant sinner above all others, it would be a good idea to sin, then repent so that the Almighty might love one all the more. This was the likely rationale behind Rasputin's equal capacity for carnal sin and selfless devotion.

The Tsarina Alexandra was immediately charmed by the rough peasant ways of this mysterious Siberian. To her, Rasputin was nothing less than a saint for, by the touch of his hands, the bleeding of her son would cease. At the sound of his voice, calm would descend upon the pain-wracked boy.

Inevitably, Rasputin's influence over the Tsarina grew and, since she was the main advisor to her husband, it was soon claimed that this lecherous

RASPUTIN PREDICTS HIS FATE

Less than two months prior to his murder by Prince Yussopov, Rasputin stated in a letter to his daughter, Maria, that the day of his death was fast approaching. He seems to have firmly believed that his fate was inextricable from that of Russia.

66 I feel that I will be dead by January 1st, 1917… and if I am killed by the Russian peasantry, Russia will remain a prosperous monarchy for centuries to come. If, however, I am murdered by Boyars (aristocrats), their hands will be stained with the blood for twenty-five years, and no nobles will remain in Russia; the Tsar and his family will die within two years. 99

---

peasant ruled the Russian Empire in all but name. It was claimed that Rasputin was the Tsarina's lover, but that cannot have been the case. In her eyes he was pure and godly, mainly because the Tsar had gone to great lengths to keep all gossip about Rasputin's outrageous escapades from his gullible wife.

The extent of Rasputin's malign influence came to light during the First World War. Tsar Nicholas had gone to the Front to take command of the troops, leaving his loving, but utterly naive wife in full control of the government. She constantly turned to Rasputin for advice, ignoring the views of her husband's ministers.

In November, 1916, Rasputin wrote a curious letter to his daughter, Maria. In it, he stated that the day of his death was fast approaching, 'I feel that I will be dead by January 1st, 1917… and if I am

killed by the Russian peasantry, Russia will remain a prosperous monarchy for centuries to come. If however, I am murdered by Boyars (aristocrats), their hands will be stained with my blood for twenty-five years, and no nobles will remain in Russia; the Tsar and his family will die within two years.'

A DEADLY PROPHECY

On 29 December, 1916, Rasputin was invited to the palace of Prince Yussupov. Having been lulled by music, dancing, copious quantities of vodka and possibly opiates, Rasputin was given chocolate cake laced with cyanide. This should have killed him within four minutes. The plotters were alarmed that the poison had no effect whatsoever and Rasputin showed no signs of expiring. Then Yussupov cast subtlety to the wind, took out a

LEFT: This Russian poster depicts Lenin speaking, and conveys how threatened the imperial family's followers felt when Rasputin served as sole advisor to the Tsarina during the First World War.

BELOW: Prince Yussopov tried to poison, shoot, and beat Rasputin to death. Finally, he threw him into an ice-covered river.

portal into the courtyard. There, Yussupov and his fellow conspirators shot Rasputin again and beat him savagely with an iron bar. Yet still, the 'mad monk' showed no readiness to die. Finally, in desperate exasperation Yussupov and his cohorts threw their still-living victim into the river through a hole in the ice.

A CURSE ON THE NATION?

When the news of Rasputin's death was broken to the Tsarina, she was completely devastated. It is arguable that it only served to unhinge her already fragile mind further and accelerate the revolution which, true to the mad monk's prophecy, swept the imperial family from power and resulted in their brutal murder at Ekaterinburg on 16 July, 1918 – in less than the two years predicted by Rasputin. The October Revolution which brought in Lenin's Bolsheviks also caused a mass exodus of Russia's nobility. This included Prince Yussupov, who lived out the rest of his long life in the USA as the man who murdered the mad monk. Yussupov died in 1968.

revolver and shot the monk at point blank rage, using the crackling sound of a gramophone record of 'Yankee Doodle Dandy' in order to cover the noise of the gun. The trembling Yussupov then left the room to find a sheet with which to cover the prone body. On his return, the horrified prince saw Rasputin get up and stagger to the door. Even when wounded, Rasputin's strength was so great that he broke right through the locked

Civil strife was the lot of the Russian people right up to the German invasion in June, 1941 – exactly twenty-four years and six months after Rasputin's gruesome death. So we are left with one simple question: was the statement in Rasputin's letter to his daughter a prediction, or a curse on the nation that detested him?

THE SLEEPING PROPHET

The gaunt, balding man with a receding chin and twinkling eyes loosened his collar and tie and undid his shoelaces before relaxing on the couch in his study. His arms folded across his chest, he breathed deeply before drifting off into slumber. However, it was not a deep dreamless sleep that he embarked upon, but a hard day's work – seeking the guidance of universal forces which spoke through him while he was in an unconscious state. His name was Edgar Cayce (pronounced Kay-see) and he was one of the twentieth century's most famous and influential psychic healers and clairvoyants.

The unassuming, good-natured Edgar Cayce was born in 1877, the son of a Kentucky farmer. He worked as a travelling salesman, married and generally lived an ordinary life. But all was not as it seemed, because Cayce had the ability to go into trance, or rather, to fall asleep and diagnose his own and other people's ailments. In this state, he would prescribe some very odd treatments and provide spiritual healing for the 14,000 people who consulted him.

This strange ability had first manifested itself when he was hypnotized by a travelling huckster named Al Layne. Edgar had previously suffered with a peculiar loss of voice. But once under the influence of hypnosis, he spoke normally and prescribed a cure for his own malady. Layne was so impressed that he

The American psychic and healer (and ex-travelling salesman) Edgar Cayce (1877-1945) prophesied in his sleep – or a sleep-like mediumistic trance.

soon put Cayce under again, this time to discover what the entranced salesman could tell him about his own medical problems. Again Cayce spoke in complex medical terms, later found to be completely accurate.

It was the beginning of a brilliant career, but his talents did not stop at 'spiritual diagnosis'. Cayce also delved into patients' past lives and predicted the future. He advised his clients on how to resolve their relationship difficulties and career problems. He also successfully pinpointed the location of oil reserves, and even of buried treasure, and was paid well for these latter services.

Financial success did not detract from what Cayce regarded as his spiritual mission. He answered the needs of as many people as he could until, for him, sleeping became as arduous as any other manner of earning a living. The pressures exhausted him to the point where a nervous breakdown became a real possibility.

THE END OF CIVILIZATION?

In 1932, he learned that he had been talking about reincarnation while in a trance state. Because he regarded this as a pagan concept, his fundamentalist faith was rocked. However, he eventually came to terms with the concept and thereafter firmly believed that he had been 'Prince of Atlantis' more than 10,000 years before. This led him to take an interest in the cataclysm that he believed overtook the lost continent, and he became convinced that a similar fate awaited our civilization. His trance states informed him that the very poles of the earth would shift, and massive continental changes would occur, with devastating effects.

Cayce prophesied that this massive disaster awaited the world at the end of the twentieth century or at the start of the twenty-first. Its first sign would be a huge earthquake which would destroy San Francisco and plunge California into the ocean. Thereafter, New York and much of Britain would be destroyed, and the islands of Japan would sink into the Pacific.

HITS AND MISSES

In many ways, Cayce's prophecies are reminiscent of those of Nostradamus, and, like the old 'Seer of Salon', the 'Sleeping Prophet' has scored many hits. He was certainly committed to his predictions, and moved himself and his family to Virginia Beach because it would be unaffected by the coming cataclysm.

Cayce also predicted the original Wall Street Crash, the assassination of J.F.K and the death of F. D. Roosevelt. He prophesied the formation of the state of Israel, India's independence and the 'rebirth' of Russia after the fall of the Soviet Union.

Although it has been claimed by his biographer, Jess Stearn, that Cayce's 'batting average' on predictions was incredibly high – close to one hundred per cent', this does not seem to be borne out by the facts. It is true that, on historical subjects, Cayce seems to have been weirdly accurate, even with the most obscure details, and that many of his forecasts have indeed come true. However, many others have not. Despite Cayce's prophecies, China and Japan have not adopted Christianity, General Franco of

> 'Watch New York, Connecticut and the like. Many portions of the East coast will be disturbed, as well as many portions of the west coast, as well as the central portion of the United States.'
>
> EDGAR CAYCE

Spain did not massacre his people, even though his forty-year regime was repressive, and the British Empire did not grow to govern the world but declined rapidly after the Second World War.

Notably, some of Cayce's statements about Atlantis have prefigured some modern theories which are still not widely accepted in the refined atmosphere of academia. He boldly stated that the Great Pyramid of Egypt had been planned in 10,400 BC, a ridiculously early era in the view of most archaeologists, but a date which is now gathering support. To back this claim, Cayce also stated that the 'hall of records' of lost Atlantis lay concealed in a chamber beneath the left paw of the great Sphinx of Giza, and that this chamber would be discovered between 1996 and 1998. It was actually found in 1997, but, at the time of writing, has not been opened, so the predicted evidence of the drowned continent as yet remains unproven.

The Sleeping Prophet died in 1945, long before his doom-laden prediction of the end of civilization as we know it was due to come to pass. We who will live through the era of the rest of Edgar Cayce's dire warnings must hope that he was mistaken – either that or seek higher ground!

THE SOCIETY PALMIST

When Count Louis Hamon received the Order of the Lion and the Star from the hands of the grateful Shah of Persia in 1900 as a reward for a timely warning of an impending assassination attempt, he may well have reflected on how far he had come since his childhood in rural Ireland. In fact, Count Louis Hamon was not his real name, but an invented one. Born William John Warner in 1866, he had sensed a grander destiny from an early age. It was a fate that would make him the confidant of princes and kings, and one of the world's most celebrated clairvoyants.

Warner's mother, an otherwise conventionally religious woman, had been intensely interested in astrology – a passion that she passed on to her precocious son. However, in his mid-teens young William decided that the poverty of old Ireland was not for him, so he literally ran away to sea. Subsequently, he travelled the world picking up occult knowledge wherever he could find it. In the Indian city of Bombay, he learned the ancient art of 'cheiromancy' – more commonly known as 'palmistry'. It was also about this time that he refined his astrological expertise and added numerology to his repertoire. A visit to Egypt's Valley of the Kings yielded for him a macabre keepsake – a mummy's hand – that Warner kept as a mystical charm to ensure his success. He

Count Louis Hamon (1866-1936), a palm reader known as Cheiro, was born William John Warner in Ireland. He escaped poverty there to charm the famous and titled of Europe and America.

later claimed that this hand had once belonged to the wife of Tutankhamun, although this was probably just a good romantic story. Nevertheless, the grim memento must have had some effect because by the age of twenty-four, William Warner – now universally known as Louis Hamon, was the best-known clairvoyant in fashionable London. Professionally, he adopted the name of Cheiro and set about dazzling the glittering world of the West End with his phenomenal psychic accuracy.

His good looks and charm did him no harm at all, and he was soon to be pleasurably embroiled in love affairs with some of the most beautiful ladies in the land. He had acquired the polish of a fine gentleman and, possibly through the intervention of some of his well-connected lady friends, Cheiro was soon consulted by the greatest names in the Empire. A particular ally was the actress Lillie Langtry, who happened to be the mistress of the Prince of Wales. His association with her opened the doors to the artistic as well as the political elite.

When, for instance, he read the palm of the famous playwright and poet Oscar Wilde, Cheiro grimly foretold a sad end for him. Later, in 1895, Wilde was condemned to Reading gaol for immorality. In

Cheiro's good looks and psychic and acting abilities enabled him to reinvent himself as a gentleman and consultant to both royalty and the stars of the time, impressing them with his glamour and the accuracy of his predictions.

contrast, the struggling politician Arthur James Balfour learned that he would one day become Prime Minister – an event that duly occurred in 1902. Impressed by this prediction, the statesman Sir Austin Chamberlain, a member of one of Britain's political dynasties, actually invited Cheiro to read his palm in the House of Commons.

FORTUNE TELLER TO THE STARS

Realizing that, for him, America was a land of opportunity since it did not possess anyone with his own particular talents, Cheiro crossed the Atlantic. His reputation had preceded him, and he found himself at the centre of a circle of devoted fans – the most prominent of whom was the operatic diva, Dame Nellie Melba. Cheiro astounded President Grover Cleveland and even amazed the arch-cynic Mark Twain with the accuracy of his character readings and predictive statements. Twain was so agog that he felt obliged to re-examine his views on the mystic arts that he had previously described as 'so much hokum'.

Back in Britain, Cheiro broke protocol at the request of the Prince of Wales by divining the exact date of his mother, Queen Victoria's death. He gave the prince the precise length of his reign as king and accurately predicted the month and year of his death, too.

Now the crowned heads of Europe sent envoys to Cheiro's door. As early as 1900, he

foretold a gloomy fate for the imperial family of Russia. He also predicted the assassination of King Umberto of Italy (this monarch's life seemed to be as full of omens as a Roman emperor's). Upon encountering the child who would later become King Edward VIII, Cheiro prophesied an abdication due to an unsuitable marriage. The affair of the King and Mrs Simpson did not begin until 1936. He also cautioned newspaper magnate W. T. Stead not to travel by water in April of 1912. Stead took his advice and cancelled his ticket for the maiden voyage of the 'unsinkable' Titanic.

Mata Hari (1876-1917), a spy who probably worked for both German and French intelligence services, is said to have been one of Hamon's conquests, or, possibly, co-spies.

The London consulting room of 'Cheiro, Palmist and Clairvoyant', where William John Warner established himself as the most famous fortune teller in Europe and advisor to the rich and famous.

It is odd to think that Cheiro may have been responsible for the enduring legend of the 'Curse of the Pharaohs'. Using his mummified hand as a focus, Cheiro warned Lord Carnarvon not to enter the newly discovered tomb of Tutankhamun in 1922, 'or it will cost you your life'. Carnarvon ignored his dire words and died mysteriously shortly thereafter, while all four power stations in the city of Cairo suffered a blackout simultaneously.

Palmistry and mysticism were not the only strings to Cheiro's bow. He was also a newspaper editor, a popular author on a variety of subjects, and eventually a radio presenter. While acting as a war correspondent during World War I, he was rumoured to have had an affair with the notorious double agent Mata Hari, whose real name was Gertrude Zelle. It is

even possible that he, like Dr John Dee and other mystics before him, also indulged in espionage for a good cause. If this is so, then he was either luckier, or more astute, than his exotic paramour. Mata Hari was executed by a French firing squad in 1917.

He ended his days far from the land of his birth, dying in Hollywood in 1936. He never lost his love of working, and had begun to perform weekly on the radio – being perhaps the first person to give psychic readings over the airwaves.

Count Louis Hamon, Cheiro or William John Warner seemed to straddle two worlds and two ages. He began his illustrious career in Victorian London and ended it in Hollywood, lauded by all who knew him as the greatest palmist who ever lived.

THE BEAST HIMSELF

In the awesome darkness of the King's Chamber at the heart of the Great Pyramid of Egypt, a man and a woman stood beside the enormous granite sarcophagus. By the light of a candle, the gorgeously robed man intoned ancient formulae, calling upon the wisdom of the gods to reveal the future.

As the words of power were spoken, the man saw that he no longer had to stoop into the circle of the candle's light to read. The chamber was illuminated by some other, more pervasive light source. Trembling, he blew out the candle and continued his invocation.

The man was not a priest of ancient Egypt, nor was his wife a princess of the house of the Pharaoh. He rejoiced in a multitude of names and titles. He was an Englishman, originally named Edward Alexander Crowley. He soon changed his name to Aleister Crowley in the belief that that particular

The Pyramids at Giza, Egypt – in the Great Pyramid, Crowley supposedly met a spirit called Aiwass who dictated to him *The Book of the Law*, which became his dark philosophy.

arrangement of syllables would ensure fame. He was also known as the Laird of Boleskine, Oliver Haddo and Count Vladimir Svareff. He was convinced that there was an element of divinity about him and that in previous lives he had been many magicians and seers including Count Cagliostro, the eighteenth-century charlatan, and Edward Kelly, the necromantic associate of Dr Dee (see pages 84-87).

THE SEARCH FOR AIWASS

On this occasion in March, 1904, Crowley was posing as the Prince Chioa Khan, although he usually preferred to be known as 'To Mega Therion', the Great Beast 666. For many years Crowley had sought an elusive mystical union with his higher self, which he believed was a divine intelligence. This quest he called 'the search for the knowledge and conversation of the Holy Guardian Angel', which was, presumably, connected with these alter-egos of his.

In Egypt, Crowley felt that his efforts to unite with a more powerful divinity would be rewarded. His wife Rose was badly treated by her irresponsible husband as she trailed around the world with

'Do what thou
wilt shall be the
whole of the Law.
The word Sin is
a restriction ...'

ALEISTER CROWLEY

him. However, during their travels she had begun to experience dream-like visions in which she was told: 'They are waiting for you, all about the child, it is all Osiris'. This had led the pair to Egypt – the mention of the Egyptian god of the dead, Osiris, had prompted Crowley to invoke the deity within this vast, mysterious pyramid.

No god appeared to Crowley on that night, but in a trance Rose told him that he was to sit quietly for an hour at noon on three consecutive days, April 8, 9 and 10, and he would receive a 'direct voice'

Aleister Crowley (1875-1947) – writer, drug addict, artist and occultist – was known by many, including his mother, as 'the Great Beast'. He believed himself to be the reincarnation of Edward Kelly and Count Cagliostro, among others.

communication from the Holy Guardian Angel. Crowley instantly dubbed Rose 'Ouarda the Seer', and prepared to wait.

In those three days, Crowley wrote *The Book of the Law* – which became the basis of his philosophy and life's work. Crowley later claimed that, just as his wife had predicted, a voice had spoken from just behind him, commanding him not to turn around. It introduced itself as Aiwass, a being who, with great economy, combined the roles of Holy Guardian Angel and emissary of the gods. Aiwass then went on to command that Crowley take up 'pen and parchment and write'. So Crowley took dictation through the heat of the Egyptian afternoon. By his words, Aiwass revealed himself to be far short of the angelic ideal, emerging as a more infernal persuasion.

Among his followers, *The Book of the Law* became the Bible of a new faith – one that would supersede all others and proclaim Aleister Crowley as the prophet of a new age. 'Crowleyanity' was to be a religion of self-fulfilment: 'Do what thou wilt shall be the whole of the Law,' wrote Crowley. 'The word Sin is a restriction ... find a way that is most compatible with your innermost desires and live it to the full.' Thus Aleister Crowley became the prophet of the hedonistic lifestyles of the late twentieth century.

The Book of the Law postulates three universal ages called Aeons, each named after a god of the ancient Egyptian triad. The first, the Aeon of Osiris, was patriarchal. The second, the Aeon of Isis, exalted feminine virtues and had been evident since the advent of Christianity. However, the cusp of the age had arrived and the dictation of the *Book* ushered in the Aeon of Horus, an age of youthful force, violent exuberance and self-will.

Crowley (or Aiwass) expressed the view that the new religion was not for the masses, but for 'kingly men' and not the weak of mind (a description that appeared to include nearly everybody). Neither did compassion play a large role in his vision of the future: 'These are the dead, these fellows; they feel not. We are not for the poor and sad; the lords of the earth are our kinfolk. We have nothing to do with the outcast and unfit: let them die in their misery'. It was an ignoble sentiment worthy of a Fascist dictator, but to Crowley nothing less than the perfect truth.

A MESSAGE FROM AIWASS

The statement below is said by Crowley's followers to prophesy the coming destruction of the Second World War and the Cold War thereafter, and is attributed to a spirit called 'Aiwass':

66 The warrior Lord of the Forties; the Eighties cower before me, and are abased. I will bring you victory and joy: I will be at your arms in battle and ye shall delight to slay. Success is your proof; courage is your armour; go on, go on, in my strength; and ye shall not turn back for any! 99

Other more specific predictions were included in his book. In the words of Aiwass, Horus would be 'the warrior Lord of the Forties; the Eighties cower before me, and are abased. I will bring you victory and joy. I will be at your arms in battle and ye shall delight to slay. Success is your proof; courage is your armour; go on, go on, in my strength; and ye shall not turn back for any!'

Many admirers of Crowley have claimed that this passage is an accurate prophecy of the carnage of the Second World War and of the Cold War that followed it. Devotees of Crowleyanity, therefore, confidently expected a third world conflict to occur in the 1980s, from which only they would emerge unscathed. As we have seen, they were disappointed.

Crowley died from bronchitis and cardiac degeneration in a boarding house in Hastings, England, on 1 December, 1947. Shortly before his passing, his capacity for drinking copious quantities of gin and injecting himself with large amounts of heroin was the only remarkable trait left to the Messiah of the Aeon of Horus. His last words were 'I am perplexed'.

This ceremonial seal was designed for Aleister Crowley for use in the Temple of the
A.A. (Order of the Silver Star), his own association of occultists, and combines
symbols of the beliefs and magic which eventually destroyed his health, mind and life.

THE EYES OF THE RIPPER

The fiendish crimes of the serial murderer called Jack the Ripper, or the Butcher of Whitechapel, appalled Victorian society in the autumn of 1888. The horrific killings of five poverty-stricken London prostitutes – Mary Ann Nicholls, Catherine Eddowes, Long Liz Stride, Mary Jane Kelly and Annie Chapman – between August and November in that year sent a shudder of horror from the lowliest hovel to Buckingham Palace itself. As everyone knows, the Ripper was never caught, but that is not to say that he was never detected and stopped. Indeed, there are some who believe that the famous psychic and medium Robert James Lees, rather than the sleuths of Scotland Yard, did just that. It is possible that Lees solved one of the world's most mysterious criminal cases with the first example of psychic detection.

Later, Edwin T. Woodhill, an ex-Scotland Yard inspector who was involved with the case, was later to write, 'He [Jack the Ripper] was never brought to justice but it is a mistake to think that the police didn't know who he was. It was proved beyond doubt that he was a physician of the highest standing who lived in a fine house in the West End of London. To most people he was the most refined and gentle of men, both courteous and kind. But he was also an ardent vivisectionist and a cruel sadist who took a fierce delight in inflicting pain on helpless creatures'.

None of the preceding statement is borne out by the evidence in official records, so how did a hard-nosed policeman like Woodhill arrive at such a conclusion? The answer lies with Robert Lees. Robert Lees was a remarkable clairvoyant with some

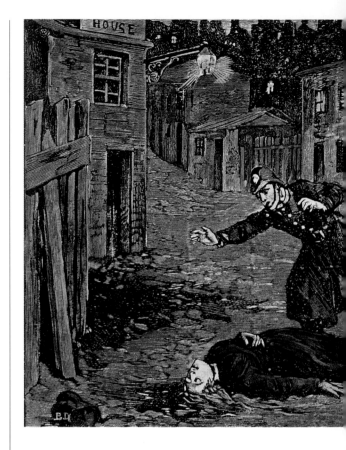

exalted clients. Queen Victoria herself had received him more than once at Balmoral, and Lees was rumoured to have put the 'Widow of Windsor' in touch with her long-deceased, yet no less beloved, Prince Albert. In fact, so obviously gifted was Lees that the queen had summoned him when he was a mere nineteen years of age.

According to some sources, the Ripper crimes began on 7 August, 1888, when the first of a series of women was horribly murdered in London's East End. Since life was cheap in such a slum area at that time, no one paid much attention to the crime. However, after a killing on the night of 6 September, counted by many Ripper-ologists as the first murder, pressure mounted on the authorities to find the attacker. This was easier said than done. The police had no clues and were understandably frantic and willing to use

THE EYES OF THE RIPPER

LEFT: The murders shocked Victorian society. They were attributed to an unknown attacker, who the newspapers called 'Jack the Ripper'. News of the killings spread around the world.

BELOW: The English clairvoyant Robert James Lees identified a doctor named Gull as 'The Ripper'. Lees found his home psychically and took the police there, who discovered that Gull was suffering from mental problems. His prediction was never proven.

any method to track down the maniac. It was at this stage that the Royal Clairvoyant entered the picture. Almost a week after the second murder, Robert James Lees was sitting peacefully in his study when he was overwhelmed by a harrowing clairvoyant vision of a man and a cheaply dressed, drunken woman leaving a dingy pub at night. The rest of the horrific story may be left to our lurid imaginations. There is no doubt that Lees was devastated by a psychic experience which had been so vivid that he even remembered the time on the clock which hung behind the bar. Still shaken by his 'second sight', Lees hastened to report it to the Metropolitan Police the next morning. Not surprisingly, he was treated like an idiot or a hoaxer. A condescending

desk sergeant said, 'There, there sir, what a terrible experience. Could you tell me when the next murder will take place?'

The uncomprehending Lees replied, 'Tomorrow night', and then furnished circumstantial details of the future crime scene. Realizing that he was not believed, Lees then made his way home. As Lees had predicted, the murderer did indeed leave his bloody mark on the East End once more the following night. The day after the crime, Lees claimed he was taken to the site of the grisly deed and recognized the location immediately.

This close encounter with the grim reality of his clairvoyant impression so disturbed Lees that he could not sleep. His doctor ordered Lees and his family to depart for Europe in the hope that his terrible visions would cease with distance. Lees afterwards wrote, 'The visions made such an impression on me that my whole nervous system was seriously shaken'; so accurate was his description of the crime scene that the police were beginning to think of Mr

Lees as a prime suspect in the case. However, to his immense relief the visions ceased as soon as Lees was in France. Encouraged by this, he decided to return to London hoping that the whole dreadful business was finally over.

AN ENCOUNTER WITH JACK

Unfortunately for him, one afternoon in late September it happened again. Lees and his wife caught an omnibus at Shepherd's Bush in West London, and he immediately began to experience exactly the same horrors that he had endured during previous visions.

At Notting Hill, a gentleman boarded the omnibus and met the psychic's gaze. At that moment Lees went cold and numb and ever afterwards was convinced that he had looked into the cold eyes of Jack the Ripper himself.

The man got off at Marble Arch and a panic-stricken Lees told his wife, 'I'm going to follow him, I'll be home soon.'

At an extremely cautious distance, the medium followed his quarry across Hyde Park in the centre of the city. Encountering a constable along the way, he harshly whispered, 'Look there, that's Jack the Ripper. I demand that you take him into custody.'

The officer laughed and advised him to go home and to 'take more water with it'.

'I'm telling you the truth,' the agitated Lees replied.

The constable became serious. 'I'll take you in if you don't get on your way and stop all this nonsense.'

But by now it was too late. The suspect, oblivious to Lees' pursuit, had hailed a cab and was being driven away from the scene.

TO CLIP THE LADY'S EARS

That night, Lees, still disturbed by the events of the day, had yet another vision. Fortunately for him, it wasn't as vivid as the first. However, he did see the face of the victim and the gory fact that her ears had been savagely removed.

Once more Lees went to Scotland Yard. Again he was treated as a harmless crank – until he mentioned the detail about the ears. The timing of his visit had coincided with a letter, supposedly from Jack the Ripper, which stated that he would 'clip the lady's ears off'. The Ripper had struck twice on that night of 30 September. As Lees had predicted, one of the victims had had her ears severed. When Lees was told of this, he suffered a collapse.

THE HOUSE OF THE RIPPER

It was after the murder of Mary Jane Kelly in November that the desperate police decided to use Lees as something analogous to a psychic tracker dog. He followed the Ripper's trail through Whitechapel to the West End, and to the house of the unnamed notable physician spoken of by Inspector Edwin Woodhill.

'Inside is the murderer, the man you are looking for,' stated Lees.

The police, led by Inspector Woodhill, were not completely convinced of the psychic's veracity.

'Impossible,' replied Woodhill. 'I'm telling you the truth,' insisted Lees.

'Then give me some information. If this is Jack the Ripper's house and I ring the bell, what will I see when the door opens?' demanded the inspector. 'If you truly have second sight, I'll go after the doctor.'

Lees then described a black chair to the right of the door, a stained-glass window at the far end of the hall and a bull mastiff sleeping at the foot of the stairs. At these words, Inspector Woodhill rang the bell. As the door opened, Woodhill saw the black chair and the window, but there was no dog at the foot of the stairs. He asked the maid if there was a dog in the house. 'Why no sir,' she replied, 'I just let him out in the garden.'

Then the inspector demanded to see the lady of the house. Tearfully, the lady confirmed that her husband had been behaving oddly and exhibiting a sort of split personality. At times he was thoughtful and considerate, but on occasion he would be actively cruel, almost evil. Once she had caught him in the act of torturing the family cat. He had also beaten his young son almost to unconsciousness. Recently, he had periodically vanished, each disappearance apparently coinciding with a Ripper murder.

At this moment, the doctor came downstairs. There was blood on his shirt and he seemed confused. In a shocked state, the doctor said that he had been suffering from memory lapses. A search of the doctor's wardrobe turned up a tweed suit and overcoat identical to the descriptions given of the murderer. According to Woodhill, the unnamed doctor was declared insane and confined to a private asylum, thus ending the reign of terror of Jack the Ripper.

Suspected of being 'Jack the Ripper', the respectable Sir William Withey Gull was subject to memory loss and fits of cruelty. He ended his days in an asylum.

Later sources confirm that a certain Sir William Withey Gull, a surgeon in attendance on Her Majesty, was identified as a suspect in the case. He fits Lees' account, at any rate. Gull was, in fact, confined to an asylum before his subsequent death in 1890. However, there is no hard and fast recorded evidence that he was the Butcher of Whitechapel. Sir William is but one of a number of named suspects who were identified as possible perpetrators long after the events in question.

For his work in tracking the Ripper, Robert Lees is said to have received a generous life pension from the privy purse and to have been sworn to secrecy. Whatever the truth concerning the identity of the infamous Jack, Robert J. Lees kept his word and remained silent for over forty years.

In the final analysis, the story of Robert James Lees is as suspect as the identification of Sir William Withey Gull as the Ripper. After a period of forty years, the most reliable memory may be found to be faulty. There is no reason to dismiss Lees as a police informant – Scotland Yard was desperate, after all.

The twentieth century has taught us that serial killers are rarely, if ever, men of distinction. They generally kill to fulfil a need for importance that daily life cannot provide. Most likely, Jack the Ripper has never been found since the art of detection was in its infancy in 1888, and he was probably a nobody.

THE WRECK OF THE TITAN

On the night of 28 April, 1912, the great and 'unsinkable' liner the RMS Titanic, collided with a North Atlantic iceberg while sailing at full speed south of Newfoundland. The impact tore a huge gash across its bow. The water of the frigid ocean poured into the interior. The mighty ship was up-ended and ripped in two. With a roar that sounded like the scream of a wounded leviathan, the Titanic slipped beneath the waves taking at least 1013 people to their deaths. It was the vessel's maiden voyage, and its tragic fate has been the subject of books, films, documentaries and TV scripts ever since. It could be argued that the sinking of the Titanic was the first great disaster of the twentieth century.

The catastrophe was also the subject of one of the most astounding prophecies ever made. However, when Morgan Robertson of New York made his prediction he thought he was just writing a prospective best seller! He imagined himself as an author in the style of Rudyard Kipling, and although not many other people shared his opinion, he persevered. Since he had had some experience as a merchant marine, he decided to try his hand at a nautical yarn, and sell it in instalments to a magazine.

The editor realized that Morgan Robertson possessed an immediate and exciting style which engaged the readers and made his stories extremely popular. All went well and, as the episodes spilled forth, Morgan earned the princely sum of twenty-five dollars a week. From Morgan's point of view, this was an excellent fee, especially considering that creative writing did not come easily to him, hampered as he was by a lack of education.

Then, in 1897, Robertson had a highly original idea. He was inspired to write a novel about the wreck of a huge ocean-going liner. This British ship would be the pinnacle of nautical engineering. Its owners would claim that it was so advanced as to render the vessel unsinkable. It was to be the largest craft on the sea. Its name was to be the Titan and it would strike an iceberg and go down into the freezing depths with tremendous loss of life. The novel was entitled *The Wreck of the Titan* and sub-titled *Futility*. The book was published in 1898 and, years later, was to ensure the fame of its author – not as a great writer but as an amazingly accurate prophet.

The tragic fate of the real Titanic is well known, but when one compares the fictional Titan to the real ship, some inexplicable coincidences come to light. In the case of both, the disaster struck in the North Atlantic in the month of April. Each ship weighed 75,000 tons, and had a length of 882 feet, with nineteen watertight compartments, three propellers, and 2224 people on board. It was the lack of lifeboats (twenty-two in the case of the Titanic and twenty-four aboard the fictional Titan) in both cases that made the disaster so appalling. Both ships also struck a fateful iceberg at a speed of twenty-three knots and sank on their maiden voyages.

FROM PROPHECY TO PERISCOPES

After the publication of his book, Morgan Robertson carried on writing, but even he admitted that his punch had gone. Debts, worry about an ailing wife, and lack of literary success took their toll until he admitted himself to a psychiatric ward at Bellvue Hospital. There, a psychiatrist advised him to give up writing and become an inventor instead.

Eventually, Robertson did so, coming up with the idea for a practical periscope for submarines.

Unfortunately this did not make his fortune, because he could not obtain a patent. He remained philosophical about this setback, however, stating that he wouldn't give up and 'When I go, I won't go lying down.'

Accurate details about the sinking of the Titanic were recorded fifteen years before it happened by American writer, Morgan Robertson.

How can Robertson have failed to experience a terrible chill when he realized that he had predicted it word-for-word fourteen years before it occurred? Whatever his feelings about his astounding literary prediction, Morgan Robertson lived until 1915 when he died of a heart attack at the age of sixty-three. When they found him, he was still on his feet.

THE LADY OF FATIMA

On the evening of 25 January, 1938, a weird glow was seen in the heavens all over western Europe. In some areas, the glow was so bright that night workers had no need of lighting, and one newspaper speculated that the 'fires of hell' were being seen on earth. That very night, Adolf Hitler formulated secret plans for the incorporation of Austria into the Third Reich, an event which took place in March of that year and which led inexorably towards total war. More than twenty years before, a vision known as 'Our Lady of Fatima' had predicted:

'When you see the night lit up by a great unknown light, know that it is a sign that God gives you that punishment of the world by another war, famine and persecution of the Holy Church and of the Holy Father.'

A VISION OF THE MADONNA

Fatima is a small, unremarkable Portuguese village. On 13 May, 1917, while World War I – the so-called 'war to end all wars' – was raging, an apparition of the young and beautiful 'Lady of the Rosary' appeared to three children. Lucia de Jesus dos Santos (aged ten), and her cousins Jacinta (seven) and Francisco Marto (eight) were the only three people ever to see the vision although visiting pilgrims reported a bright, hazy cloud during the lady's appearances.

Though the children themselves could not have been expected to take an interest in politics, Portugal at that time was on the verge of revolution. Anti-Catholic feeling was strong and there were elements within the

government who had sworn to wipe out religion entirely. This faction was particularly alarmed when news of a vision of the Madonna arose. They were even more appalled to discover that the children were regarded as saints and a devoted cult had started to form around them. By 13 July, more than 5000 people were gathered at Fatima in the hope of seeing the Lady. On this occasion, the apparition informed the children that pilgrims should gather on the thirteenth day of every month to receive her wisdom. She added, 'In October I will say who I am and what I desire, and I will perform a miracle all shall see so that they believe.'

The three children who saw the 'Lady' in Fatima, Portugal are shown here a few days before her final apparition on 13 October, 1917.

KIDNAPPED

However, the children were not present to meet the Lady on 13 August. They had been kidnapped by the authorities and threatened with beatings, and 'boiling alive' among many other unpleasant possibilities, if they did not renounce their vision. Alhough very frightened, the children would not cooperate and were eventually released. The Lady then appeared to them on 19 August and repeated her promise, adding that 13 October would be her last visit.

The great day arrived, and with it, 50,000-80,000 people, all of whom were agog at the prospect of a miraculous prophecy at such a specific time. Not all present were believers, though; there was a large number of reporters and sceptics who were there to debunk the whole episode as an example of mass hysteria.

THE DANCING SUN

Then the miracle occurred. The sun began to dance. It seemed to rotate on its axis, sending out multi-coloured rays in full view of everyone. Then the heavenly orb seemed to descend and turn to blood red before 'bouncing' back to its regular position. These strange motions were repeated three times. Reporters, unable to believe their eyes, described the phenomenon as a 'mysterious solar occurrence'.

Only after the crowd had been dazzled did the Lady make herself known to the children. Invisible to all others, she declared herself to be the Virgin Mary. She then said that she wanted humanity to change its ways, and delivered three prophecies of events which would occur if her wishes were not met. The first, couched in traditional religious terms, a detailed description of the fate that awaits sinners in Hell. The second referred to the odd lights in the sky and the horrors of a second world war which would occur 'within the next pontificate'. (The next pontiff, Pope Pius XI, died in 1939, one year after the mysterious lights.) The third prophecy has remained a source of controversy since the children related it to their elders in 1917.

THE PAPAL TRUST

The third prediction was sealed and entrusted to the Vatican with the instruction that the seal be broken and the message read only by the Pope in 1960. Pope John XXIII is said to have told trusted friends that he had read the third prophecy of Fatima and had 'trembled with fear and almost fainted with horror'. A German newspaper claimed to have access to the full text and printed this account in a 1963 edition: 'A great war will break out in the second half of the twentieth century. This will be a holocaust in which several entire nations will be exterminated, and persecution of the Catholic Church will occur which will involve the assassination of a reigning pope.'

The Vatican neither confirmed nor denied the veracity of this, although other predictions (notably those of St Malachy and the Papal Prophecies) are said to agree with the Lady's alarming oracle.

STARGAZERS UNDER THE SWASTIKA

On a winter's night in early 1940, while the triumphant German forces were marching through the fair fields of France, far away in Berlin Frau Magda Goebbels lay in bed reading a book entitled *Mysterien von Sonne und Seele* (or 'Mysteries of the Sun and Spirit') by Dr H.H. Kritzinger, which had been printed in 1922.

Frau Goebbels was suddenly startled by her reading matter and called out to her husband, 'Joseph, did you know that over 400 years ago, it was prophesied that in 1939, Germany would go to war with France and Britain over Poland?'

Her husband, Dr Joseph Goebbels, showed an immediate interest and asked to be shown the passage that described the events. Smiling, he read:

*'Seven times you will see the
British nation change,
Tinged with blood for 290 years:
Not at all free through German support,
Aries fears for his 'pole' Bastarnien.'*

This was *Quatrain 3.57* by Nostradamus (see pages 152-161), which the author, Dr Kritzinger, had correctly interpreted as specifically referring to the events of 1939, which took place exactly 290 years after the time Nostradamus wrote of them. For most couples, this curious fact would have been marvelled at, then forgotten, but for Joseph Goebbels the passage contained a fine opportunity. Goebbels was Nazi Germany's 'Minister of Propaganda and Enlightenment', an avid supporter of the policies of Adolf Hitler, and one of the most astute politicians of his age.

The next day, Goebbels summoned the forty-year old Karl Ernst Krafft to his office. Krafft was by birth a Swiss citizen, but now he had become German and a committed Nazi. Krafft had earlier predicted great things for the rising Nazi party and its leader Adolf Hitler by means of astrology.

RISING STAR

Krafft's recent advancement from penniless fortune teller to advisor to the elite had been the result of a memo delivered to Heinrich Fesel of Himmler's secret intelligence service on 2 November, 1939. The warning stated that, between the 7th and 10th of that month, 'there is a possibility of an assassination attempt through the use of explosive material.' Fesel kept the memo, but did not pass on its contents officially. The assassination attempt duly took place on 8 November when a bomb concealed behind a pillar on Hitler's rostrum in Munich

Joseph Goebbels, Germany's Minister of Propaganda during the Second World War, used the predictions of Nostradamus to dismay Hitler's enemies.

exploded. The Führer himself was not there, having left early – so it is possible that Krafft's warning had indeed reached him.

Krafft wrote to Hitler's deputy Rudolph Hess, informing him that he had known of the attempt on the Führer's life before it had happened. This letter was seen by Hitler and Goebbels who, at that stage, misunderstood its import. The unfortunate result was that Krafft was arrested by the Gestapo for suspected complicity in the plot. However, in a stunning reversal of fortune, and despite some extreme interrogation methods, Krafft managed to convince these brutal men that he was indeed innocent and from that moment he gained the confidence of Hitler's 'inner circle'.

Bearing these facts in mind, Goebbels was anxious to find verses by Nostradamus that would serve the German war effort and dismay Hitler's enemies. It was to be Krafft's task to 'reinterpret' the verses of the old Seer of Salon to serve this end.

The most pressing reason for this deception was to cause French civilians to take to the roads as refugees, in order to block the highways and restrict the mobility of the remaining French forces. It was Goebbels' idea that leaflets containing a suitably perverted Nostradamus quatrain, plus a new inter-pretation by Krafft, could be dropped by the Luftwaffe to help spread panic. After all, Nostradamus had been the French national prophet, and his words still carried weight.

Krafft immediately set to work, but was unable to find a verse to suit his purpose. Undeterred, the astrologer began to write his own, rather clumsy, forgeries which fooled no one. Even so, various members of the Nazi elite such as Heinrich Himmler

Adolf Hitler with the deputy leader of the German Nazi Party, Rudolf Hess, who secretly parachuted into Scotland to negotiate peace with Britain – apparently on the advice of an astrologer.

and Rudolph Hess now began to consult Krafft on a variety of questions which they believed could be answered by the ancient art of astrology. Both these prominent figures were convinced of the efficacy of astrology, which inspired a joke circulated at the time that Goering only cared about the stars on his epaulettes, while Himmler only cared about the stars in his horoscope.

For the moment, the personal star of Karl Ernst Krafft was in the ascendant, but it was not to last. The mysterious flight of Rudolph Hess and his subsequent capture in Scotland on 10 May 1941 was blamed on his obsession with horoscopes. Hitler raged, 'He has been crazed by astrologers.' At the order of the Führer's new deputy, Martin Bormann, all 'astrologers, fortune tellers and swindlers' were rounded up and confined to labour camps. The unswerving loyalty of Karl Ernst Krafft did not exempt him from this order and he was herded into a cattle wagon along with his fellows.

Contrary to popular belief, Krafft was not consulted by the Führer himself. Hitler apparently had little interest in astrology, even though some of his beliefs were heavily influenced by an odd mixture of dubious racial theory and cranky mysticism.

However, the London *Times* correspondent in neutral Switzerland wrote on 14 May, 1941, 'They say that Hess has always been Hitler's astrologer in secret. Up to last March, he had consistently predicted good fortune and had always been right. Since then, notwithstanding the victories Germany has won, he has declared that the stars showed that Hitler's meteoric career was approaching its climax.'

It has also been suggested that Hess was prompted to embark on his abortive peace mission by Ernst Schulte-Stathaus, an administrator on his staff. When arrested, Schulte-Stathaus understandably denied being an astrologer, but indicated that May would be an unlucky month for Hess. Schulte-Stathaus was imprisoned until 1943.

Krafft was not so fortunate. Condemned to hard labour, he still tried to worm his way back into favour. His long drawn-out efforts were unsuccessful, even though he warned Hitler of another assassination attempt and provided an unrealistically optimistic prediction of Germany's ultimate victory in May 1945. Hitler escaped the new bomb plot, but ignored Krafft's plight. As much a prisoner in his bunker as Krafft was in the labour camp, Hitler had more pressing matters on his mind.

Shortly before the Russians stormed Berlin, Krafft died of typhus, which he had contracted in the prison's unsanitary conditions. He died en route to the Buchenwald death camp.

Another astrologer, Wilhelm Wulff, was somewhat more fortunate. He, too, had been incarcerated in 1941 after Hess's flight but was released four months later on condition that he stopped casting horoscopes. Wulff was a true eccentric; a soldier in the First World War, he later became a sculptor and took up astrology as a hobby. He specialized in the horoscopes of missing persons and helped the authorities to trace them.

After his release Wulff was taken to a top-secret military establishment and found himself in a bizarre assembly of psychics, spiritualists, astrologers, mathematicians, astronomers and ballistics experts. In his autobiography *Zodiac and Swastika*, Wulff wrote, 'Day in and day out, the pendulum practitioners squatted with their arms stretched out over nautical charts'. Evidently, they were trying to locate convoys of Allied supplies in the North Atlantic. 'The results were pitiful,' stated Wulff, at least proving that no one works well with the pressure of a Luger against one's temple.

One of his 'ridiculous commissions' was to use Hindu astrology to find Mussolini, who had been abducted on 26 June, 1943. Wulff informed his masters that 'Il Duce' was not further than seventy-five miles south-east of Rome. Italy's dictator was indeed a prisoner on the Island of Ponza at the time.

Wulff was convinced that Hitler would die in 'enigmatic circumstances', that the stars favoured Stalin in 1945-46, and the American President Roosevelt would die in office very soon. In fact, Roosevelt died in 1945, three weeks before the German surrender. The military setbacks did not

prevent Reichsmarschall Goering exulting 'It is written in the stars. The second half of April will be the turning point for us. It is the turning point!'

To prevent defeat, Wulff then advised SS chief Himmler to have Hitler arrested. Himmler told him 'That would be difficult', but indicated he would think about it. He evidently thought about it for too long because, when Allied troops had devastated German resistance and Russian tanks were poised to enter Berlin, Himmler phoned Wilhelm Wulff with the cry 'Tell me what I am to do'. His astrologer could not offer any advice and was making his own arrangements for flight. Wilhelm Wulff was later taken into American custody and disappeared into the obscurity of one of their security organizations.

Interestingly, Allied forces, too, had their own 'occult espionage' campaigns. Perhaps astrologers and psychics once in the service of the Third Reich were used for the benefit of American and British intrigues. After all, Werner von Braun, the mastermind behind the V1 and V2 missiles, became one of the founding fathers of NASA.

JEANNE DIXON AND THE DAY IN DALLAS

Prophetic inspiration can occur at the most unexpected moments, as housewife and amateur clairvoyant Jeanne Dixon found out in 1952. In front of the statue of the Virgin Mary, outside St Matthew's Cathedral in Washington, DC, she experienced a vision that was to mark her as one of the most notable psychics of the twentieth century. The setting was apt enough, for Mrs Dixon, a committed Catholic, was convinced that her prophetic abilities were a gift from God.

The scene of statue and cathedral before her melted into a 'dazzling' vision of the White House, with the numbers 1, 9, 6 and 0 superimposed upon it. She then saw a young man with remarkable blue eyes in the doorway. This clairvoyant vision was then complemented by an 'inner voice' which informed Jeanne that the young man was a Democrat and would suffer a violent death while in office. Unknown to Jeanne, the figure in her vision was John Fitzgerald Kennedy who was elected in 1960 on the Democratic ticket.

AN UNBELIEVABLE PROPHECY

This was not to be the last time that Jeanne Dixon was to have intimations of impending disaster. In the eleven years between her vision and the assassination of J.F. Kennedy in Dallas on 22 November, 1963, she gained more knowledge of the details of the shooting and the identity of the future president.

In fact, she became something of a nuisance to an enormous number of federal officials and well-connected Washington grandees – so much so that her prediction of that day in Dallas is the only one which is thoroughly documented.

In 1956, Jack Anderson, a reporter for *Parade* magazine, published an account of Mrs Dixon's ominous foresight. However, this received little attention, since its speculation of events seven years hence held little interest for the magazine's readers. It was a different matter when Jeanne repeated her prediction to columnist F. Regis Riesenman in October, 1963, barely a month before the events were due to occur.

Additionally, Jeanne had clairvoyantly seen the perpetrator of the crime, only as a shadowy figure, but she had more luck with his name, which had two syllables and five or six letters. The first was either an 'o' or a 'q', the second definitely an 's'. The last letter had an upright line which curved a little like a 'd'. The name 'Oswald' certainly fits the bill.

In the month leading to the Kennedy assassination, Mrs Dixon tried to warn the president repeatedly via mutual acquaintances but J.F.K. had no time for what he considered to be occult mumbo-jumbo. He was also a fatalist and was

Jeanne Dixon, a committed Catholic, was a housewife when she experienced her first vision of catastrophe for the President of the United States.

John F. Kennedy, Mrs Kennedy and Texas Governor John Connolly ride through Dallas, Texas, moments before Kennedy was assassinated on November 22, 1963.

'No, the President's dead ... you will learn that he is dead'

JEANNE DIXON

quoted as saying, 'If they want to get you, they're going to get you.'

On the fateful day, Jeanne Dixon was at dining at Washington's Mayflower Hotel. Noticing her preoccupied manner, her companion, Mrs Rebecca Kaufmann urged her to wake up. Jeanne replied, 'I can't. I'm sorry. It's just that something dreadful is going to happen to the President today.'

At precisely that moment the presidential car was driving into Dealey Plaza in Dallas. It was only seconds later that a bullet pierced the back of Kennedy's neck, closely followed by a second which entered his brain.

At the hotel, the orchestra conductor stopped the music to tell the stunned throng that, 'Someone has just tried to take a shot at the President'. Gossip flew around the room to the effect that though there had been an assassination attempt, Kennedy had escaped injury. The gloomy Jeanne said, 'No, the President's dead ... you will learn that he is dead.'

PROPHET OF DOOM

Later, Jeanne Dixon developed a reputation as a prophet of doom. Specializing in the violent deaths of the great and good, she also foretold the deaths of Mahatma Gandhi and Martin Luther King. However, she saw nothing but good things around President Nixon, and maintained that the Russians would be the first to put a man on the moon but, reverting to doom-laden warnings, she foresaw a world war started by China in 1958 (when in fact it over-ran Tibet).

For the future she seemed to be in general agreement with Nostradamus. She expected the third world to rise up against the United States and a catastrophic war in 1999 to lead to appalling casualties from chemical and plague weapons, with America's defeat being due to moral degeneracy, while in Rome, the heart of the Catholic church, a pope would be assassinated.

it through something that something person want to

CHAPTER SIX

6

MESSAGES FOR THE MILLENNIUM

*W*e stand poised at the threshold of the new millennium — a new cycle of time that will either propel us into the vast reaches of space, bring us back into touch with the earth itself and unite humanity in peace, or quite simply signal the end of mankind's tenure of this planet and lead us to extinction. The question is, which is it to be?

Nostradamus was in little doubt. In 'The Centuries of Nostradamus' (pages 152-161), he foresaw terror the like of which the world has never experienced before, but as for the end of the world — according to his prophecy we are safe for the next 3400 years at least.

A coloured copper engraving from seventeenth century France, depicting Nostradamus, the Jewish astrologer-physician.

Before we get too complacent, the 'Seer of Salon' makes sure that we are well aware of the many trials and tribulations which may be coming our way.

There have been plenty of prophecies that point towards the fateful year of 2000 and the decades following it, which paint a gloomy picture of our future prospects. Pessimists point to ominous words in the Book of Revelations, and the new self-styled 'Messiah' cults. However, modern-day saviours are not like the Biblical prophets of old, nor are they 'voices crying out in the wilderness' – these are sophisticated, charismatic figures with a powerful line in persuasion, often with views that would make Nostradamus look quite optimistic. Characters like David Koresh or Marshall Applewhite are quite prepared to remove themselves from this sinful world, but what right do they have to organize members of their respective organizations to accompany them on that final journey? And can it be true that advanced alien beings travel in vast starships concealed in the tails of comets? These questions and more are raised in 'The Countdown to Doomsday' (pages 162-165).

The controversy surrounding gene manipulation is explored in 'Gene Genie' (pages 166-167). The problems and benefits of experimenting with the building blocks of life have ramifications that go far beyond the obvious and are the source of many doomsday prophecies, some of which strike a chillingly truthful chord.

Cult leader David Koresh died in a siege in Christian Baptist-dominated Waco, Texas. He was killed by American government agents sent to take control of his group's weapons.

'The New Age' has been a fashionable phrase since the Love Generation of the 1960s, but its meaning is open to misinterpretation. What exactly does it mean? Does the year 2000 mark the beginning of a new era, an enlightened 'Age of Aquarius'? And if so, will this be any different from the 2000 years we have lived in the 'Age of Pisces', which we are leaving behind?

Humanity's perceptions changed dramatically once we saw satellite images of Earth, such as the one pictured.

In contrast to the dire warnings of doom and contamination, we can only hope that 'The New Age' (pages 168-169) heralds a happier and more optimistic forecast for our future.

THE CENTURIES OF NOSTRADAMUS

Of all the prophets whose words we might heed as we move into the next millennium, perhaps the most respected is Nostradamus, doom sayer *par excellence*. This seer's view of the future seems to be one of war, plagues, famine, earthquakes and revolutions. Calamity piles onto calamity in a never-ending series of misfortunes. This does not necessarily imply that the old prophet Nostradamus believed the entire future of humanity was to be one of misery. But it does seem that his gift, like that of so many other prophets through the ages, sought out dramas and crises which he illustrated in verse portraits of eloquent despair, some of which came to pass, and others which are perhaps still on the horizon…

It would not be true to say that Nostradamus considered the future to be fixed and immutable. He may even have thought that there were certain pivotal times when the history of mankind could go one way or the other. When considering these occasions, Nostradamus gives two possible outcomes in a manner suggesting that both are equally valid. Critics of the old seer claim that Nostradamus is merely hedging his bets. But this is missing the point of his basic philosophy, which holds that history and indeed, destiny, are created from the actions and beliefs of the collective soul of mankind, which is played out in accordance with the will of God. This destiny is shown by signs, visions and the courses of the stars and planets to those gifted enough to see it. However, if God does not deign to show his will, then destiny becomes malleable, and various mutually contradictory outcomes may be perceived.

Nostradamus published his ten books of prophecy between 1555 and his death in 1566. These volumes are known collectively as *The Centuries*, not because he predicted in hundred-year batches, but because there are one hundred verses in each book. In all, he completed nearly 1000 four-line verses, composed several prophetic letters to King Henri III and was also said to have penned fifty-eight six-line verses known as 'sixtains', as opposed to his more famously ambiguous 'quatrains'. However, there is no record of the sixtains before 1605, so they may be forgeries.

THE MYSTERIES OF NUMBER

Nostradamus's letters to King Henri III of France are far more revealing than his notoriously cryptic verses. In one of these missives, the prophet informs the king that he has predicted the fate of France, and also the world, for the next 3700 years. In this mysterious number lies the key to Nostradamus's motive – why, during a time of personal ill-health, he expended so much energy on prophecy, when an accusation of heretical teachings could lead to execution.

From the cultural perspective of Michel de Nostredame, the world had been created by God in seven days, exactly 3300 years earlier. Therefore, using logic, Nostradamus concluded that, since there were seven days in a week, seven (known) planets, seven colours in the rainbow, seven perfect virtues and seven deadly sins, the number seven must be absolutely significant on an absolute level. For was it not by sevens that God had ordered the universe? We must remember that Nostradamus was of Jewish origin, and also strongly influenced by the mystical teachings of his two grandfathers. These two men had instilled in Michel the number symbolism of his

LES
VRAYES CENTURIES
ET
PROPHETIES
DE MAISTRE
MICHEL NOSTRADAMUS.

Où se voit représenté tout ce qui c'est passé, tant en France, Espagne, Italie, Allemagne, Angleterre, qu'autres parties du Monde.

Revûës & corrigées suivant les premieres Editions imprimées à Paris, Roüen, Lyon, Avignon, Troyes, Hollande, & autres.

Avec la Vie de l'Auteur.

Et plusieurs de ces Centuries expliquées par un Sçavant de ce temps.

A LYON,
Chez ANTOINE BESSON, Marchand Libraire rue Tupin.

AVEC PERMISSION.

Dieu se sert icy de ma bouche
Pour t'anoncer la verité
Si ma prediction te touche
Rends grace a sa Divinité

The title page from the 1690 edition of *Les Vraies Centuries et Phropheties de Maistre Michel Nostradamus*, one of the first copies of the books of prophecies which were published by Michel de Nostredame.

Hebrew ancestors. Through his own experience, Nostradamus confirmed these doctrines and, over the course of many years' research, became convinced of the tradition that the Lord had given mankind dominion over the earth, and all that was on it, for a total period of 7000 years.

Nostradamus believed that he lived at a point approximately half-way through this 'Long Dominion'. He may have thought he was writing his prophecies of the next segment of time as a new addition to, or at least a set of books associated with, The Holy Bible.

A particularly well-educated man, Nostradamus was not only a doctor, but a herbalist and a surgeon. His occult disciplines included astrology, augury, alchemy and the complex number system of mystical Judaism known as the Cabala. The Cabala is the reason that there are ten books of prophecy, and that he intended that there should be a hundred prophecies in each. The number ten is another significant number in Cabalistic belief, because according to that system, God created the universe in ten stages, each one flowing into the next in a kind of smooth evolution.

Nostradamus was familiar with many belief systems, which was unusual at a time when the Catholic Church dominated the hearts and minds of Europe. His frames of reference included Greek, Roman, and Celtic mythologies. Nostradamus was aware of the history of Europe and the ancient world, and had a thorough knowledge of the devious politics of his time. He was a scholar of Latin – the language of the learned, Greek, Hebrew, and also possibly various Celtic tongues. With all these sources to draw upon, it is unsurprising that his prophecies are unbelievably complex. Add to this his capacity for puns, anagrams and wordplay, and each verse could have a volume devoted to its explanation – the work of a genius.

ANALYZING THE ANAGRAMS

The puns that are part of Nostradamus's verses have given rise to more speculation over the centuries than any other part of his work. To conceal identities, Nostradamus used a complex anagram system, in which a change of a single letter was permitted. He also occasionally added or subtracted a letter from the name. For instance, the name Chyren occurs more than once in the prophecies. It points to a future ruler or 'king' who will restore harmony to much of the world after a time of crisis. This Chyren could be interpreted as someone by the name of Henry. By transposing the letters and adding a 'C' to the beginning, his message is encoded.

In a letter to King Henri III, Nostradamus explained that he purposely made his prophecies ambiguous, lest any who sought to do him ill should find cause in his writings. This sounds as if the officers of the Church were a constant worry to the ageing prophet.

THE FATE OF FRANCE

Michel de Nostredame was a patriotic Frenchman, therefore many, if not most, of his prophetic verses are concerned with the destiny of his homeland. Therefore, the future Revolution, the advent of Napoleon Bonaparte, the fall of the monarchy, the Franco-Prussian war, and of course, the two world wars, were of paramount importance. Other states were also important. Nostradamus speaks of Britain as 'the Ancient Dame', reflecting its long history, or as 'the Sea Monster' – a powerful maritime nation posing

King Henry III of France (1551-1589) on horseback. Nostradamus explained in a letter to him that he had made his prophecies ambiguous on purpose to avoid attacks from his enemies.

a threat to French interests. 'The Ancient Dame' was a fascination for the seer, because soon British history would call into question one of Nostradamus's cherished beliefs – that of the divinity of a king.

THE BLOOD OF THE JUST

As a devoted monarchist, Nostradamus was appalled by the prospect of the deaths of kings at the hands of their subjects. He, in common with many others before and since, believed that there was something sacred about the 'Blood Royal', and that it was not fitting that mere commoners should spill it. His vision of the execution of Charles I of Great Britain filled him with horror, as indeed did the prospect of rule by Oliver Cromwell:

> *'More a basket of meat than a king in England –*
> *Born in obscurity, he will gain rank through force;*
> *Coward without faith, he will bleed the land;*
> *His time approaches so near that I sigh.'*

CENTURY 8.76

Cromwell came to power as Lord Protector after the English Civil War. His lack of 'faith', simply meant that he was not a Catholic. The reference to him as a 'basket of meat' implies that he would be a butcher, and that also his ancestors worked in an abattoir.

According to Nostradamus, this martyrdom of the king laid a curse on the British people, which would be expressed by disasters falling on the city of London.

> *'The great Plague of the maritime city*
> *Shall not lessen until death has taken vengeance*
> *For the blood of the just, condemned for no crime;*
> *The Great Dame is outraged by pretenders.'*

CENTURY 2.53

> *'The blood of the just shall be required of London,*
> *Burned by fire in thrice twenty and six,*
> *The Ancient Dame shall fall from her high place,*
> *And many of the same sect shall fall.'*

CENTURY 2.51

In both of these quatrains, vengeance for the 'blood of the just' (Charles I) is required to even the score – firstly by plague, which occurred in 1665, and secondly by the Great Fire, which raged in 1666. The 'Great Dame' is Britain itself, which would indeed be 'outraged by pretenders' – in other words, monarchs who were not of the true Royal bloodline – in times to come. But Nostradamus also believed that the curse that had fallen on the British people at King Charles's death would not be lifted until rulers of seven different family names had occupied the throne.

> *'Seven times you will see the British nation change,*
> *Tinged with blood for 290 years:*
> *Not all free through German support,*
> *Aries fears for his 'pole' Bastarnien.'*

CENTURY 3.57

The beheaded Charles I of the House of Stuart was followed by Oliver Cromwell, then his son Richard, and the Restoration of King Charles II occurred in 1660. That king's family, the Stuarts, were followed by the House of Orange, Hanover, Saxe-Coburg, and then Windsor. The curse apparently ended in 1917 when King George V, previously of the House of Saxe-Coburg, changed the family name to Windsor because, being at war with Germany, the name seemed inappropriate.

An alternative count would begin with the royal line current in Nostradamus's time, namely: the House of Tudor (1485–1603), Stuart (1603–1647),

Cromwell (1647–1660), Stuart again (1660–1714), and then the 'German' Houses of Hanover (1714–1901), Coburg (1901–1917) and Windsor (1917-). However, the 290-year period that Nostradamus speaks of brings us to 1939, when 'Aries fears for his 'pole' Bastarnien'. Aries is the astrological sign governing England, who 'fears for' Poland – once known as the Land of the Basarnae.

This was the quatrain that so excited Frau Magda Goebbels, the wife of the Nazi propaganda minister, as a prophecy that Britain and Germany would go to war over Poland. It was, of course, the German invasion of Poland that triggered the Second World War.

THE NEW LAND

The formation of the United States may well be prophesied in *Quatrain 1.50*:

'From the aquatic triplicity shall be born
One who has Thursday for his holiday
(or holy day).

His fame, praise, rule and power will grow,
By land and sea to trouble the east.'

CENTURY 1.50

At first sight, the 'aquatic triplicity' may seem to be a reference to the astrological signs of Cancer, Scorpio and Pisces, the three 'water' signs of the zodiac. In fact, it refers to the Atlantic and Pacific oceans and the Gulf of Mexico, which form the three bodies of water around the USA. The 'holy day of Thursday', is probably Thanksgiving Day.

THE THREE ANTI-CHRISTS

Several times, Nostradamus mentioned three future villains whom he described as Anti-Christs. These figures would cause great suffering through their insane, boundless ambitions, and persecute the church. Two of these three have already come and gone. The first was to follow the 'Great Disorder' of the French Revolution; the second was likened to a beast or an unruly, destructive child.

Napoleon seems to figure as the 'First Anti-Christ' in the quatrains in various forms. The word 'noir', which is French for 'black' occurs more than once, and is possibly an anagram of 'Roi N', or 'King N'. Nostradamus also speaks of three small, insignificant towns in Western France: 'PAU NAY LORON'. It is interesting that he sets them in capitals in the following verse:

A map of North and South America created by Lullier, 1731, shows Europeans' view of the New World shortly before the time of Napoleon Bonaparte I (1769-1821), who sought to create an empire.

TEMPEST, FIRE AND BLOODY SLICING

Given Nostradamus's views on the sacredness of monarchy, the prospect of the French Revolution, or 'Great Disorder', filled him with horror and brought the prospect of the royal curse to the people of France.

66 At night will come through the forest of Reines

Two partners, by a roundabout way, the Queen,

the white stone,

The monk-king at Varennes,

The elect Capet, resulting in tempest,

fire, bloody slicing 99

CENTURY 9.20

In 1791, King Louis XVI, surnamed Capet, and his wife Marie Antoinette, fled the Parisian mob and, by a circuitous route, went to the town of Varennes. The King had disguised himself as a monk. The first 'constitutional' monarch of France, Louis could be described as 'the elect Capet'. Recognized from his portrait on a coin, the royal pair were arrested and sent back to Paris, later to be guillotined.

'PAU NAY, LORON, will be more of fire than blood.

To swim in praise, the great man will swim to

the confluence.

He will deny the magpies entrance.

Pampon and the Durance will keep them confined.'

CENTURY 8. 1

This suggests that the three towns will burn and that blood will flow at a time of terrible upheaval. Perhaps the magpies in line three are looters whom the great man will keep at bay, or at least that is how it was read when first published. However, the verse has nothing whatever to do with those three small towns. If we apply the rules of the Nostradamian anagram, the words rearrange as NAYPAULORON or even as NAPAULON ROY – a close enough approximation of 'Napoleon' or 'Napoleon the king', from a distance of over two hundred years. The 'magpies' mentioned in the verse may be a reference to two successive popes whom Napoleon imprisoned. In French, magpie translates as 'Pie', wordplay could also make 'Pie' mean pious, and both pontiffs were named Pius.

'An emperor shall be born near to Italy

Who shall cost the empire dear

They shall say, with what peoples he keeps company!

He shall be found less a Prince than a butcher.'

CENTURY 1.60

There is no ambiguity in this verse. The Corsican-born Napoleon is positively identified, since he was the first French ruler to adopt the title of Emperor and to be born on an island of Italian stock. Napoleon is again indicated in *Century* 8.57.

'From a simple soldier, he will attain to Empire,

He will exchange the short robe for the long,

Brave in arms, much worse towards the Church,

He vexes the priests as water soaks a sponge.'

CENTURY 8.57

The short robe exchanged for the long refers to the small cloaks worn by military cadets, which Napoleon once wore. The long robe is the splendid purple cloak of an emperor. All to go well for Napoleon – his retreat from Moscow in 1812 is revealed in *Quatrain* 4. 75:

'He who was ready to fight will desert,
The chief adversary will obtain the victory.
The rear guard will make a defence,
Those faltering, dying in a white country.'

QUATRAIN 4.75

Nelson's naval victory at Cape Trafalgar in 1805 and Napoleon's final fall at Waterloo in 1815 are shown in verses 1.77 and 1.23:

'Between two seas, a promontory will stand;
By him who will die by the bit of a horse.
Neptune will fold a black sail for his own.
And a fleet shall be near Carpre (Gibraltar) and
Rocheval (Cape Roche).'

QUATRAIN 1.77

The most interesting point about this verse is the man 'who will die by the bit of a horse'. This can only be Admiral Villeneuve, commander of the French forces at Trafalgar, who was strangled to death by a horse's bridle.

'In the third month, at the rising of the sun,
The wild boar and the leopard battle
   in the fields of Mars.
The tired leopard lifts his gaze to heaven,
And sees an eagle flying around the sun.'

CENTURY 1.23

Three months after Napoleon's return from exile, French and British forces met at Waterloo. After a hard day of battle, the tide seemed to be turning in Napoleon's favour.

However, the sight of Prussian troops under the banner of the German Eagle ended French chances. Napoleon, stripped of his power and titles, was forced to flee the field.

HISTER, THE PRIEST OF THE PARTY OF MARS

The second Anti-Christ, Adolf Hitler, is also called the 'Captain of Greater Germany', 'the bird of prey', and 'the unruly child'. But the most controversial identification of the 'Second Anti-Christ' is as 'Hister' in *Century* 2.24:

'Beasts ferocious from hunger will swim across rivers.
The greater part of the forces will be against Hister.
The great one will cause him
   to be dragged in an iron cage.
When the German child will observe nothing.'

CENTURY 2.24

The objection has been raised that before the Second World War, the word 'Hister' was taken to refer to the River Danube itself, which translated into Latin as 'Istria'. However, this may be just another example of Nostradamus's subtlety, since Hitler was born in the Austrian border town of Braunau, near to the Danube. If the fourth line refers to Hitler's childhood, it should be noted that the young Adolf abandoned any religious convictions early, preferring his own twisted vision of the world. An alternative translation of that line is: 'When the child of Germany follows no law' – save his own, that is.

The Danube connection of the 'Hister' quatrain is even more complex; because it also seems to refer both to Hitler's annexation of Austria to the Reich in 1938, and to the imprisonment of Admiral Horthy, ruler of Hungary (another country through which the Danube flows), and the subsequent rule of the 'Iron Guard', a pro-Nazi organization. Hitler's takeover of Hungary is described in the following verse:

158

Adolf Hitler, who led Germany into the Second World War (1939-1945), whom Nostradamus is said to have referred to as 'Hister', the 'Second Anti-Christ', 'the bird of prey' and 'the unruly child'.

'A Captain of Greater Germany
Will deliver counterfeit help,
A King of Kings to support Hungary,
His war will cause great bloodshed.'

CENTURY 9.90

More references to Hitler are found in other verses:

'In the farthest depths of Western Europe,
A child will be born of a poor people,
Who by his speeches will seduce great numbers,
His fame will grow even greater
    in the eastern dominion.'

CENTURY 3.35

'He will transform into Greater Germany,
Brabant, Flanders, Ghent, Bruges and Boulogne
The truce feigned the Grand Duke of Armenia
Will assail Vienna and Cologne.'

CENTURY 5.94

The 'Armenia' referred to in line three is not the country of that name, but a semi-legendary Germanic hero of the AD 1st Century. This prophecy indicates that the non-aggression pact with Stalin and the USSR enabled the 'Captain of Greater Germany' to expand his empire westward. History has shown that the 'truce feigned' was broken by Germany in 1940, as described in this verse:

'The great priest of the Party of Mars
Who will subjugate the Danube
The Cross harried by the crook
Captives, gold, jewels more than
    a hundred thousand rubies.'

CENTURY 6.49

The Party of Mars, god of war, is easily identified as the Nazi Party. However, the 'Cross harried by the crook' may have a triple meaning. Firstly, the 'crook' who persecuted the Church or 'Cross' is Hitler himself. Secondly, the combination of cross and crook gives the idea of a crooked cross or swastika, and finally, the people of the crook or sickle, the Russians, harried those of the swastika mightily.

As might be expected, the Second World War figures largely in the quatrains. *Century 1, verse 31* refers to the Allied invasion of Sicily in 1943:

'In Naples, Palermo, Syracuse and throughout Sicily,
New tyrants come, with great noise
    and fire in the heavens,

A force from London, Ghent, Brussels and Suse,
A great slaughter, then triumph and festivity.'

CENTURY 1.31

The reference to 'new tyrants' should not be taken as a criticism of the Allied forces. Nostradamus was referring to the ancient rulers of Sicily, the tyrants of Syracuse who came to the island and established good government. A Nostradamian pun is also to be found in the word 'Suse', which with one letter changed and another dropped, forms USA.

'Liberty shall not be recovered,
A black, fierce and wicked villain shall occupy it,
When the material of the bridge is completed,
The republic of Venice shall be annoyed by Hister.'

CENTURY 5.29

The fact that Nostradamus writes of the 'material of the bridge', rather than construction, indicates that the seer knew that it would be makeshift, rather than built of stone.

On 21 February, 1941, the *New York Herald Tribune* reported that a temporary pontoon bridge had been built across the Danube in order to facilitate Nazi troop movements. Within one month, evidence was gathered that Nazi agents had infiltrated Italian government positions, much to the annoyance of Italy's dictator and Adolf Hitler's half-hearted ally, Mussolini. The fall of France is also predicted:

'The bird of prey flies to the window.
Before conflict with the French, makes preparation.
Some will take him as good,
    others as evil or ambiguous.
The weaker party will hold him as a good sign.'

CENTURY 1.34

However, across the English Channel:

'Those in the Isles long besieged
Will take vigorous action against their enemies.
Those outside dead, overcome by hunger,
They will be put in greater hunger than ever before.'

CENTURY 3.71

Hitler's plans to starve Britain into submission are also dealt with in *Century 4.15*:

'Where he thought to breed famine,
There will come plenty,
While the eye of the sea watches like a greedy dog;
For one to the other will give oil, wheat.'

CENTURY 4.15

The assistance of the USA foiled Hitler's scheme, despite the Nazi U-boats watching and waiting 'like a greedy dog'.

Second World War gun soldiers using an aircraft weapon are wearing gas masks that make them look somewhat pig-like. Nostradamus's description of the 'pig-half man' in *Century 1.64* could have been referring to them.

The London Blitz and the Battle of Britain are foreseen in a bizarre quatrain that seems to show the seer's confusion about his vision of war in the air.

'They will think they have seen the sun at night,
When they see the pig-half man:
Noise, battle, fighting in the sky perceived:
And brute beasts will be heard to speak.'

CENTURY 1.64

The 'pig-half man' has been taken as a description of a fighter pilot in his gear of helmet, goggles and oxygen mask, while the 'sun at night' is thought to correspond to explosions and searchlights.

It also may be that the present fame of the Nostradamian prophecies dates from the Second World War. Magda Goebbels persuaded her husband, the Nazi propaganda minister, that they could be used to undermine the morale of the allies (see pages 144-147).

THE THIRD ANTI-CHRIST

Of the terrible 'Third Anti-Christ', he who apparently is to be more monstrous than either of his predecessors, Nostradmus has this to say:

'The Anti-Christ very soon annihilates the three,
Seven and twenty years his war will endure,
The heretics are dead, imprisoned, exiled,
Red hail, water, blood and corpses cover the earth.'

CENTURY 8. 77

Interpreters of *The Centuries* have speculated that this prophecy is due for fulfilment at some point in the early years of the new millennium. If this is the case, then we shall all soon see the emergence of this new 'messiah of evil' – to our cost.

A NOSTRADAMIAN EPITAPH – OR TWO

The great prophet Michel de Nostredame died on June 25, 1566. It was a shock to his family but not, apparently, to him, since he had predicted the circumstances of his death some time before. He was buried upright within the wall of the Church of the Virgin in Salon; though this was not specified in his will, Nostradamus apparently expressed a horror of being trodden on. His grieving widow placed an inscription on his peculiar tomb, which stated:

'Here lie the bones of Michel Nostradamus, whose near-divine pen was alone, in the judgement of mortals, worthy to record, under the inspiration of the stars, the future events of the whole world. Posterity, invade not his rest.'

Later, posterity did indeed disturb the seer, but it appears that the wily prophet was prepared for his disclosure. Legend attests that an unruly mob sacked the Church in 1791, at the height of anti-papal feeling during the French Revolution. After stripping the building of its valuables, the mob turned their fury on the grave of Salon's most famous resident. Breaking through the wall, they tore the lid from the prophet's casket. There within, his dessicated corpse still stood. Upon its chest was a lead plaque bearing the inscription '1791'. However this did not deter the rioters, who scattered the bones, only ceasing their wanton vandalism when the town mayor bravely faced them to say that Nostradamus had predicted the Revolution, and in his day, had been a healer. The bones were returned, and have been treated as relics ever since. Oddly, the rioter who had laid hands on them was killed the next day in an ambush.

COUNTDOWN TO DOOMSDAY

With the advent of the new millennium, the prophets of doom are having a field day, just as they did at the dawn of the last millennium when they inspired riots all over Europe. However, the more apocalyptic of the religious and crank cults have shown a worrying tendency which has not previously been seen. Increasingly, they are engaged in either encouraging the end of the world or trying to pre-empt the final strike. Even though the rest of us would vastly prefer to avoid potential calamity, some cultists actively court a doomsday scenario, sometimes mixing in the Old Testament idea of the wrath of God, with modern innovations and a strangely optimistic Ufology in their preaching.

We have numerous examples of how a charismatic leader can influence and control the thought patterns of his followers. The Reverend Jim Jones was an example of this type of leader, as was David Koresh – both of whom considered themselves to be incarnations of the Messiah and both of whom were responsible for the deaths of not only themselves, but also their followers.

The 'survivalists' are another example of people who follow this doomsday idea. A distrust of organized government, religion and convention has been particularly obvious in the United States, where the old ideal of self-sufficiency has been given a darker, more sinister interpretation by survivalist adherents. It could be argued, however, that being armed 'to the teeth', planning to protect your home and property 'to the death' and a total distrust of strangers makes you a terrorist rather than a true believer. Indeed, in recent

The Reverend Jim Jones captured on video, in this still taken from poor-quality footage filmed just before his cult's mass suicide by poisoning – even children were forced to swallow sweet drinks laced with poison.

years, several terrorist bombing outrages in America have been linked to extremist survivalist groups.

THE CULT OF THE COMET

Still, the USA is not the only western nation to experience cult-inspired doomsayers. Members of the 'Solar Temple' committed ritual mass suicide in Switzerland, Canada and many other countries when the comet Schumaker-Levi was sighted. Solar Temple cultists believed that the arrival of Schumaker-Levi heralded the end of the world. They were of the opinion that the comet concealed a vast spaceship sent to collect their souls and transport them to eternal bliss. The death toll numbered fifty-three in 1994 and was followed by five further cult suicides in Canada in 1997. However bizarre this sounds, it is not unique. In 1997, thirty-nine members of the 'Heaven's Gate' movement, under the benign guru-ship of the patriarchal Marshall Applewhite, described themselves as an 'away team', and committed mass suicide. Having been convinced by Applewhite that they were not wholly physical beings, but originated from another point in time and space, the 'away team' decided to go home. Apparently the only way to do this was to leave their physical bodies and astrally journey to a conveniently positioned spaceship which was concealed at the core of a comet. This one was called HaleBop, which was then passing through our sector of the solar system. They knew that their action might be misconstrued, so they left a farewell video which explained their position. It would be laughable were it not so tragic.

This belief that comets portend catastrophe is not a new one. The word 'disaster' literally means 'bad star' and originally referred to the appearance of a comet.

Imagining that some external force will save one is also not a unique idea. In January 1998, a group led by German psychologist Heidi Fittkau-Garthe was rounded up by Spanish police on Tenerife, thus foiling the second suicide bid in one week by nineteen people, including three children, who had chosen to die by poison. The authorities were apparently alerted to the second attempt when a farewell call to a relative was intercepted. The followers of Heidi Fittkau-Garthe are well-educated and affluent, but this does

The comet West came near the Earth on March 9, 1976. The trail of dust and rocks behind it is white, and its gas tail is blue. Cults like Heaven's Gate and the Solar Temple incorporate natural phenomena like comets and earthquakes into their beliefs.

not stop them from regarding their leader as semi-divine and calling her 'The Source'. They, too, believe that the end of the world is nigh, and, like the acolytes of the Solar Temple and Heaven's Gate, are convinced that a flying saucer will come to rescue their souls from the Tenerife mountain side at the point of death. This, they claim, will save them from the approaching apocalypse, which they believe will cause the Earth's axis to shift and continents to move as Edgar Cayce predicted (see pages 126-127). Contrary to the views of the 'Sleeping Prophet', how-

In the 1990s, David Koresh was the leader of a doomsday cult in Waco, Texas, which the American government placed under siege. Cult members were charged with amassing weapons that they would not give up.

ever, the followers of Fittkau-Garthe firmly believe that this signals the end of mankind.

Doom watching isn't a new phenomenon. Prophets have been predicting the end of the world for centuries. One of the most notorious of these dubious seers was Johann Stoffler (see page 181), who predicted a disastrous flood that would sweep away the remnants of mankind. This was set to occur on 20 February, 1524. Whatever one might say about Stoffler's incompetence as an oracle, he was a superb publicist, because many people in Germany built arks to preserve themselves, their families and livestock from the rising waters. As the fated day approached, the hysteria of the populace reached fever pitch. Count von Iggleheim, who had constructed one of the most comfortable and roomy arks, was trampled to death by an ugly mob trying to seize his vessel. Needless to say, the rains never came, the seas remained calm and the rivers did not rise to cover the land. Stoffler then stated that his calculations were somewhat adrift – unlike the

assembled arks. He revised them and came up with the year 1588 as the correct time for the predicted flood. Of course, the time passed without event, but by then Johann Stoffler was safely dead and beyond reproach.

In a more Biblical vein, a native of New England, William Miller, stirred up a mob with his prophecies of imminent doom in 1843. As a student of the scriptures, Miller became obsessed with the visions of the prophet Daniel (see pages 52-55). With apocalypse in mind, Miller worked out the precise date of the end of the world to be 21 March of that year. He was not alone in predicting this, as a certain Joseph Woolf had calculated the year for it as being 1847, as had Harriet Livermore. Miller was the most popular of these prophets by far, however, and soon found himself elevated to the status of Messiah. As if on cue, a comet appeared in the sky, and thousands of hysterical people climbed to the top of the mountains dressed in shrouds. But they experienced nothing except the night's chill. Miller extended his prediction to encompass Christmas and the New Year and lost his followers overnight, subsequently drifting into obscurity.

TWENTIETH-CENTURY APOCALYPSE

Of course, one can only predict what one can imagine. Stoffler forecast doom by flooding, whereas Miller and others predicted earthquakes and

huge conflagrations that would consume the earth. Before the twentieth century, the only forces capable of such devastation derived from nature itself. It has taken the brilliance of some of the finest minds on the planet to ensure that mankind is now quite capable of creating its own doomsday scenarios without any help from nature 'red in tooth and claw', or even the will of a wrathful God.

The so-called 'Millennium Bug', which could affect computer systems across the globe is the source of another, hopefully mistaken, prediction. It involves a system named Y2K. Apparently, this computer network controls the firing codes for the nuclear arsenal of the free world. Were the Bug

There are fears that the computer systems across the globe which control the world's nuclear arsenal will be set off in the year 2000 by a 'Millennium Bug'.

to grip this system, we would very likely experience the kind of apocalypse that Nostradamus is often, mistakenly, thought to have predicted. As if Y2K were not enough, another paranoid, yet currently fashionable, idea is that the earth could be struck by an asteroid – a suggestion that we can hardly ignore given that our solar system is fairly crowded with whirling lumps of rock the size of mountains. And it has happened before, last time with tragic consequences for the dinosaurs.

If there's one thing that the last millennium should have taught us, it is that prophets of doom are rarely, if ever, correct, and that so-called messiahs are very dangerous people who invite us to share their delusions. We do so at our peril.

GENE GENIE

The increased influence of genetic engineering is about to change our lives for good or ill in the new millennium. This subject, which many find troubling, has been the focus for a number of self-styled prophets. In the early 1970s, for example, Dr Paul Segall predicted that genetic engineering will allow us to be replicated, and by the year 2020 we will exchange entire bodies or swap vital organs.

Genetic engineering is seen by some as a science that will improve the lives of millions. It is argued that the manipulation of basic cell structures could eradicate malnutrition in the Third World, provide medical advances which could end disease, and possibly even improve humanity itself. Others counter that genetic research and gene manipulation is nothing more than meddling with nature and evolution in the manner of Dr Frankenstein, ignoring all signs of imminent catastrophe.

The early years of the third millennium are likely to bring us both good and bad effects from this form

Dolly the Sheep made headlines in 1997 as the world's first sheep to be cloned from an adult sheep cell – the cloning of humans may not be far behind.

of cellular research. On the one hand, new varieties of rice will be developed to replace the existing staple diets of over two-thirds of the earth's population. These new plants will be resistant to insects and disease and will be easier to propagate, possibly even producing a greater number of crops annually. This factor alone will lead to population growth in the poorer areas of the world.

Thus, the manipulation of rice genes could lead to a circular problem. The more rice produced, the more people are fed; the more people are fed, the larger the population will grow – leading to more rice production. Alongside this, food gene cells may be altered to increase the life of foodstuffs, thereby lengthening storage times. Food may also be made more nourishing, as plants may be induced to produce more amino acids, the building blocks of proteins – effectively banishing malnutrition from the face of the earth.

Gene manipulation is also being used to create new and more potent vaccines for the treatment of existing diseases as well as those which will appear in the future.

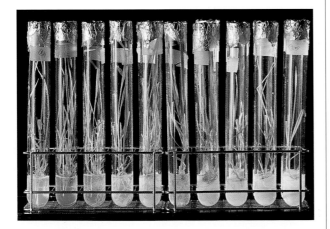

Micropropagation – in which single cells from a 'parent' plant are grown in test tubes until they are ready to be planted outdoors – allows the mass agricultural production of genetically identical or 'cloned' plants.

Even taking all of these benefits into account, many people are worried that scientists have opened a Pandora's box and will soon be creating new species from scratch, some of which could even end man's tenure on earth prematurely.

Although this attitude smacks of science fiction rather than fact, the cloning of Dolly the sheep may open the door to more sinister possibilities. Recently, bones from the long-extinct moa bird have been scoured for DNA samples, the idea being to culture these remains into a viable genetic matrix which would then be mingled with the genes of an ostrich in order to create a new hybrid bird which would stand well over seven feet tall and have enough meat on one vast drumstick to feed an entire city block! How long, then, before the sabre-toothed tiger or the woolly mammoth reappear?

There could be little to stop unscrupulous scientists from creating monsters if the world's governments choose to protect the money markets rather than nature.

DIPPING INTO THE GENE POOL

However, before we lose sight of the facts as we venture into the seas of speculation, this sort of DNA splicing may help to preserve presently endangered species. After all, why create a sabre-toothed tiger when we already have tigers on the verge of extinction – ones whose genes are far more readily accessible than those of their long-dead cousins. The same may be said for the rhinoceros, the elephant and all other endangered life-forms.

And what of the human gene pool? This sort of manipulation could ultimately prove to be one of the most terrible dangers that man has ever faced. Consider the views of racial purity held by the Nazis. Had genetic engineering been around in the 1930s and 40s, what would they have done to create a 'master-race' and eliminate the weak and unacceptable? Only constant vigilance can prevent a dictator from using such methods to further his own agenda.

One thing is certain: the genetic genie is now out of the bottle and no amount of pushing is going to put it back in. The ball is in our court. If we really don't like what is being done with DNA manipulation, then it is up to us to stop it. If, on the other hand, the benefits outweigh the dangers, as some people claim is the case with nuclear energy, then we will have to be prepared to adapt to the new – or in some cases, like the moa, the very old.

THE NEW AGE

For Millennia, astrologers have divided time into blocks of 2000 years known as 'Ages', which are refered to by their related signs of the zodiac. This astrological cycle lasts over 24,000 years and is known as the 'Precession of the Equinoxes'. For example, 332 BC, the time of Alexander the Great, was known as the Age of Aries, ruled by Mars the God of War, and a time of war and battle. Alexander himself was often to be portayed with the horns of a ram. After this came the Age of Pisces, represented by the fish, also the symbol of Jesus, and a time of great faith.

From May 2000, we will enter a new, more enlightened age dominated by the star sign of Aquarius, said to herald a time of compassion, peace, love and scientific advancement for the benefit of all. Aquarius's influence indicates that fair dealing and humanitarian values should be strongly featured over the coming years, and indeed, centuries. This Age also suggests that we will encounter a lot of ecological, economic and political problems that need to be resolved if global harmony is to be achieved.

We have lived through an age which depends on progress, yet paradoxically, we also crave stability and cling to the hope that chaos will not overwhelm our lives. Instability is exactly what we create by constantly changing our frames of reference – this is not to say that progress is wrong or that we should creep meekly back to a simpler, more agricultural way of life, but we need to bear in mind that the future cannot simply consist of a series of eternal improvements, neither need it spell out doom and disaster at every turn.

This kind of view of a US astronaut floating freely in the space above the Earth in his 'manned maneuvering unit' encouraged the emergence of the 'one-earth' ideal whose proponents believe will unite the world's disparate nations in peace.

A TIME FOR CHANGE

Nostradamus predicted world events for 3,700 years into the future. Subtracting the 500 years since his death, there are still 3,200 years of prophecies remaining, suggesting his prophecies do not necessarily indicate the end of time as we know it.

As the twentieth century has seen far-reaching changes – technological advancement, the demise of most European monarchies, and world conflict – the twenty-first century is set to bring about more intense change and insecurity. One could say that we are now in an age of transition; those among us who have experienced upheaval on a personal level can imagine what this could feel like in global terms. Recently, a computer-generated study measuring the rate of technological advancement arrived at the same conclusion as the ancient Maya, who predicted a major 'time of change' by 21 December 2012. In other words, the rate of progress will have reached saturation level by that date. We are already aware that new products can be obsolete by the time they are put on the shelves, and it becomes increasingly difficult to keep up with innovation. Society is under pressure to deal with much change in a short time. This is not an argument for a 'slow down', just the need to acquire new coping mechanisms.

Unscrupulous politicians and would-be dictators who were able to control what their people saw and heard and thought now have the internet and instantaneous satellite communication to contend with. While control of this network could pose a huge threat to freedom of speech, on an individual basis, news and views can no longer be as easily censored.

LIFE ON ANOTHER PLANET

Science-fiction writers such as Isaac Asimov and Arthur C. Clark have long held views on the development of human life beyond earth. Clarke, for eaxmple, predicted that by the year 2060, space colonies will exist. As history has proved, one way to unite people is through a grand project – as the Pharaohs found when they built the pyramids. The new project for our age could be the colonization of Mars, to be followed by the Moon – possibly acting as a staging-post – and then the more distant reaches of our solar system such as the moons of Jupiter. A thorough understanding of our own ecosystem will lead inevitably to the creation of ecosystems elsewhere. The trapped water on Mars and the moon may be the starting point for any such venture.

THE AGE OF AQUARIUS

It has been said that the Age of Aquarius will provide us with an unparalleled opportunity to evolve. This is true – every age does, bringing new issues to the fore. The alternative is not to be contemplated – some of the verses of Nostradamus seem to suggest an alliance of the Western powers with Russia, which will turn on China and bring terror to the world. Could the isolated 'sleeping giant' of China be awakened as Napoleon feared and Nostradamus foresaw?

We have also the prospect of Nostradamus's Third Anti-Christ to contend with, set to make an appearance on the world stage in the early years of the twenty-first century. Fortunately for us, so is 'Chyren', the anagramatic name of a prince who will battle against the Anti-Christ and save us all. Could this be interpreted as Prince Henry, second son of the Prince of Wales, who will become the prophesied leader?

One thing is certain – we cannot possibly hope to foresee the future without having an good understanding of the past. As the great Swiss psychologist Carl Gustav Jung once remarked, 'He who forgets the past is condemned to relive it'. Whatever the interpretations of Nostradamus' remaining verses, we can be sure that only time will tell what the future holds.

Humanity has a profound and wonderful destiny, but we should not forget that the responsibility lies with us to make it so, and to repeat the mistakes of the past would be a betrayal of our true potential. The future is out there, and we need to embrace it with courage and optimism.

A SYMPOSIUM OF SEERS
FROM A TO Z

Evangeline Adams
1865-1932

Astrologer

Originally an amateur astrologer, Mrs. George E. Jordan was so successful in making predictions that she decided to take it up professionally. Assuming the name Evangeline Adams, she went on to promote her then obscure art in the first-ever astrological radio broadcasts from New York. On her first visit to the Big Apple she informed the owner of her hotel that he was 'under the worst possible combination of planets, bringing conditions terrifying in their unfriendliness'. Later that night, the hotel burned to the ground and the resulting publicity catapulted Evangeline to stardom. She was prosecuted for fraudulent fortune-telling in 1914, and as part of the court proceedings was given an anonymous horoscope to interpret. From the dock, she read the horoscope chart, to the utter amazement of the judge, who announced that the horoscope belonged to his son, and that Evangeline's reading had been astoundingly accurate. The case was dismissed and the judge gave his ruling that 'she has raised astrology to the dignity of an exact science'. She began a regular radio programme in 1930. A *New York Times* review stated that it was 'radio and astrology dancing hand-in-hand to victory'. Like Nostradamus, whom she admired, Evangeline predicted the date of her own death long before the actual event in 1932.

Apollonius of Tyana
First century AD

Philosopher, Wizard and Seer

Apollonius was a wandering holy man and miracle worker who impressed the Empress Julia Domna. He must have had a long life, since he was present at the court of Nero (reigned AD 54-68) and yet again in the time of Nerva (reigned AD 96-98). He travelled all over the known world as far as India, and some of his feats had much in common with the skills of Indian fakirs. He is said to have defeated the wiles of a vampire lady and performed feats of levitation, clairvoyance, healing and raising the dead. Over a century after his death, Apollonius was said to be a divine prophet and was a pagan saviour rivalling Christ.

Ascletarion
Died AD 96

Imperial astrologer

Ascletarion was foolish enough to tell the Emperor Domitian how and when he would die. In response, the emperor asked how Ascletarion himself was doomed to perish. On being told that the astrologer was fated to be savaged to death by wild animals, Domitian determined to prove him wrong by condemning him to be burned at the stake and his ashes scattered. However a sudden downpour extinguished the flames and Ascletarion was indeed devoured by beasts.

A concert party in Naples attended by Kenneth Mackenzie, 1st Earl of Seaforth, whose family's doom was predicted by Coinneach Odhar, the Brahan Seer.

Elizabeth Barton
1506-1534

*The Holy Maid of Kent
Christian Mystic*

The Holy Maid of Kent's prophecies were used as political propaganda by those who opposed King Henry VIII's ecclesiastical and marital policies. Prompted by elements within the Catholic Church, Elizabeth Barton claimed to speak 'in the name and authority of God'. However, her prophecies failed to materialize and she was condemned to hang. Her moving speech from the gallows convinced many that she had been a mere dupe in the whole affair, although her final prophecy concerning the fate of the king did come true (see pages 64-65).

The Black Doves Oracles

c. 1200 BC–AD 394

Oracles of Zeus at Dodona
Priestesses

The Black Doves were the priestesses who presided over the oracle of the king of the gods in Northern Greece. The historian Herodotus claimed that the oracle was founded in remote times by a dark-skinned Egyptian girl, though the legend states that a black dove which spoke with a human voice was the founder. Herodotus was of the opinion that both stories were at least symbolically true. In his day, the Black Dove priestesses were named Promeneia, Timarete and Nicandra. There was another so-called 'Black Dove oracle'. This was the famous Oracle of Ammon at Siwa in the western deserts of Egypt. Alexander the Great consulted both.

Guido Bonatti

Thirteenth century AD

Astrologer

The most famous astrologer of his day, Bonatti's reputation was such that if he favoured a particular cause in the interminable civil wars which wracked Italy, that side's victory was assured, the opposing party assuming that it was fated to inevitably lose. The poet Dante placed Bonatti among the sorcerers consigned to hell; his punishment was to have his head twisted around for all of eternity so that he could only look backward – for daring to look to the future.

The Brahan Seer

Died 1665

Coinneach Odhar
'The Warlock of the Glen'

The one-eyed crofter gifted with second sight, Coinneach Odhar prophesied many of the trials and tribulations which would afflict his native Scotland. He was put to death at the command of the third Countess of Seaforth. As his doom was pronounced, he retaliated by uttering a prediction which has since become known as the 'Doom of the Seaforths', every detail of which has been fulfilled (see pages 112-115).

Jerome Cardan

1501-1576

aka Gerolmo Cardano
Mathematician, Physician and
Astrologer

A person of renowned intellect, Jerome Cardan was greatly respected by other great minds of his time like Dr John Dee. His talents were so manifest that he was asked to cast a horoscope for the youthful King Edward VI of England. Unfortunately, Cardan's gifts did not run in the direction of astrology and, as a seer, he was indifferent. Nevertheless, he set about the task with vigour. Finally he announced that His Majesty would enjoy a long and happy reign. Misfortune would only occur when King Edward, at the age of fifty-five years, three months and seventeen days, would fall dangerously ill. This prophecy became so well-known that Cardan was a laughing stock when the king died at the age of sixteen. Cardan's reputation never recovered and he is said to have taken his own life to prove the accuracy of a fatal prediction he made concerning himself.

Count Alessandro del Cagliostro

1743-1795

aka Giuseppe Balsamo,
'The Grand Copht'
Alchemist, Numerologist,
Astrologer, Clairvoyant, Charlatan,
Masonic Enthusiast

According to Aleister Crowley (who claimed to be the count's reincarnation, see pages 132-135), Giuseppe Balsamo was born in a brothel in Palermo, Sicily. Balsamo developed into an argumentative, ungovernable person. He was sent to a seminary school but continually ran away. Forced to become a novice monk, he got himself thrown out of the church and trained as an artist, a profession for which he showed great talent. Typically, he soon turned this gift to forgery. Where he acquired his knowledge of numerology, astrology and alchemy is unknown; however, he did display clairvoyant gifts from an early age. Teaming up with fourteen-year-old

Lorenza Feliciani in Rome, Balsamo adopted the spurious title of Count Cagliostro and set about conning the rich and gullible with potions of immortality and methods for turning lead into gold. However, he did also make many accurate predictions, both for private individuals and on matters of state. In 1776, Cagliostro, calling himself Colonel Joseph Cagliostro of the Third Regiment of Brandenburg, was admitted to the Freemasons at the King's Head Inn, Gerard Street, Soho, London. He then devoted his life to promoting masonic ideals around Europe. He rediscovered or invented 'The Egyptian Rite' as a higher degree of Freemasonry and founded his own lodges, taking the title of 'The Grand Copht'. Now claiming to have twelve lives and astounding occult powers he also appeared to be rich, and the doors of the courts of Europe were open to him. Later, conned into the notorious 'Affair of the Diamond Necklace', which is cited as one of the causes of the French Revolution, he was imprisoned in the Bastille for a year. His spirit broken, he and Lorenza fled back to Italy, only to be arrested by the Papal Inquisition for prophesying the fall of the French monarchy, the beheading of the king and queen, and that the hated Bastille would be made into a public promenade. Imprisoned in the Castel San Leo, Cagliostro was almost literally buried alive in darkness, dying in 1795. Invading French soldiers under Napoleon's command searched for him in 1797, intending to proclaim 'The Grand Copht' a hero of the revolution.

Calanus

Died 321 BC

Hindu Seer

An ancient Brahmin, Calanus entered the service of Alexander the Great in India and travelled west with him after he had failed to conquer the sub-continent. Sensing the approach of death, Calanus burned himself alive on a pyre in Indian fashion and prophesied Alexander's own end at Babylon from the midst of the flames.

Calpurnia

First century BC

Wife of Julius Caesar

Julius Caesar's official Roman wife (even though he may have gone through an Egyptian marriage ceremony with Cleopatra), Calpurnia was said to 'be above suspicion'. She must have had great affection for her errant husband and always spoke in his defence. On the night before he was assassinated in the senate on the Ides of March, 44 BC, Calpurnia had a precognitive dream in which she saw her husband soaked in blood, dying at the feet of his now-deceased rival, Pompey. Her dire prophecy was ignored and Julius Caesar did, in a sense, expire at Pompey's feet – his body came to rest at the base of a statue dedicated to the general.

The Grand Cameo of France, AD 20, shows Germanicus, Julius Caesar, Augustus, Aeneas, Tiberius, Livia and Caligula – some of the luminaries of the Roman Empire.

Tommaso Campanella

1568-1639

*Dominican Friar, Philosopher,
Heretic Magician and Astrologer*

Campanella was a Dominican friar whose philosophy and often radical views offended the church authorities. His opinions were based on the so-called 'Emerald Tablet of Hermes Trismagestus', a magical treatise which described the basis of alchemy and astrology. He was often imprisoned and, on one occasion, had to feign insanity to escape execution. He was well-connected, even though he was regarded with suspicion. Both King Louis XIII and his chief minister Cardinal Richelieu proclaimed him a great astrologer. Despite his unsavoury reputation in ecclesiastical circles, Campanella was employed by the heretical Pope Urban VIII to magically preserve his life. In his book *The City of the Sun*, Campanella advocated a theocratic form of government based on religion rising from the forces of nature rather than on dogma.

Cassandra

Eleventh century BC

*Legendary Prophetess
Princess of Troy*

Cassandra was the favourite daughter of King Priam of Troy. Extremely beautiful, she attracted the attention of Apollo, the god of prophecy, who gave her second sight. Unfortunately, she did not reciprocate his feelings, and rejected his advances. Since he could not take back a gift that he had already given, Apollo cursed Cassandra – so that, even though she saw the future clearly, she was always disbelieved. According to the Roman poet Virgil, she vainly tried to warn the Trojans of the folly of bringing the Wooden Horse into the city but was thought by many to be insane. After the Greeks had sacked the city, Cassandra was taken as a slave to Mycenae by the victorious Agamemnon, who she warned of a plot against his life. Again she was not believed and Agamemnon was murdered by his scheming wife. Cassandra also met a violent death on that day. Her awareness of the future and inability to alter it have made 'Cassandra-like' warnings proverbial.

Edgar Cayce

1877-1945

'The Sleeping Prophet'

The most famous and influential psychic healer and clairvoyant of the twentieth century, Edgar Cayce had the ability to go into trance, or fall asleep, and diagnose his own and other people's ailments. In this state, he would provide spiritual healing for the 14,000 people who consulted him. Cayce would also delve into his patients' past lives and predict the future. Very interested in the cataclysm that he believed overtook the lost continent of Atlantis, he prophesied that a similar fate awaited the world at the end of the twentieth century. This would be signalled by a huge earthquake which would destroy San Francisco and plunge California into the ocean. His other famous predictions include the original Wall Street Crash, the assassination of John F. Kennedy and the death of F. D. Roosevelt, as well as the formation of the state of Israel and the independence of India.

Jacques Cazotte

1718-1792

Poet

A well-known figure in the fashionable salons of pre-revolutionary France, Cazotte is known to have made only one detailed prediction in his lifetime, but one so chillingly accurate that it turned him into a legend. In 1788, one year before the start of the French Revolution, Jacques Cazotte was the guest of the Duchess de Gramont. In her salon, he casually predicted the eventual fates of all of those there. To the philosopher Condorcet, Cazotte predicted death by poison to cheat the executioner; to the playwright Chamfort a cold vision of suicide by razor; to the astronomer Bailly, beheading; a fate which he calmly remarked was also reserved for himself as well as all others present. The notorious atheist Jean de Laharpe laughed and asked if a similar end was reserved for him. Cazotte replied in the negative, adding that Laharpe would convert to Christianity and escape the blade. All happened as Cazotte had predicted and he went to the guillotine during 'The Terror' of 1792. Laharpe was so affected that he converted to the Catholic faith immediately, and survived the Revolution to record his remarkable friend's words.

Cheiro

1866-1936

*aka Count Louis Hamon
and William John Warner
'The Palmist to Princes'
Palmist, Numerologist,
Astrologer, Clairvoyant*

William Warner was taught the art of astrology by his mother, and by his mid-teens had travelled extensively. In

Bombay, he learned the arts of palmistry or 'cheiromancy' and adopted the professional name 'Cheiro'. He was also known as 'Count Louis Hamon'. By the age of twenty-four Cheiro was a well-known clairvoyant in fashionable London, and was consulted by the great names of the day. For example, he foretold the fate of Oscar Wilde, who was condemned to Reading Gaol for immorality in 1895, and became the confidant of the rich and famous of the day, impressing amongst others, operatic diva Dame Nellie Melba, President Grover Cleveland, and amazing the arch-cynic Mark Twain with the accuracy of his predictions. Cheiro predicted the death of Queen Victoria by numerology and the month and year of the death of her son, King Edward VII. He warned the envoy of Tsar Nicholas II of Russia of the fate that was in store for the imperial Family, and predicted the assassination of King Umberto of Italy.

Coratus

Sixteenth century BC

Legend states that the shepherd Coratus discovered narcotic fumes rising from a cleft in the rock at Delphi. The first to be overcome by the 'mephitic vapours', he was thus the first to prophesy at that spot. Unfortunately, his words are lost to posterity.

Aleister Crowley

1875-1947

'The Great Beast' and 'The Wickedest Man in the World' Occultist, Black Magician, Mountaineer, Chess Master, Poet

Aleister Crowley embraced occultism at an early age, and was obsessed by

contacting a higher power he called 'The Holy Guardian Angel', which eventually manifested itself to him under the name of Aiwass in Egypt in 1904. Aiwass seemingly dictated *The Book of the Law* to Crowley, which provided the foundation of his new religion called 'Crowleyanity', its basic dictate being 'do what thou wilt'. In this book, Aiwass predicted the eras of both the First and Second World Wars, according to Crowleyites. The third and final war was, according to Crowley, to have occurred in the 1980s. His own worst enemy, Crowley's bizarre sense of humour, publicity seeking and drug abuse led to his slow decline. He lived long enough to see the defeat of the fascism, which he believed was to have led to the establishment of his new faith worldwide. Crowley became a cult figure in the 1960s as a precursor of the 'free love drug culture'.

Dr John Dee

1527-1608

'The Wizard of Mortlake' Mathematician, Inventor, Geographer, Philosopher, Spy, Seer, Alchemist, Astrologer Royal

Dr Dee was probably the original for Shakespeare's king-magician Prospero from *The Tempest*. He was certainly an influential advisor to Queen Elizabeth I, and had set the date and time for her coronation. He also acted as a spy in Germany for his monarch and was referred to as 'Agent 007'. Dee's support of the last Tudor monarch had led to his imprisonment under her predecessor, and it was only Bloody Mary's timely death that saved him from being burned at the stake. His unwise association with the sinister

Edward Kelly (see pages 84-87) tarnished his historical reputation; however, his predictions helped ensure the smooth succession of the Stuart dynasty, even though Dee personally suffered persecution under the new King James I. Dee is the only person in history to actually demand to be tried for witchcraft and to escape with his life. His 'Magic Mirror' (given to him by King Phillip II of Spain), and a crystal ball allegedly given to Dee by an angel are still to be seen in the British Museum, London.

Jeanne Dixon

1918-1997

Palmist, Crystal Gazer, Clairvoyant, Prophet

Jeanne Dixon, née Pinckert, is most famous for her prediction of the assassination of J. F. Kennedy in 1963. She also claimed to have had forebodings of the deaths of both Mahatma Gandhi and of Martin Luther King. Though she had some notable successes, many of her prophecies failed to prove themselves. Her prediction of a world war in 1958 failed to materialize, as indeed did several other disasters. As time went on, her pronouncements became more apocalyptic in nature. Dixon maintained that the Anti-Christ had been born on 5 February, 1962, in the Middle East. She also claimed that where would be nuclear war in 1999 and that Jesus would return to earth in 2020. Despite her shortcomings as a prophetess, Jeanne Dixon maintained the favour of Washington's great and powerful. Her last prominent client was allegedly Nancy Reagan.

The mixture of European pagan and Egyptian symbols in this painting offers an impression of the kind of manipulative philosophy which Crowley espoused.

The Witch of Endor

Eleventh century BC

Biblical Sorceress and Spirit Medium

Even though the teachings of the Biblical prophets forbade the calling up of the spirits of the dead, King Saul, in desperation, turned to the sinister Witch of Endor to make contact with his deceased advisor Samuel (*The First Book of Samuel* 28) on the eve of battle with the Philistines. The Witch duly summoned the spirit, who was very angry about being disturbed. Samuel's enraged ghost then informed the terrified king that God was displeased with him and that victory would go to the Philistines. The last we hear of the Witch is when she served calf's meat to the sorrowful King Saul and his followers before he went off to fight his hopeless battle.

The Lady of Fatima

1917

Apparition

The Lady of Fatima is the name given to an apparition of the Virgin Mary apparently seen by three Portuguese children – Lucia de Jesus dos Santos, Jacinta Marto and Francisco Marto – in 1917. The apparition uttered three dire prophecies to the children which are now in the keeping of the Holy See in Rome (see pages 142-143).

Gordius

Founder of the City of Gordion

The semi-mythical Gordius was a peasant with an excellent sense of

Louis DeWohl

1903-1961

Astrologer to Winston Churchill and the War Cabinet

German-born Louis DeWohl fled Nazi persecution to settle in London in 1935. When the Second World War broke out, he was drafted to provide an astrological insight into the personality and motivations of Adolf Hitler and to ascertain what Karl Ernst Krafft (see pages 144-147) and other Nazi astrologers were telling the Führer.

DeWohl held the honorary rank of Lieutenant Colonel for the remainder of the war, and was responsible for forging copies of German astrological magazines to be smuggled into the Nazi block, which gave negative predictions. DeWohl also may have had an influence on choosing the date for D-Day because he knew that Hitler had a morbid fear of the number 6. Thus, D-Day, the Allied invasion into mainland Europe, occurred on the sixth day of the sixth month.

timing. Just after the oracle of Didyma had predicted that the next man to enter the gate would be king, Gordius arrived with his family, pulling a simple farm cart. Gordius was immediately acclaimed king. Before he died, he said that any man who could unravel the complex knot which held the yoke to the shaft of his cart, would conquer the world. This task baffled many who came to attempt it, but its mystery was eventually solved by Alexander the Great (see pages 26-31).

Joan of Arc
1412-1431
The Maid of Orleans

Born in Domremy in Lorraine, at the age of thirteen this simple peasant girl experienced angelic visions, telling her to restore the throne of France to its

Joan of Arc became a mythical heroine for the French. This contemporary depiction, *Joan of Arc Attacks Paris Unsuccessfully*, **was painted in 1429.**

rightful claimant, the Dauphin Charles. As most of France was under the control of the English and their allies the Burgundians, the only way to complete her mission was by force of arms. Joan proved her divine credentials at Chinon when she successfully identified Charles, even though he had concealed himself among his courtiers. Joan was armed as a knight at the Dauphin's expense and placed at the head of an army, though it is unlikely that she was actually in charge. Joan soon became a sort of lucky mascot to the French forces who came to believe that they could not be

defeated while 'The Maid' was with them. Bolstered by this confidence, the long siege of Orleans was relieved and Joan led a force of 12,000 men through the English-held territory to crown the dauphin as King at Rheims. However, the Burgundians sold Joan to the English, and she was tried for witchcraft at Rouen and burned at the stake on 30 May, 1431. She was canonized as the patron saint of soldiers in 1921.

Joseph, son of Jacob
Eighteenth century BC
Hebrew Patriarch found in the Book of Genesis

Joseph was favoured by his father over his other twelve sons and was given a coat of many colours, which caused his brothers considerable jealousy. This was made worse by Joseph's prophetic dreams that indicated his own future greatness. His brothers sold him into slavery and Joseph eventually found himself in an Egyptian prison with the pharaoh's butler and baker. His accuracy in foretelling their fates led to his interpretation of the pharaoh's dream (*Genesis 41*). He later ruled Egypt in the pharaoh's name and was reconciled to his family (see pages 50-51). Joseph's use of a 'divining cup' is mentioned in Genesis 44.5.

Julia

First century BC

Niece of Julius Caesar, Mother of Octavian Augustus

While pregnant, Julia had a dream in which she gave birth to the god Apollo. This was taken as an omen that her son would be an incarnation of this god. Her son Octavian was canny enough to use this prediction as a propaganda ploy during his war with Mark Anthony and Cleopatra.

Edward Kelly

1555-1595

aka Edward Talbot

Seer, Necromancer, Alchemist

An associate of Dr John Dee, Edward Kelly was an accomplished crystal-gazer. He was also a cheat and a con-man. His origins are obscure, but at some early point in his colourful career, Kelly had one ear chopped off as a punishment for fraud. However, his occult talents were genuine, and Dee found him an invaluable ally in his work, even though Kelly's morality left much to be desired. After accompanying Dee to Prague, Kelly suggested that they swap wives, hinting that this was what the spirits desired,

which provoked an infuriated Dee to promptly throw Kelly out. Dee's flight from Germany shortly afterwards left Kelly to his own devices and he returned to his old criminal habits. He was eventually imprisoned in the castle of Zerner in Bohemia, and was either murdered or killed while trying to escape (see pages 84-87). Aleister Crowley claimed Kelly as a previous incarnation.

Karl Ernst Krafft

1900-1945

The Gestapo Astrologer

Born in Switzerland, Krafft became devoted to the Nazi cause and predicted great things for the rising Hitler. Later, he was employed by Propaganda Minister Goebbels to re-interpret some of the prophecies of Nostradamus in a favourable light for the Nazis. Contrary to popular belief, Hitler was not very interested in astrology; however, other members of his clique were. Krafft was consulted by Rudolf Hess and other high-ranking Nazi officials such as Heinrich Himmler. After Hess secretly flew to Britain to negotiate a peace settlement in 1941, Hitler was of the opinion that Hess had been 'crazed by astrologers' and that they were to blame for his successor's defection. Krafft and many other astrologers then fell victim to a purge and were detained in concentration camps. Krafft tried to worm his way back into favour by sending a message to Hitler that his life was in danger from assassination. The Führer escaped the threat to his life but ignored Krafft's plight. Even a carefully phrased prediction of German victory set for May, 1945, did not warm the dictator's heart. Karl Ernst Krafft

eventually died of typhus while being transported to Buchenwald in a cattle wagon.

Marie Lavaux

c.1794-1881

'The Bosswoman'

The Voodoo Queen of New Orleans

Probably born in Haiti in 1794 or in New Orleans in 1796, it is believed that this enigmatic figure arrived in New Orleans after a slave revolt in Haiti in 1809. She proceeded to exert a tremendous influence over everyone with whom she came into contact. Governors, politicians, judges and businessmen who wanted curses to be laid or removed came to her and paid considerable amounts for the privilege. Possessing an eye for the great and for those who would become great, Marie became a personal friend of the Marquis de Lafayette, General Jean Humbert, future president General Andrew Jackson and the pirate Jean Lafitte, telling their fortunes readily. Legend claims that the spirit of Marie Lavaux rises on St John's Eve, 23 June, and her tomb is still revered by voodoo cultists.

William Lilly

1602-1681

'The English Merlin'

Astrologer and Prophetic Pamphleteer

The son of a yeoman farmer, Lilly found that he 'could not endure the plough', so in 1620 he travelled to London to seek employment. He became the secretary of the wealthy but illiterate Gilbert Wright. After Wright's death, Lilly promptly married the widow Wright and thereby increased his fortune considerably. He took lessons in astrology from a quarrelsome Welsh mystic named Mr Evans and in 1633 he set up in business – publishing pamphlets containing predictions. He became very successful, having few rivals, and certainly none who could match his turn of phrase. Often libellous, Lilly usually had several lawsuits pending at any given time. The English Civil War between the King and Parliament put Lilly in a difficult position, since he was consulted by both sides in the dispute. Lilly tried to please everyone by claiming that he 'loved and approved of the monarchy but engaged body and soul in the cause of the Parliament'. This statement was never to be forgotten by disgruntled royalists who eventually took their revenge in 1666. When his enemies accused Lilly of being an arsonist, following the Great Fire of London, he had great difficulty in persuading the court that he was innocent. Sadly his reputation never recovered and he eventually died in obscurity.

St Malachy
Died 1148
Healer and Papal Prophet
Born in the Irish state of Armagh, Malachy O'Morgair was a devout and humble man. He first gained fame as an accomplished healer, and his

prophetic abilities may be linked to the fact that he rarely, if ever slept. A series of riddles chronicling the succession of future Popes has been attributed to him (see pages 56-59).

The return of Quetzacóatl, the plumed, white-skinned god, was prophesied by the Aztecs. Montezuma believed Cortés to be Quetzacóatl, particularly as the Spanish soldiers had plumes on their helmets.

Montezuma
Died 1521
aka Moctezuma II
Emperor, or more properly, First Speaker, of the Aztec Empire
This last powerful ruler of the Aztec Empire was considered a mystic by his own people. He was heavily influenced by the prophetic nature of the ancient Mayan Calendar, and was an accomplished astrologer. He read omens from nature and also consulted the 'magic' mirror of Tezcatlipoca which eventually ended up in the hands of Dr John Dee. Montezuma was a fatalist and considered himself doomed from the moment that news of Cortés's landing reached him (see pages 72-75).

Jacques de Molay
Died 1314
Grand Master of the Order of the Knights Templar
The last Grand Master of the illustrious Order of the Knights Templar was accused, along with all of his followers, of heresy and many other unspeakable crimes by King Philippe IV of France and Pope Clement V. From the stake, de Molay prophesied the deaths of these two powerful men, and also laid a curse on the next thirteen generations of French kings (see pages 76-79). His final prophecy was fulfilled in 1794 when Louis XVI was executed on the same spot as Molay was burnt at the stake, at which point someone in the mob shouted 'Jacques de Molay, you have been avenged'.

Robert Nixon

1467-1485

'The Cheshire Idiot'

Robert Nixon, better known as the Cheshire Idiot, was an illiterate peasant boy who was retarded and incoherent for most of the time. He came to the notice of the powerful noble Cholmondely family for his occasional predictions concerning the state of the English nation and historical events, among them the Plague, the Great Fire of London, the beheading of Charles I, the Restoration, the reign of William of Orange, the French Revolution and the Napoleonic wars. He also said that when a raven built its nest in the mouth of a stone lion, a King of England would be cast out of the country. This unlikely event took place just as James II was deposed and fled the country over two centuries later.

Nostradamus or Michel de Nostredame

1503-1566

'The Prophet of Salon'
Physician, Astrologer and Seer

The inexplicable Nostradamus, though outwardly Christian, was of Jewish origin and was educated by both of his grandfathers, who instilled in him a love of learning and a healthy disrespect for dogma. His early career won him renown as a successful doctor specializing in the treatment of plague victims. In 1556, he was consulted by Queen Catherine de Medici of France, who persuaded him to gaze into a magic mirror to foretell the destinies of her sons. The Queen must have protected him from the fanatics of the Inquisition. Nostradamus also predicted the glittering future of a boy fated to become King Henri IV of France by reading the moles on his body (see page 185). Nostradmus's posthumous fame rests with ten volumes of his prophecies known as *The Centuries*, (see pages 152-160). Many people have tried to decipher his enigmatic verses, known as quatrains, ever since he committed them to paper. Nostradamus has been acclaimed as a genius and true prophet, and, conversely, has also been vilified as being an insane deceiver, a drunkard and a drug addict. The last accusation may have some truth behind it since he, like the witches of the time, certainly employed some dubious mixtures in pursuance of prophetic visions. His verses are as mysterious and compelling now as they were in the sixteenth century. After the death of Nostradamus, his wife had inscribed on his monument a startling claim describing him as 'the only one in the judgement of all mortals worthy to write with a pen almost divine under the influence of the stars of future events of the entire world'.

Olympias of Epirus

Died 316 BC

Queen of Macedonia

Mother of Alexander the Great, Olympias was rumoured to be a prophetic witch. She certainly indulged in weird orgiastic cults in which she danced naked entwined with serpents. Though married to Phillip II of Macedonia, she is rumoured to have slept with Nectanebo, last pharaoh of Egypt, although this may merely have been propaganda designed to give her son a claim to the Egyptian throne. Olympias predicted the divine nature of her son Alexander by augury and may have helped things proceed by murdering her husband King Phillip and one of his other sons. After Alexander's death in Babylon, Olympias made his posthumous son king, but the pair were eventually murdered by Cassander, a Macedonian general who then usurped the crown.

Pe-Har, Devil King

Founded in 1648

Oracle to the Dalai Lama

Pe-Har is the name of a devil enchanted and forced to serve the Buddhist hierarchy of Tibet. The oracle was established in the seventeenth century and a succession of specially trained monks are said to be possessed by this entity and to utter prophecies. Some of Pe-Har's pronouncements have been wide of the-mark. The devil-king now predicts that the Dalai Lama will eventually return to Tibet.

Pythia

1600 BC—AD 394

Greek title given to the oracles of Delphi

The Pythia of Delphi was a title for an oracle priestess who was part of the line of otherwise unnamed priestesses who, in a manic trance state were possessed by the god Apollo. The prophecies of Pythia were extremely influential throughout the entire period of Greek, and, later, Roman civilization. The Christian dominance which followed tended to demonize the Pythia and oracles in general. The line of Pythias is said to have begun in the sixteenth century BC and continued until the fourth century AD. Often the demand for the prophetess's services was so great that three Pythias would work a shift system to satisfy their clientele. It is untrue that the Pythia's clients were made up only of kings and emperors. Often the priestess would sit on the steps of her temple to answer the questions of the humbler classes.

Grigori Efimovitch Rasputin
1871-1916

Mystic and Healer

Considered a sinister influence on the last Tsar of Russia and his family, Rasputin maintained his position by easing the bleeding of the haemophiliac Tsarevich Alexei. His magnetic personality ensured that he kept a firm hold on the imperial family, and thus gained many powerful enemies who feared and objected to a peasant being so close to the throne, particularly one so salacious. The story of Rasputin's prophecy of his own death and of the fate of Russia is told on pages 122-125.

Morgan Robertson
Died 1915

Author and Inventor

Morgan Robertson's sole claim to fame is that he appeared to predict the sinking of the Titanic long before the event took place. In his novel *The Wreck of the Titan or Futility*, Robertson set out in great detail the fictional equivalent of the tragedy that was to occur some fifteen years later (see pages 140-141).

Mother Shipton or Janet Ursula Southiel
c. 1488-1561

Witch and Prophetess

The archetypal hag-like witch, Mother Shipton, was a native of Knaresborough, Yorkshire. She was thought to be a child of the devil and was renowned as a sorceress and

People took to the streets in Russia in November, 1917 and the Tzar and his family were assassinated immediately after Rasputin's death, as the latter prophecied.

prophet. Her reputation is based on a prophecy in appalling doggerel published long after her death. However, there have been so many versions of this that her credibility has not stood the test of time (see pages 102-105).

Sibyl
616 BC–AD 394

Mythical Prophetess

The Roman name given to the oracular priestesses of Cumae

The sibyls were a line of prophetesses who served the god Apollo. Tradition holds that there was but one Sibyl, who requested Apollo immortality from Apollo but did not ask for eternal youth. Thus,

she lived on and on, becoming older and older for eternity. The Roman state relied on manuscripts from a sibyl, called the Sibylline Books, which were sold to King Tarquinius Priscus in the fifth century BC. The most celebrated of these documents is called *The Succession of the Hairy Ones*.

Vitricius Spurinna
First century BC

Augur

The man who prophesied 'beware the Ides of March' to Julius Caesar, Spurinna probably divined this ominous date from reading the entrails of sacrificial animals (see pages 32-35). Though Spurinna was obviously a well-born Roman citizen of senatorial class, he remains obscure, apart from this one fateful prophecy.

Johannes Stoffler

Sixteenth century AD

Astrologer

Johannes Stoffler has gone down in history as the worst astrologer who ever lived. His pronouncements have been ridiculed as much as those of Jerome Cardan. However, during his lifetime, they were taken very seriously indeed. He published an almanac in 1499 which stated that the world was destined to be destroyed by a great flood on 2 February, 1524, due to a malevolent line-up of planets in the sign of Pisces. As the fateful date approached, many people in Germany began to emulate Noah and build arks. Ships were requisitioned in ports and the local population moved into them. Panic was rife when the day arrived and a desperate mob stormed an ark prepared by Count von Iggleheim, trampling the unfortunate nobleman to death in the process. But the storm clouds did not gather; the rivers did not rise. In short, nothing happened. Stoffler then announced that he had made a mistake in his calculations and that the real date for doomsday was due in 1588. Nothing happened then either, but Stoffler didn't care as, by then, he was long dead.

Teiresias of Thebes

Twelfth century BC

Legendary Seer

According to myth, the blind seer Teiresias had, as a youth, struck a pair of mating serpents and had been transformed into a woman. Seven years later, he again saw two serpents mating and struck them again, and was turned back into a man once more. Some time later, Zeus and his queen, Hera, argued over who got the most pleasure from

sex – men or women. Since Teiresias had been both, the two divinities decided to ask him. Teiresias answered that women experienced the most pleasure at a ratio of nine to one. In anger, Hera blinded him, but in compensation, Zeus granted Teiresias a long life and the gift of prophecy. Teiresias is a key figure in the story of Oedipus and appears in the tragedies of Sophocles and Euripides. Homer mentions that his shade was consulted by Odysseus on his visit to the underworld, a story repeated by Ovid. The medieval poet Dante places Teiresias in the Eighth Circle of Hell in his Inferno 20. Both Tennyson and Swinburne wrote poems about the ambiguous Teiresias. The transsexuality of this mythical prophet may be a folk memory of an ancient shaman who 'stood between the worlds', neither good nor bad, alive nor dead, male nor female, but encompassing all contradictions within himself as the source of prophetic power.

Thomas the Rhymer

Thirteenth century AD

Seer

A renowned prophet, Thomas the Rhymer was a bard who is said to have enchanted the 'Queen of Elfin' with his songs. She took him into her kingdom and gave him the gift of second sight. Thomas was long thought to be an incarnation of the sixteenth century Merlin. Archbishop John Spottiswood (AD 1565-1639) wrote of him, 'He may be justly admired, having foretold to many ages before the Union of England and Scotland in the ninth degree of Bruce's blood, with the succession of Bruce himself to the crown, being yet a child, and other

divers particulars which the event hath satisfied and made good.' The Bruce referred to in the above passage was Robert the Bruce (AD 1274-1329), the Scottish hero who became king in 1306. The ninth in succession from the Bruce was James VI of Scotland who inherited the throne of England in 1603.

Thrassylus

BC 42–AD 37

Astrologer and Augur

Thrassylus was a Greek-educated Arab who came into contact with Tiberius on the island of Rhodes, remaining with him for the remainder of his life. Thrassylus had the reputation of never being wrong, even when he lied. Infinitely bribeable, Thrassylus would tell anyone anything if he was paid enough, then pretend that his visions had been mystically inspired. Amazingly, his prophecies, fake or otherwise, always seemed to come true. He died in AD 37 after being visited by a lizard, in the same year as his imperial employer – just as he had predicted (see pages 36-37).

Wovaka son of Numitaivo

1858-1932.

aka Jack Wilson

Paiute Medicine Man and Prophet

Born near the Great Salt Lake, Wovaka was strongly influenced by both the native traditions of his people and by his adopted father, 'white man' rancher David Wilson. Wovaka brought a message of hope to Native Americans through his prophecy of their eventual victory in the ongoing war with the White Man. The Ghost Dance cult which he founded united the tribes until their massacre at Wounded Knee in December 1891 (see pages 66-69).

PARTING THE VEIL
A Glossary of Divinatory Techniques

Aeromancy ∞ divination from atmospheric conditions such as haloes around the sun and moon and the appearance of comets. A comet presaged the invasions of Julius Caesar in 44 BC and of William the Conqueror in 1066. Sightings of the aurora borealis in 1914 and 1939 were said to portend world war.

Alectryomancy ∞ created by the philosopher Iambilichus in the fourth century AD and still used in some places, for example Andorra. It is a divination requiring a rooster to peck at grains of wheat laid over a circular alphabet in order to spell out messages. The ancient Egyptians used a similar technique with their sacred animals.

Aleuromancy ∞ predictions are written on slips of paper and then baked in cakes. Chinese fortune cookies are the modern equivalent.

Alomancy ∞ reading the future in the fall of salt. This survives in the form of the tradition of throwing spilled salt over the left shoulder to ward off evil.

Alphitomancy ∞ used to determine an accused person's guilt or innocence by making him swallow a blessed barley cake. Earl Godwin of Wessex fatally succumbed to this test in 1053.

Amniomancy ∞ predictions made concerning a child born with a membranous caul.

Anthropomancy ∞ a messy process involving human sacrifice and then divination from the victim's entrails. The Druids often used this form of divination, according to Julius Caesar, although some say this was just propaganda.

Apantomancy ∞ omens are observed in chance encounters with certain animals and unexpected occurrences. A modern example of apantomancy is having a black cat cross one's path. The ancient British queen Boudicca (or Boadicea) released a hare which had been nestled in her bosom before a battle with the Roman Legions at Colchester. The pattern of the animal's movements provided a good omen and indeed her forces were victorious.

Arithmancy ∞ fortune-telling by numbers, as in numerology (see pages 128-131).

Armomancy ∞ a method of divining a person's suitability for a post by close physical inspection that is very similar to moleoscopy.

Aspidomancy ∞ divination of future events by means of possession by a spirit or demon.

Astragalomancy ∞ divination with dice, bones or dominoes.

Astrology ∞ an area where divination meets science. Dating from at least the second millennium BC in Babylon, astrology is known worldwide in various forms. It is the study of the movements and relative positions of celestial bodies that influence humans, and other beings, their affairs and the world. Best known is tropical astrology which is based on planetary positions and aspects against a background of the zodiac which begins at the vernal equinox. Sidereal astrology takes as its basis the zodiac of the fixed stars and constellations. The sidereal form of astrology is widely used in India in the form of Vedic astrology. Oriental astrology has many forms, the best known of which are the twelve animal signs of the Chinese Zodiac, based on the twelve-year cycle of the planet Jupiter. Aztec and Mayan astrology allot specific zodiac signs to individual days and are based on the movements of the planet Venus.

Astromancy ∞ primitive astrology, such as making a wish when a shooting star is seen, or worrying during an eclipse.

Augury ∞ the seeking of omens from the environment. The ancient Romans had many skilled augurs who sought the future in the entrails of beasts, the flight of birds, metereological phenomena, and so on. Vitricius Spurinna, who warned Julius Caesar of the Ides of March, was an augur.

Austromancy ∞ foretelling by the study of winds. Knowing which way the wind is blowing is pretty important after all.

Axinomancy &) used in judicial proceedings. An axe head was heated, set upright and a marble set thereon. Whichever way the marble rolled determined guilt or innocence.

Belomancy &) tossing arrows to determine which direction to take.

Bibliomancy &) a well-known form of divination performed by opening a book (usually the Bible) at random, pointing to a verse and then reading it.

Botanomancy &) divination by the properties of various plants and herbs.

Cabalism &) originally a Hebrew form of number mysticism, it was later adopted by the neo-Platonists of the Renaissance and magicians of the nineteenth century. It can be applied to numerology, astrology and tarot, amongst many other systems. Nostradamus may have used it as the basis for his *Centuries*.

Capnomancy &) divination by smoke. If it rises straight then good fortune will come, if it hangs in the air then ill news is due.

Cartomancy &) a common form of divination using cards. Tarot cards, ordinary playing cards or indeed any other might be used.

Catoptromancy &) divination with the aid of a magic mirror. Originating in ancient Persia, it was widely used by such mystics as Dr. John Dee and Nostradamus. The Mirror of Dr. Dee can be seen in the British Museum.

Cattabomancy &) divination by ringing brass vessels.

Causimomancy &) a form of divination in which articles are thrown into a fire. If any fail to burn, it is a good omen.

Cephalomancy &) boiling a donkey's head in brine and noting which orifice produces bubbles.

Ceromancy &) adding melting wax to water and divining by the shapes it produces – an ancestor of tea-leaf reading.

Chalcomancy &) used at the Oracle of Dodona, it was similar to cattabomancy and also involved ringing brass vessels. Tibetan traditions also use chalcomancy.

Chaomancy &) divination by the weather, which often inspired folk wisdom and sayings like 'Red sky at night, shepherd's delight; red sky in the morning, shepherd's warning'.

Chartomancy &) divination by writing or the interpretation of mysterious inscriptions.

Cheiromancy &) palmistry or, more correctly, the interpretation of a person's character and predicting their future by examining the lines and features of their hands.

Chresmomancy &) divination from the utterances of a person in a frenzy or trance. The Delphic oracle was chresmomantic.

Chrystallomancy &) crystal gazing. Like the use of a magic mirror (see also Cataptromancy), this is also known as scrying.

Clairaudience &) the ability to hear spoken messages from the spiritual realms.

Clairvoyance &) literally 'clear seeing' and is a term applied to many forms of psychic awareness, especially those involving visions.

Cleidomancy &) divination by using a key. A key is suspended on a string. Questions are asked and the key is said to respond.

Cleromancy &) the casting of lots, stones, beads or pebbles to foretell the future.

Coscinomancy &) a sieve is held between the blades of a pair of shears so that two people must press the handles of the shears until the sieve begins to move, then questions can be asked. If it doesn't move, then pronounce the words 'Dies, Mies, Jeschet, Benedoefet, Dowima, Enitemaus,' a demon will then urge the process along.

Crithomancy &) divination using corn or grain or methods of fortune-telling by using cakes, bread or dough.

Cromniomancy &) divination through using onions: name each onion, plant them and wait until the first sprouts – this will be your man. (Could be good for predicting election results.)

Cyclomancy ෨ a lottery or roulette wheel is used in this form of divination to find winning numbers. It is known as the wheel of fortune.

Dactylomancy ෨ divining the meaning of rings worn on the fingers. The metal of the ring, any gemstone and indeed the finger itself are taken into account.

Daphnomancy ෨ an ancient Greek practice in which laurel leaves (sacred to Apollo) were thrown into a fire: if they crackled loudly then good would come; if quietly or not at all, then it boded ill.

Demonomancy ෨ a dangerous practice in which the demons of hell were summoned to answer questions.

Dowsing ෨ often called water-divining, it can also be used to find almost anything. The most common forms involve using either a forked twig such as that from a hazel tree, or a pendulum. This art is still very much alive in rural areas.

Eromancy ෨ muttering questions at the surface of water; if any ripples occur, then this is interpreted as a positive answer.

Felidomancy ෨ divination arising from the movements of a cat, ranging from predicting changes in the weather to unexpected visitors – an ancient Egyptian survivor.

Floromancy ෨ divination with flowers and plants; finding a lucky four-leafed clover would be positively floromantic.

Gastromancy ෨ divination by the sounds made by the stomach. Very popular in China, this may also be a ventriloquist's technique used by dubious mediums.

Gelomancy ෨ the interpretation of hysterical laughter and convulsions.

Geomancy ෨ a highly complex art involving the interpretation of mystic figures drawn on the earth.

Graphology ෨ the study of handwriting to assess character.

Gyromancy ෨ used by Dervishes who whirl around until they are in a trance-like state when questions are then put to them.

Hieromancy ෨ divination through mishaps occurring in set religious rituals. Omens may be drawn from missed-words, or from stumbling or things not proceeding in the correct order. Weddings, funerals, coronations and presidential inaugurations are observed for such omen taking.

Hippomancy ෨ divination by observation of the gait and deportment of horses.

Hydromancy ෨ divination with water. One form of this is the contemplation of a still pool to gain visions; another involves dropping stones into water and interpreting the ripples. The way pieces of bread float has been employed to foretell the future.

I Ching ෨ Arising from Chinese philosophy, the *I Ching* or *Book of Changes* is still used as a divinatory tool, even though its conceptual basis is part of the complex philosophies of Taoism and Confucianism.

Ichthomancy ෨ divination by the examination of fish offered as sacrifices. This may also involve watching the movements of living fish.

Idolomancy ෨ the use of pagan idols to answer questions. In ancient times, hollow statues were employed to impress the credulous.

Lampadomancy ෨ lighted lamps are watched to determine the future by the appearance of their flames. During the Hindu festival of Diwali, the Rite of Lamps is performed in honour of the goddess Lakshmi.

Lecanomancy ෨ a variant of hydromancy involving dropping precious gems into water.

Libinomancy ෨ the interpretation of incense smoke – similar to capnomancy (see also page 183).

Lithomancy ෨ divination by noting the unusual appearance of stones and rocks; any divination with pebbles or gems is usually included under this heading.

Logarithmancy ෨ the use of higher mathematics to divine the future. Computer forecasts and statistics may come under this title.

Lynchomancy ෨ divination from the flames of three candles set in an equilateral triangle. If the flames waver, then a change of life is to be expected.

If they twist, then beware of double-dealing. If they rise and fall, then beware of danger. However, if one flame outshines the rest then extremely good fortune is foretold.

Macharomancy ∞ divination by swords, daggers and other sharp objects – usually undertaken before a battle. This is probably the origin of Scottish sword dances.

Margaritomancy ∞ a pearl is placed within a pot, which is sealed. The names of people suspected of a crime are then spoken; when the name of the guilty person is mentioned, the pearl (we are told) will strike the lid of the pot.

Mediumship ∞ also known as channelling and spirit possession, and usually a function of the modern spritualist movement, it has a long history in many cultures and is at the centre of Voodoo and related practices in Caribbean and African cultures. Many oracles of the ancient world can be regarded as mediums.

Meteoromancy ∞ a form of astromancy (see page 182) specifically related to shooting stars – their direction, brightness and speed are taken into consideration.

Metopomancy ∞ the practice of interpreting a person's character and prospects from the lines on the forehead.

Molescopy ∞ the study of the moles on the body, which are considered to be akin to stars in the sky. Character readings and prognostication were performed this way. Nostradamus used molescopy to discover the destiny of a boy fated to become King Henri IV of France (see 'The Prophet of Salon' on page 106).

Molybdomancy ∞ involves dropping melted lead onto a flat surface and then interpreting the shapes that result. Hot lead is also dropped into water for interpretations of hissing sounds.

Myomancy ∞ divination taken from the appearance or activities of mice, rats and other vermin –

rats abandoning a ship that is about to sink is a good example.

Necromancy ∞ a highly dubious and dangerous form of divination involving black magic. By occult rites, a fresh corpse was said to be induced to speak to reveal the whereabouts of treasure. Edward Kelly (see 'The Crop-eared Rogue' on page 84) and the Thracian witch, Erichtho, were reputed to be masters of this foul art. Modern spiritualism could be thought of as a form of necromancy, since by this means the dead are in communication with the living.

Nephelomancy ∞ divination by observing the shape of clouds.

Numerology ∞ a system in which each number is allocated a significance according to the effects of planets which rule them – Cabalistic and Pythagorean numerologies are considered to be the most complex.

Oculomancy ∞ the study of the eye, particularly the iris, for diagnosis of ailments or knowledge of the future; this is also known as irridology.

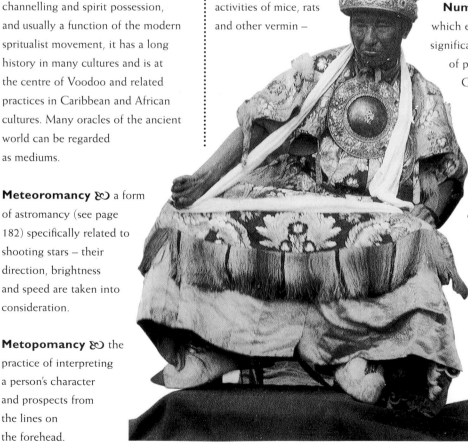

An Oracle Priest of Tibet in the final stages of a trance. Whilst using his body to channel spirit energy, the face of the Oracle-priest will lose its normal expression, becoming dark red and swollen, the lips will become blue, and the eyes bloodshot.

Oinomancy &co; the study of wines – their taste, colour and bouquet. Many modern wine tasters can tell which slope a particular grape comes from, unconscious of the fact
that this is an oinomantic process.

Omphalomancy &co; the contemplation of one's own navel to gain enlightenment – this is considered to be a branch of yoga.

Oneiromancy &co; the interpretation of dreams to gain knowledge of the future. Oneiromancy is still practised in many parts of the world today and many dream dictionaries are available.

Onomancy &co; divination by names and the letters which make them up; hence some people give children regal or impressive names in the hope that they will live up to them.

Onychomancy &co; divination involving the reflection of sunlight on someone's fingernails.

Onyomancy &co; similar to onychomancy. In this case, the appearance of the fingernails themselves is important, particularly to ascertain the health of a person. This is a branch of cheiromancy.

Oomancy &co; an ancient divination technique using eggs – either the shells or the contents. The Salem witch trials of the seventeenth century began with oomancy. The Empress Livia (first century BC) divined the exalted destiny of her son Tiberius by hatching an egg in her hands. The chick that emerged had a cockscomb proving to her that he would be emperor one day.

Ophiomancy &co; divination by observing the movements and markings of snakes, originally from ancient Egypt and Meso-America. A cult of religious snake handlers in the USA today prove their faith by holding venomous serpents, which is a form of ophiomancy.

Ornithomancy &co; a widely used divination technique from the ancient world, pertaining to the flight of birds. St. Patrick specifically forbade it in Ireland where the Druids were very adept at this art. Certain birds are still regarded as being good or bad luck. Doves and ravens come to mind. Modern equivalents include folk rhymes about numbers of magpies.

Pegomancy &co; divination by observing the colour of streams and waterfalls. A reddish hue indicates a coming war, while shapes formed by swirls of water can also be interpreted.

Pessomancy &co; divination by observing colours of pebbles, each having a different meaning. Shaking them in a bag, then withdrawing one, provides the basis for interpretation.

Phrenology &co; the study of the bumps on the head. This was a Victorian pseudo-science which grew out of the art of physiognomany.

Phyllorhodomancy &co; the practice of slapping rose leaves against the side of the hand and noting the sounds that they make.

Physiognomany &co; the study of the general conformation of the body and appearance with particular concentration on the face. A high brow and an aquiline nose would indicates intelligence, while a corpulent person is considered to be of a jolly disposition.

Podomancy &co; similar to hand analysis, although in this case the appendages under examination are the feet – specifically the soles. This ancient technique is still popular in China.

Psychomancy &co; a wide description of many varied techniques such as psychometry (holding an object to create a psychic link), the use of ouija boards and automatic writing. The ouija board connects psychomancy to necromancy.

Psychometry &co; see Psychomancy.

Pyromancy &co; divination by fire. This includes seeing shapes in flames as a sort of scrying technique and throwing some substance, such as incense or pitch, into the fire, which creates curious shapes that can foretell the future or provide omens.

Rhabdomancy &co; divination with the use of a wand – most commonly found today in the form of dowsing.

Rhapsodomancy &co; a form of bibliomancy (see page 183) in which books of poetry are used instead of sacred texts. Shakespeare's plays and sonnets are the most popular source material.

Scapulomancy &co; a technique in which omens are taken from the markings on the shoulder bone of an animal. In Europe, the sheep was the most commonly used beast, but Native Americans were known to use the shoulder bone of a buffalo.

Scarpomancy &: the unusual practice of reading character from a person's old shoes – possibly Russian in origin.

Sciomancy &: the study of shadows in which their changes, size, shape and density are taken into account. Ancient lore is full of dark stories about those whose shadows have been stolen. It was thought that communication with the dead was best performed in darkness, so sciomancy took on a necromantic flavour.

Scyphomancy &: divining by using drinking cups, most particularly with the liquid within them or with floating particles in it – obviously related to tasseomancy.

Second Sight &: a term embracing clairvoyance – usually applied to Celtic mystics of the Scottish Highlands, Ireland, Wales, Cornwall, Brittany and the Isle of Man.

Selenomancy &: can be regarded as a branch of astrology or astromancy – a specialized divinatory art concerning the shape, phase and aspects of the moon.

Sideromancy &: the art of dropping straws onto a red-hot plate and interpreting the shapes they make.

Sortes Virgilianae &: when one opens a volume of Virgil's work at random in order to make predictions.

Rabelais makes one of his characters do this and Charles I of England and Scotland is recorded as actually trying it.

Sortilege &: any method of divination that involves mixing things together or scattering them to allow fate to take a hand; e.g., shuffling cards is a form of sortilege.

Splanchomancy &: comes from the ancient Etruscans, who sought omens in the entrails of sacrificial victims.

Spodomancy &: divination using ashes. Related to pyromancy, its main concern is with the remnants of a fire rather than the fire itself.

Stareomancy &: a general term describing any divination that uses the Platonic elements of Earth, Air, Fire or Water; it can cover almost anything.

Stichomancy &: a variant of bibliomancy and rhapsodomancy, using a book which is a novel or a factual text.

Sychomancy &: the practice of writing names on the leaves of a fig tree and allowing them to dry out. If they dry slowly, the omens are good for the person named; if quickly, then the outlook is bad. There are variations of sychomancy using sycamore or vine leaves. Ivy leaves may be soaked in water for five days and then examined; if they remain green and fresh, it is an omen of good health and success. However, if they become spotted or discoloured, then misfortune and illness will come.

Tasseomancy &: divination by tea-leaves or coffee grounds. This is a traditional art – endangered by the advent of the teabag.

Tephramancy &: is another method of divining using ashes from a sacred fire. It is akin to spodomancy .

Theomancy &: directly appealing to, and hopefully getting an answer from, a god or gods.

Theriomancy &: folk wisdom taken from the actions of animals, includes folklore such as rain inevitably follows the croaking of frogs, or that a barking dog never bites.

Tyromancy &: a smelly form of divination which interprets the mould growing on cheese.

Transataumancy &: a Japanese method of fortune telling.where snippets of overheard conversations may have a meaning for the hearer which has no relation to the intent of the speaker. Such snippets are said to reveal the future.

Xylomancy &: the interpretation of fallen branches and trees. Divination by wood found on the ground comes under this heading.

Zoomancy &: where omens are suggested when an imaginary or mythical beast like the 'fire spirit' or salamander is seen, as the sculptor Cellini claimed. Sightings of the Yeti, Big-foot, the Chupacabras, sea serpents, dragons, unicorns or the Loch Ness Monster may be termed zoomantic.

The Illustrated Encyclopaedia of Mysticism John Ferguson (Thames & Hudson 1976)

Quest for Merlin Count Nikolai Tolstoy (Hamish Hamilton 1985)

Cleopatra Michael Grant (Panther 1974)

Cleopatra Michael Foss (Michael O'Mara 1977)

Elizabethan Magic Robert Turner (Element 1989)

Joan Of Arc Marina Warner (Penguin 1983)

The Nature of Alexander Mary Renault (Penguin 1975)

In the Footsteps of Alexander Michael Wood (BBC Books 1997)

Rasputin and the Fall of the Romanoffs Colin Wilson (Panther 1964)

The Occult Colin Wilson (Mayflower 1971)

The Directory of Possibilities Colin Wilson/John Grant (Corgi 1982)

From Atlantis to the Sphinx Colin Wilson (BCA 1998)

Ancient Sun Kingdoms of the Americas Victor Wolfgang von Hagen (Paladin 1973)

The Voodoo Gods Maya Deren (Paladin 1975)

Extraterrestrial Civilisations Isaac Asimov (Pan 1979)

Bury my Heart at Wounded Knee Dee Brown (Henry Holt 1970)

The Mayan Prophecies Adrian Gilbert/Maurice Cotterell (Element 1995)

Fingerprints of the Gods Graham Hancock (Mandarin 1996)

The Magical World of Aleister Crowley Francis King (Arrow 1977)

The New Apocrypha John Sladek (Panther 1974)

Millennium Prophecies A.T Mann (Element 1995)

The History of Magic, Witchcraft & Occultism W.B.Crow (Abacus 1973)

Prophecy and Prediction in the 20th Century Charles Neilson Gattey (Aquarian 1989)

Body Magic Benjamin Walker (Paladin 1979)

Transcendental Magic Eliphas Levi (Bracken reprint 1995)

The Black Arts Richard Cavendish (Picador 1967)

The Cheiro Book of Fate and Fortune Cheiro (Hamelin 1971)

The Dark Side of History Michael Edwardes (Corgi 1980)

Encyclopaedia of Myths and Legends Stuart Gordon (Headline 1994)

The Book of Predictions David Wallechinsky/Amy Wallace/Irving Wallace (Corgi 1982)

World Atlas of Divination John Matthews (Headline 1992)

Nostradamus and His Prophecies Edgar Leoni (Bell 1982)

Nostradamus Francis X. King (Carlton 1998)

Nostradamus and the New Millennium Michael Jordan (Carlton 1998)

Complete Prophecies of Nostradamus Henry C. Roberts (Thorsons 1994)

Nostradamus the Final Reckoning Peter Lemesurier (Piatkus 1998)

Predictions Joe Fisher/Peter Commings (Sedgewick & Jackson 1981)

The Future Now Derek & Julia Parker (Mitchell Beazley 1988)

Magick Aleister Crowley (Routledge Kegan Paul 1973)

Astrology Louis MacNeice (Bloomsbury 1989)

Santeria Migene Gonzalez-Wippler (Original Pub. 1981)

Qabalah Will Parfitt (Element 1991)

The Rosicrucian Enlightenment Francis A. Yates (Paladin 1972)

The Divine Plot A.T. Mann (Alan & Unwin 1986)

The Holy Blood and the Holy Grail Michael Baigent/Richard Leigh/Henry Lincoln (Corgi 1983)

Vicars of Christ Peter de Rosa (Bantam 1988)

The Astrology of Fate Liz Greene (Mandala 1984)

I Claudius Robert Graves (Penguin 1943)

Claudius the God Robert Graves (Penguin 1943)

Count Belisarius Robert Graves (Penguin 1954)

The Greek Myths vols 1 & 2 Robert Graves (Penguin 1962)

Julian Gore Vidal (Panther 1962)

Satyricon Petronius Arbiter (Sphere 1965)

On the Trail of Merlin Dieke Rich/Ean Begg (Aquarian 1991)

Encyclopaedia of the Unexplained Richard Cavendish (Routledge Kegan Paul 1974)

The Great Beast John Symonds (Mayflower 1971)

Anastasia Peter Kurth (Fontana 1983)

Zodiac Signs Frederick Goodman (Brian Trodd Ltd 1990)

Who's Who in the Ancient World Betty Radice (Penguin 1973)

The Histories Herodotus (Penguin 1954)

Prophets and Predictions Richard Lewinsohn (Secker &Warburg 1958)

Predictions for the New Millennium Noel Tyl (Llewellyn Pub. 1996)

Forbidden Rites Richard Kieckhefer (Sutton 1997)